IMAGES
of America

DOVER

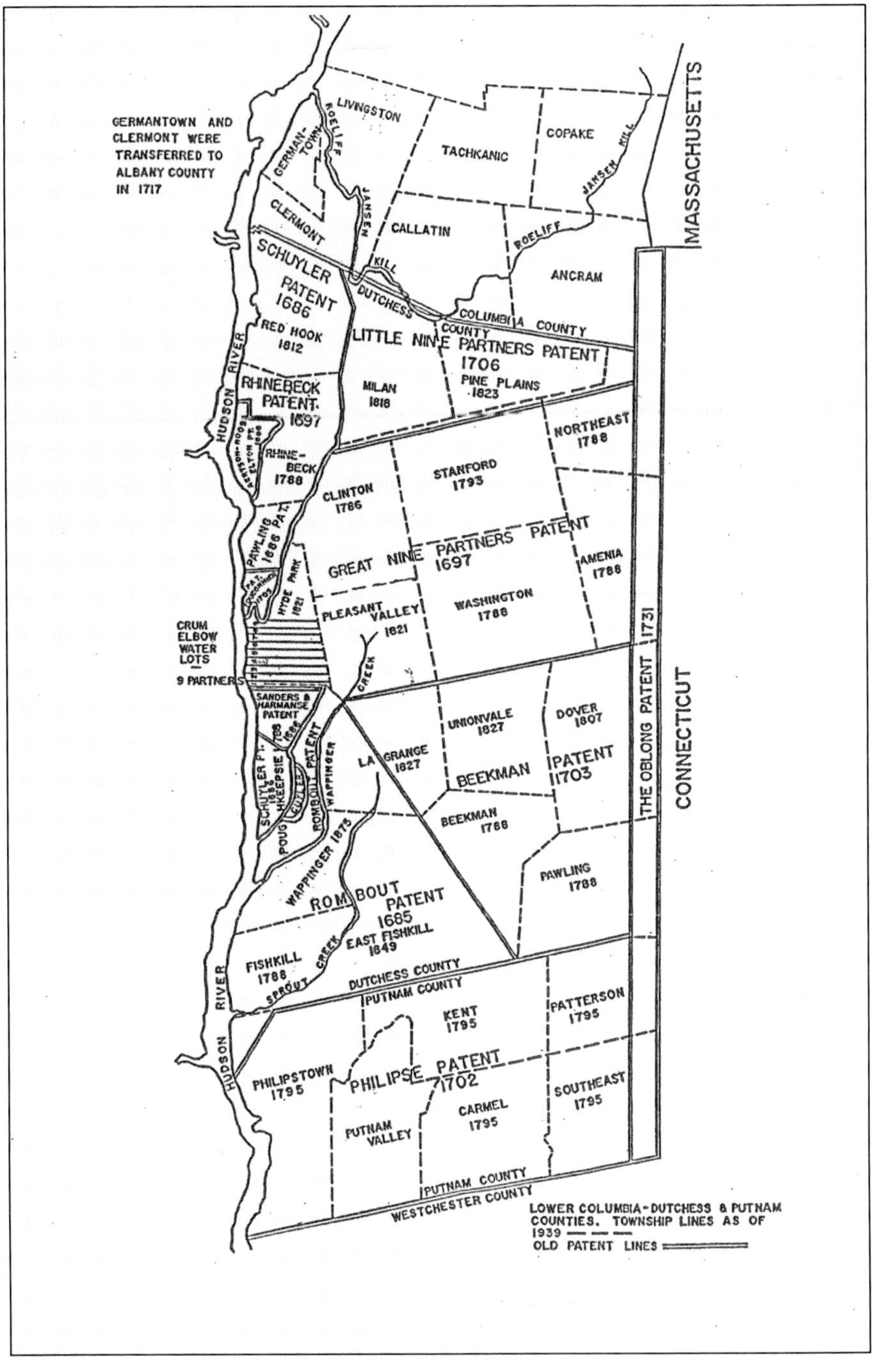

Created in 1683, Dutchess County extended from the Westchester County boundary to the Albany County boundary and east from the Hudson River to the colony of Connecticut. Initial settlements and patents bordered the Hudson River. The town of Dover occupies the northeast corner of the Beekman patent, and over a quarter of the town extends the width of the Oblong patent to the Connecticut line. (Dutchess County Historical Society.)

On the cover: Please see page 44. (William A. Reimer and Richard T. Reimer.)

IMAGES of America

DOVER

Donna P. Hearn

ARCADIA PUBLISHING

ISBN 978-0-7385-6313-8

Published by Arcadia Publishing
Charleston SC, Chicago IL, Portsmouth NH, San Francisco CA

Printed in the United States of America

Library of Congress Catalog Card Number: 2008925858

For all general information contact Arcadia Publishing at:
Telephone 843-853-2070
Fax 843-853-0044
E-mail sales@arcadiapublishing.com
For customer service and orders:
Toll-Free 1-888-313-2665

Visit us on the Internet at www.arcadiapublishing.com

To those whose words, photographs, and collections kept Dover's past alive for future generations. And to my husband and family, who patiently put up with my writing efforts.

Contents

ACKNOWLEDGMENTS

Many thanks are extended to editor Rebekah Collinsworth for her help and guidance in this endeavor.

Thanks are due to the Dover Town Board of 2007, including Jill Way (supervisor), Brian Kelly, Richard Hawthorne, Katie Palmer-House, and James Johnson; the Dover Town Board of 2008, including Ryan Courtien (supervisor), Chris Galayda, Richard Hawthorne, Katie Palmer-House, and Katherine Frame for the use of the Town of Dover Historical Collections (TDHC); the Smithsonian American Art Museum; commissioner Charles Traver and Mike Dutcavich of the Dutchess County Department of Public Works; Pres. Stephen Mann and Stephanie Mauri of the Dutchess County Historical Society; Judy Moberg-Kelley of the Friends of the Great Swamp (FROGS); director Jonathan Kuhn of the New York City Department of Recreation and Parks; Nada Davis of the Quaker Hill Historical Society; Pres. Donald B. Dedrick of the Town of Dover Historical Society (TDHS) for the use of their collections; Dover Union Free School District supervising principal Dr. Craig Onofry; the American Antiquarian Society; the Connecticut State Library; former town historians Doris Dedrick and Edward Hogan (EH), and Dover, England, correspondent Lorraine Sencicle, Dover Museum, Dover, England.

Thanks are extended to Robert Acken (RA), Richard Beebe Jr., the Benjamin Companies, Lewis and Emily Benson (LEB), Roger H. Bolomey, Frank Boscardin (FB), Denise Bryan (DB), Everett and Linda Brady (ELB), Roger and Madeline Callahan (RMC), Arthur Coe, Catherine S. Colligan (CSC), Robert Crane (RC), Kevin Cunningham (KC), Doris Dedrick (DD), Marie Feathers Darling (MFD), Kristine DaVersa (KD), Charles Diters (CD), Robert Duncan, Albert Franklin (AF), Elizabeth Fogel (EF), Joanne Mostachetti Graham, Janet Griffin (JG), Gerald Herbert (GH), Helen Walker Herman (HWH), Ian Holback (IH), Patricia Hoag (PH), Doris and Robert Hufcut (DRH), Robert V. Humeston (RVH), Brian and Cheryl Kelly (BCK), Judy Moberg-Kelly, Skip Kern (SK), Dr. Lucianne Lavin (LL), Elizabeth Crane Lawrence (ECL), Amy Lynch (AL), Brian P. Marasco (BPM), Armando and Ann Mostachetti, Leo Mostachetti (LM), Fred Murphy (FM), Joel E. Pelky, Janet Pickering (JP), Patricia Duncan Porter (PDP), Elsie Puglisi (EP), Caroline Rogers Reichenberg (CRR), Richard Reichenberg (RR), Richard T. Reimer (RTR), William A. Reimer (WAR), Richard Rennia Sr. (RAR), Bob Riley (BR), Thomas D. Rogers, Schaghticoke Tribal Nation, Chief Richard Velky, Kathleen Schibanoff, William Schreiber (WS), Lorraine Sencicle (LS), Charlotte and David Shelby (CDS), Claudia Masiero Sina (CMS), Richard Van Horn (RV), Walter A. Vincent (WAV), Philip Wathley (PW), Mary Lou Whaley (MLW), and Joanne Cutolo Zmudowsky (JCZ). Images credited with DPH are from my own collection.

INTRODUCTION

Welcome to the town of Dover, a small community located in eastern Dutchess County along the western boundary of Connecticut. Steep ridges surrounding Dover and other eastern towns created the narrow Harlem Valley, where Dover occupies the central location. There, a quarter century after Henry Hudson sailed up the river for the Dutch, Dover's earliest legend of refuge occurred amid ruins of war, betrayal, and death, as the Pequot Chief Sassacus fled New England during the first Pequot War in 1637. In a steep western hillside, Sassacus and his band found refuge in a hidden cave whose waters flowed to the Housatonic River.

Although Dover's recorded history began as a part of Beekman's patent, its eastern border with Connecticut remained uncertain. European colonization created disputes between New England and the Dutch where charters and grants overlapped. When the Duke of York conquered New Netherlands in 1664, boundary disputes began with New York, as earlier agreements failed to resolve the problem. In 1731, Connecticut and New York held a boundary conference in Dover where representatives signed an indenture swapping the equivalent lands, creating today's interstate boundary. In 1737, Connecticut organized townships east of the Housatonic River in its western lands along the boundary. On the New York side, the Beekman precinct population doubled by 1748, as Quakers settled the Oblong. Squatters and a band of Colonial counterfeiters soon inhabited the remaining mountainous lands. Colonial highways crossed in Dover. Stagecoaches traveling from New York City to Bennington, Vermont, crossed routes from the Hudson River ports in Fishkill and Poughkeepsie to Hartford. During the American Revolution, the Morehouse Tavern provided rest and respite for Gen. George Washington and other war leaders and dignitaries. There, Col. Andrew Morehouse received information from Enoch Crosby, America's first spy.

Dover separated from Pawling in 1807 and held its first town meeting in John Preston's home. Farmlands dotted the valley and sections of Chestnut Ridge, while small sustenance farms populated East Mountain. As iron demands grew, mountain farms and woodlots were coaled to feed the furnaces. Drover traffic from Vermont to New York increased, as thousands of cattle went to feed the growing city. In the 1840s, area anti-rent protests against government quitrent assessments of tenants and landowners eventually brought about change in the 1846 New York State Constitution, which abolished quitrents, making the deed holder the landowner. When the railroad came in 1850, it changed the town. Railroad transportation ended the cattle drovers traffic but moved iron, grain, and products out while bringing new people to the area. Asher Brown Durand, a founder of the Hudson River School of Art, came to Dover in 1846, captured by its tranquil beauty and verdant landscape. Durand sketched the Dover Stone Church and the plains in Dover. One view of Dover's plains by Durand is a pivotal painting at the Smithsonian American Art Museum. It visually answers the question of "where do I come from?"

During the Civil War, John Henry Ketcham organized a volunteer regiment while Theodore Timby's invention revolutionized naval warfare and changed armament strategy forever. Reconstruction requirements drove Dover's ore mines, beds, and furnaces. When the war's end demanded memorials to its fallen heroes, Dover's quarries provided monuments for battlefield cemeteries. Farming and dairy businesses expanded, sending fresh products to nearby New York City and western areas. By then, Ketcham, Dover's Civil War general, had retired and become a congressman. Locally an 1867 atlas shows numerous neighborhoods and recognized hamlets within the growing community.

During the last of the 19th century, Chestnut Ridge resident Benson J. Lossing was a journalist, editor, and engraver who created works that covered the American Revolution, the Civil War, the Hudson River, and New York State history. Locally he wrote and engraved a work about the Dover Stone Church. Dover's own congressman served his constituents as well as serving on the public lands and post office committees. His efforts to provide daily mail service to outlying areas became a reality through the rural free delivery system of the U.S. Postal Service. In 1895, Charles P. Morgan's mill on the Ten Mile River provided electric power to his Dover mill, house, and eight customers. His business provided Dover Plains with streetlights before New York City had them and became Harlem Valley's "grand-daddy" portion of the New York State Electric Company. In Wingdale, pure white marble from the South Dover quarries became fashionable as New York City expanded.

Growth continued into the 20th century. As the need for fire protection grew, the J. H. Ketcham Hose Company was organized in 1903. By 1909, the 16 local school districts in town had merged to build a high school. Radio was popular, and one trendy tune at that time was "Put on Your Old Grey Bonnet." Webatuck resident Margaret Faulkner often told folks that "Silas and Miranda," who drove up to Dover on their golden wedding day, often sat on the front porch veranda of the Faulkner farm. The area's natural beauty fostered a camp, resort, and tourism industry as families escaped the heat of the city during the summer and fathers commuted by train on weekends. The congressman's hometown area had become a showplace. Despite the effects of World War I, the area economy remained relatively stable. New York State, seeking a working farm area for a prison, chose the Harlem Valley as a site to house the lawless, provide jobs for other out-of-work New Yorkers, and expand the local economy. In 1912, modifications to the prison created a mental health institution. The Harlem Valley State Hospital doors opened for 32 patients in April 1924 and soon changed the economy of the entire valley. As young Franklin Delano Roosevelt piloted the Taconic State Parkway project and praised the Dover Stone Church to his commissioners, prohibition of alcohol brought stills to the hills. The 1929 stock market crash swelled the state hospital with patients and caregivers. Federal programs brought well-known artists such as Arthur J. E. Powell, George Glenn Newell, and Harry F. Waltman to Dover, where they remained. In the late 1930s, New York City's photography club judged the Webatuck area the most beautiful in six counties. Next door, Hunt Country Furniture was getting started. After 1941, World War II demands encouraged the federal government to build a defense plant in Dover to extract magnesium from Dover's marble. The plant employed 200 men. As farming declined, the state hospital became the major employer, caring for up to 5,000 patients. In the 1960s, two area entrepreneurs built the Dover Drag Strip in Wingdale. WABC's own Cousin Bruce Morrow advertised "Sunday drag racing," just 72 miles north of the city. By then, a local Dover teacher had turned artist and created a metal sculpture titled *Wingdale*, which is mounted in the park opposite Lincoln Center in New York City.

Dover has touched the world through its history, its natural beauty, and its people. The town proudly celebrated America's birthday in 1976 and Dover's bicentennial in 2007. It is from that celebration that the foundation of this book emerged. Although major hamlets and neighborhoods survived to the present, others merged with nearby areas, while some live on in notoriety, tradition, or disappeared altogether. *Dover* chronicles the visual history of the town, highlighting new information about its people, places, and events. It celebrates over 300 years of history in Dover.

One

A Place Called Dover

Dover's 1637 legend of Pequot chief Sassacus told of his flight from Connecticut during the first Pequot War in New England. When the militia left, Sassacus and some of his band sought refuge from the Mohawk Tribe in the north. A second Pequot War sent Native Americans to New York's Schaghticoke sanctuary northeast of Albany. By 1702, the governor divided conference gifts between two Schaghticoke settlements. Locally, historians reported that Schaghticoke and Pequot in the valley of the Ten Mile River called their river Weebutook, or "Beautiful Hunting Ground."

Beginning in 1697, the governor patented Dutchess land eastward to Connecticut. Perhaps Richard Sackett, the first white settler in the area, thought the soaring eastern hillsides reminded him of the steep cliffs of Dover, England. Henry Beekman's 1703 patent predated Sackett's 1704 Washiack patent. Although Sackett identified himself as "of Dover," his claim fell to the political power of Beekman. By 1738, Beekman's children divided his land. The northeast sector went to daughter Catherine Pauling. In 1788, Dutchess County created Pauling Township, which contained Dover.

By 1728, hunting areas had dwindled. The Schaghticoke and Pequot followed Gideon Mauwee from the valley of the Weebutook "over the mountain." Today their descendants live on their mountainside reservation in Kent, Connecticut. Records show they lived on the mountain and continued their annual rounds through Dover well into the mid-1800s.

In 1731, an intercolonial conference settled the boundary issue. Connecticut kept the towns of Greenwich and Stamford. New York received a two-mile-wide strip along Connecticut's western border. Representatives signed the document in Dover on May 14, 1731. Thomas Hawley received a 63-mile-long patent for 50,000 acres the following day, and settlements soon followed. By the 1740s, squatters, thieves, and counterfeiters inhabited the mountain areas of the equivalent lands left out of the Hawley patent.

In South Dover, the Colonial highway called the Upper Road passed the Morehouse Tavern, where Gen. George Washington met with generals Benedict Arnold, Horatio Gates, the Marquis de LaFayette, and Israel Putnam as troops connected to other destinations. There also, America's first spy relayed Loyalist names and Tory plans.

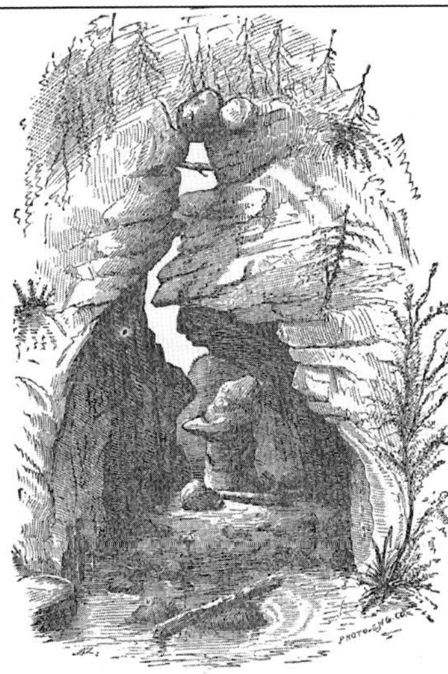

View of the Dover Stone Church.
(From the outside looking in.)

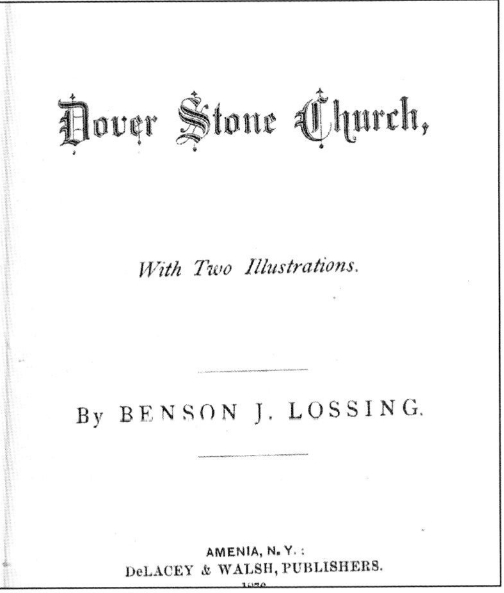

Dover Stone Church,

With Two Illustrations.

By BENSON J. LOSSING.

AMENIA, N. Y.:
DeLACEY & WALSH, PUBLISHERS.

In 1876, Dover's Benson Lossing authored a small pamphlet titled *Dover Stone Church*, emphasizing the holiness and the history of the site. Two engravings show contrasting views of the enchanting grotto. The first engraving, *From the Outside Looking In*, shows the cavern's arching, gothic, cathedral window–shaped entrance, pulpit rock, and rippling stream. Overhead, the narrow skylight lights the interior. The author explained the cavern's religious significance. (EH.)

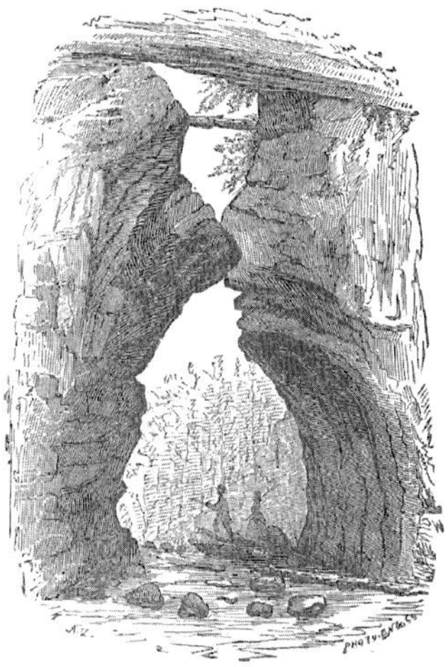

View of the Dover Stone Church.
(From the inside looking out.)

The second engraving, *From the Inside Looking Out*, reflects the site's Native American history and pays homage to the legend of Chief Sassacus. Lossing detailed how Sassacus and his followers found refuge in the Dover Stone Church in 1637. In the cavern entrance are two shadowy figures backlit by the sunlight from outside. Behind them are the rocks and greenery of the entrance way and gorge. Both engravings bear "PhotoEng.Co." (EH.)

Schaghticoke Tribe princess Eunice Mauwee was the granddaughter of the first Schaghticoke chief, Gideon Mauwee. In 1856, Lossing and a party of Moravian missionaries interviewed her on the Schaghticoke Reservation. She often visited and stayed at the Lossing farm on Chestnut Ridge in Dover, and she often told stories of the Schaghticoke during her rounds throughout the valley. Eunice and other Schaghticoke sold handmade white-ash baskets to supplement their income. (Schaghticoke Tribal Nation.)

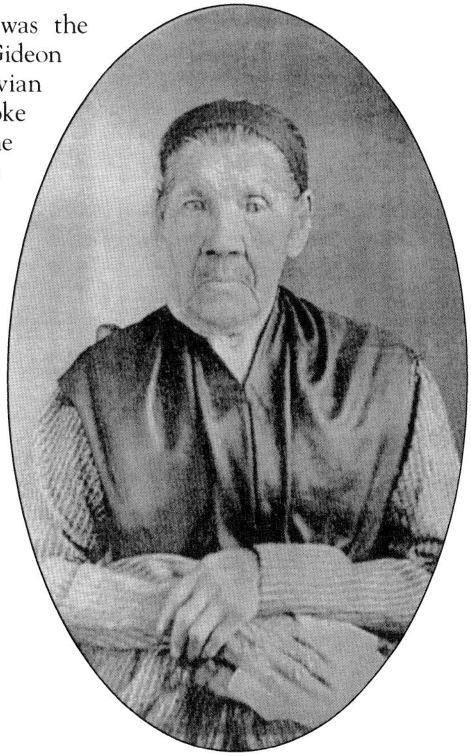

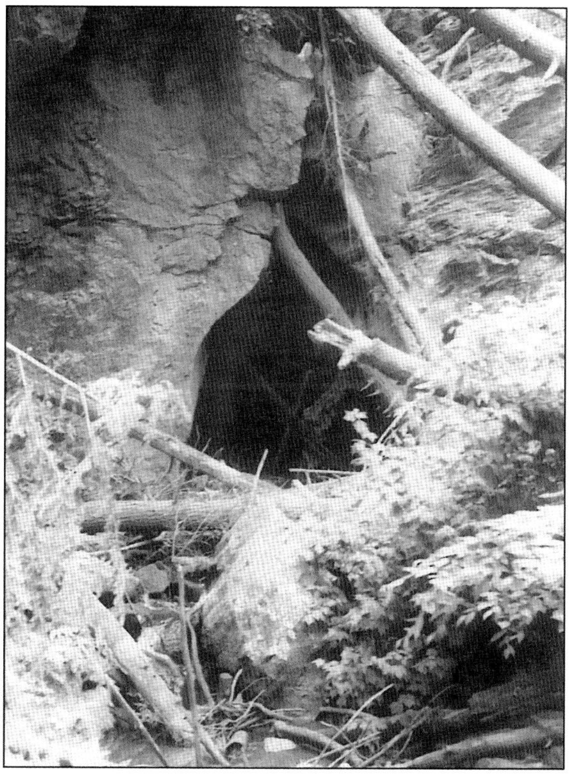

In 1997, author Donna P. Hearn took tribal council members and Schaghticoke elders Paulette Crone-Morange and Toni Hoffmann and Schaghticoke archaeologist Dr. Lucianne Lavin to the Dover Stone Church. Overgrown and strewn with brush and dead hemlocks, the ravine and stream area were a tangle. Inside the cavern though, sunlight still danced on water and reflected off the walls just as it had some three centuries earlier. (LL.)

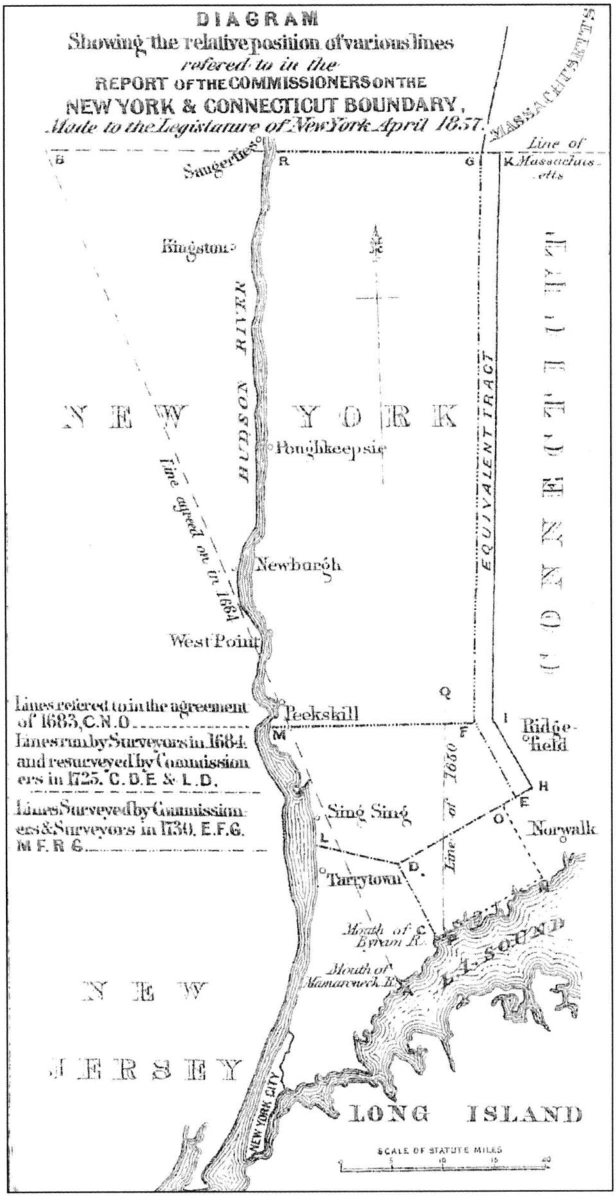

In 1855, the first major boundary dispute since 1731 erupted between Connecticut and New York when Connecticut found that the boundary line was crooked. Commissioners were appointed in New York, and they met with the representatives of Connecticut. Despite several attempts, no solutions evolved, and the dispute grew over the next two years. New York, in an attempt to have its legislators understand the historic issues, created this map to show the equivalent lands surveyed and set off for Connecticut in 1683 along with the several lines of agreement. Connecticut disregarded the 1650 line agreement and continued to settle in Dutch territory to the west. The 1664 line mapped by Connecticut did not conform to the agreement, and New York refused to sanction it. The 1683 line was agreed upon and confirmed by the king in 1700, but the parallel lines required in the 1731 survey were recently found to be crooked. As the agreement language ran the line through the bounds, and both states signed the agreement, New York felt Connecticut's desire for a new survey was unjustified. (DPH.)

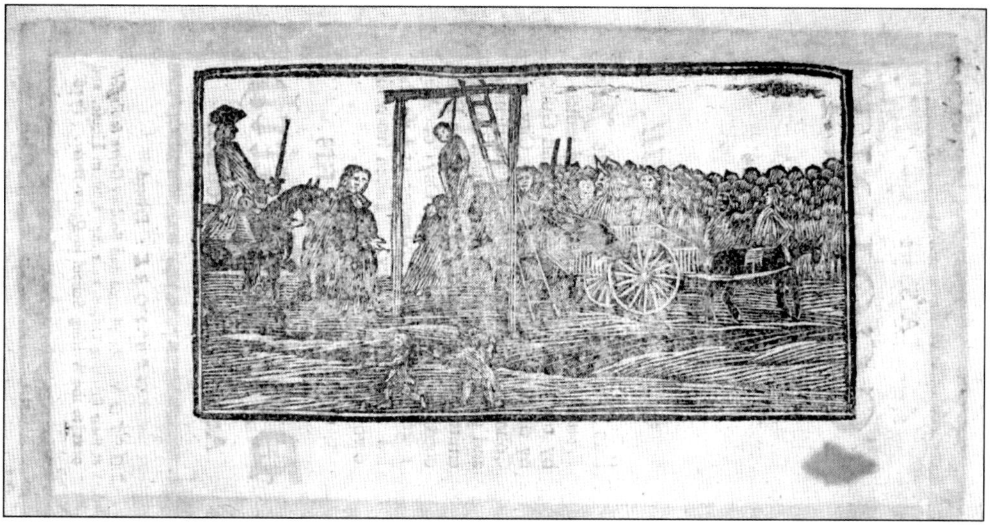

Author Kenneth Scott documented Owen Sullivan as leader of the Dover Money Club, a Colonial-era counterfeiting gang. The villains operated in the Oblong and counterfeited bills of credit for the northern American colonies. Convicted for counterfeiting in New York, Sullivan was hung New York City. William Jones created this woodcut image of the hanging of the counterfeiter on May 10, 1756, as part of Sullivan's life story. (American Antiquarian Society.)

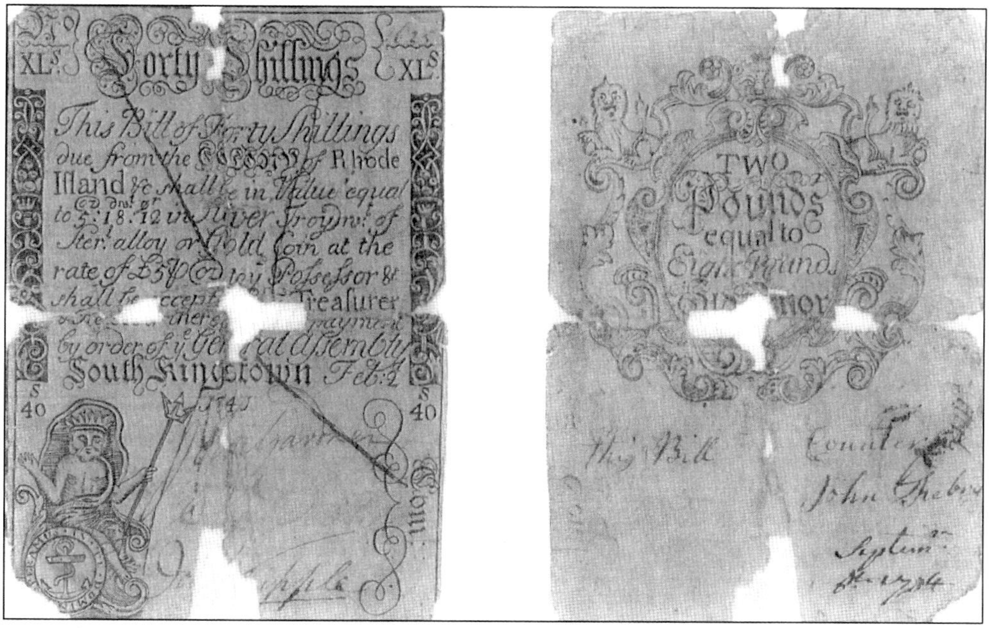

From the safety of the New York Oblong lands, the Dover Money Club counterfeited money from Connecticut, Massachusetts, New York, and Rhode Island. Joseph Steel of Beekman's precinct was associated with the Dover Money Club. At his August 1756 trial in Litchfield, Connecticut, Steel admitted passing this counterfeit 40-shilling note from Rhode Island to the wife of Benjamin Gaylord of New Milford. (Connecticut Historical Society.)

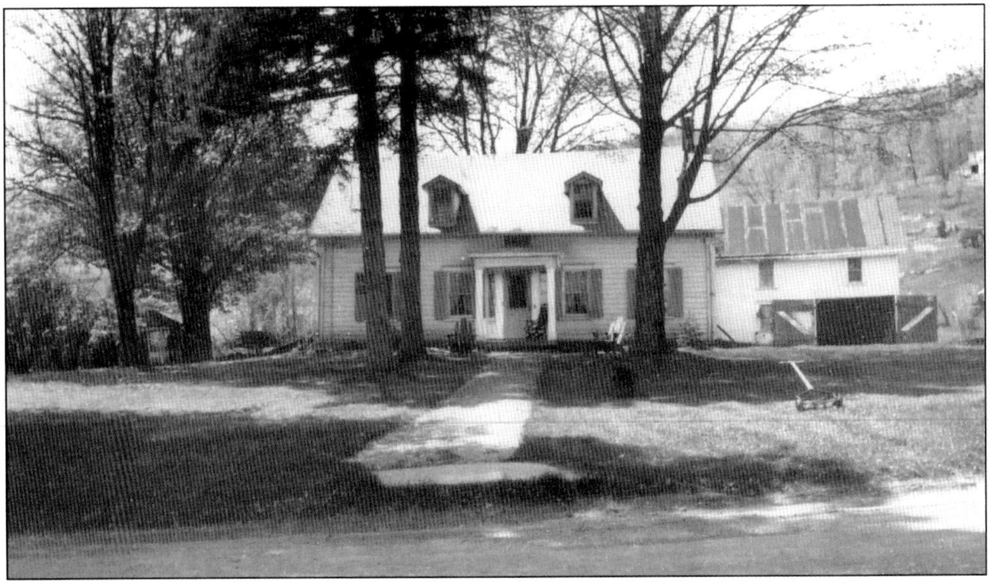

In the 1750s, a tenant family in the eastern Beekman patent built a home and, according to Caroline Rogers Reichenberg, the Dutchers carved their name into the doorway frame. This early home, built at the foot of Plymouth Hill, was noted by local historians. Shown in 1958, Benjamin Duncan's house was demolished in the 1980s for a Cumberland Farms, which now occupies the site. (HWH.)

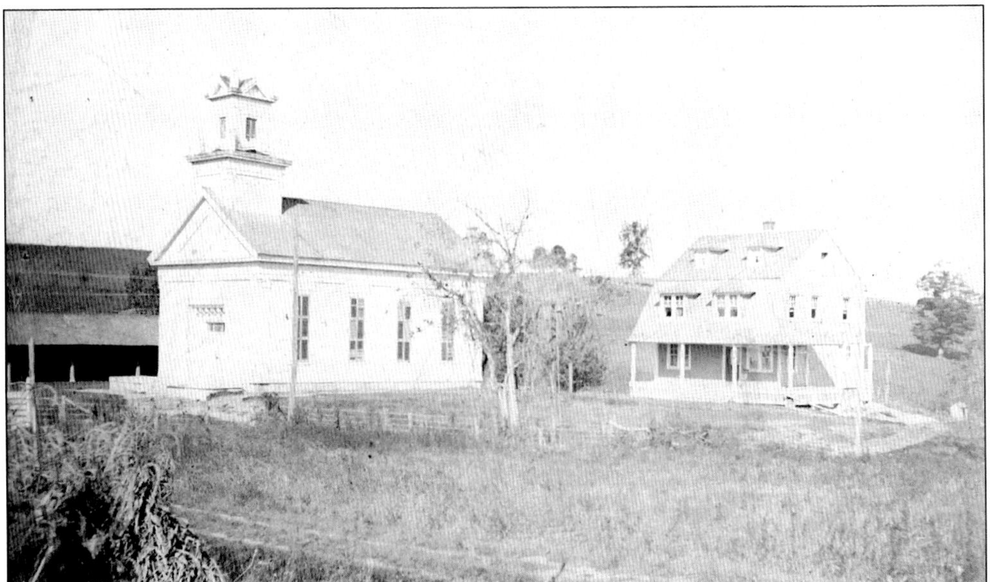

The area's first place of worship was the Dover First Baptist Church, built on the grounds of the South Dover Rural Cemetery in 1757. The present church was built in 1855 and the parsonage in 1898. In 1909, the building was painted and repaired in preparation for a state convention on Baptist church needs. The entrance was redesigned when Route 55 was upgraded in the late 1950s. The church is currently celebrating its 250th anniversary. (DRH.)

In 1761, the Province of New York assessed the lots in the Oblong for King George III's quitrent tax. The assessment list for Oblong No. 3 to No. 44 shows Wing Kelley listed under "Owners, Freeholders & Proprs [Proprietors] Names." Kelley was assessed for 4£ 9s. for his 100 acres of the 250 acres of lot 41. Nearby neighbors included Zebulon Ross, Mattius Mash, John Wing, David Preston, and Benjamin Pierce. (Quaker Hill Historical Society.)

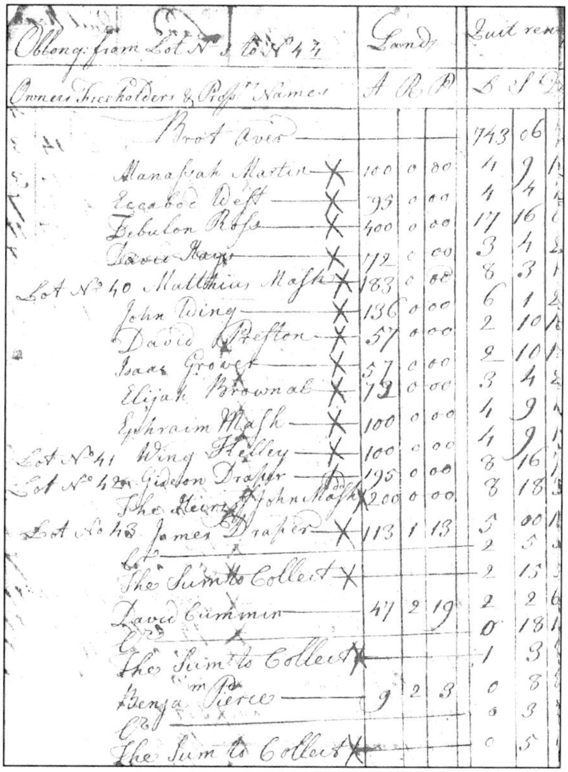

Oblong: from Lot No 3 to No 44

	Owners Freeholders & Proprs Names	Lands A	R	P	Quit rent £	S
	Brot over				743	06
	Manassah Martin	100	0	00	4	9
	Eccabod West	95	0	00	4	4
	Zebulon Ross	400	0	00	17	16
	[illegible]	72	0	00	3	4
Lot No 40	Matthias Mash	183	0	00	8	3
	John Wing	136	0	00	6	1
	David Preston	57	0	00	2	10
	Isaac Grover	57	0	00	2	10
	Elijah Brownal	72	0	00	3	4
	Ephraim Mash	100	0	00	4	9
Lot No 41	Wing Kelley	100	0	00	4	9
Lot No 42	Gideon Draper	195	0	00	8	16
	The Heirs of John Mash	200	0	00	8	18
Lot No 43	James Draper	113	1	13	5	00
	Cr				2	5
	The Sum to Collect				2	15
	David Cummin	47	2	19	2	2
	Cr				0	18
	The Sum to Collect				1	3
	Benja Pierce	9	2	3	0	8
	Cr				0	3
	The Sum to Collect				0	5

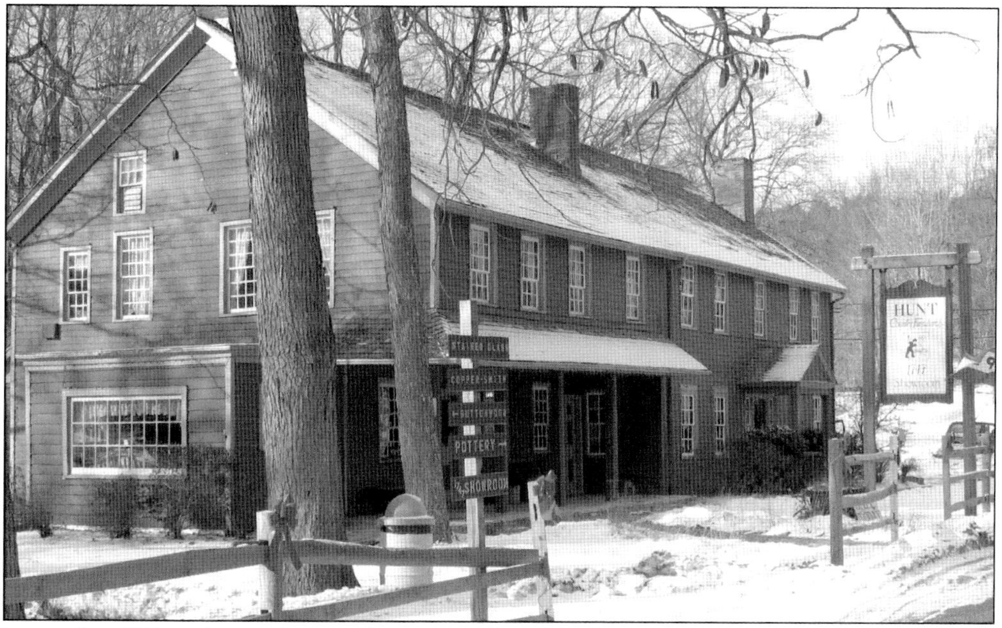

Located in Oblong lot 41, the parcel was owned by Hawley patentee and attorney William Smith in 1731. By 1761, Wing Kelley owned the land and eventually operated a mill on the Ten Mile River. The house was constructed with massive, hand-hewn beams and wide plank floors. In 1924, when the Hunt family moved to Wingdale from Pelham, the Preston family had owned the building for decades. (DPH.)

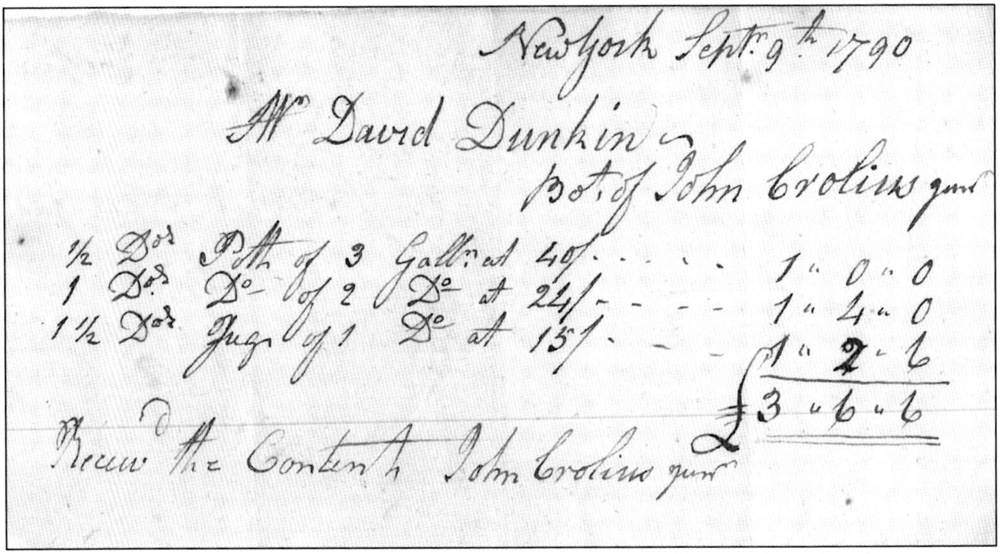

New York Septr 9th 1790

Mr David Dunkin

Bot. of John Crolius junr

½ Dos Potts of 3 Gallns at 40/ . . . . 1 " 0 " 0

1 Dos Do of 2 Do at 24/ - - - - 1 " 4 " 0

1½ Dos Jugs of 1 Do at 15/ - - - 1 " 2 " 6

£3 " 6 " 6

Recd the Contents John Crolius junr

On September 9, 1790, John Crolius received payment on a note by David Dunkin for numerous "potts" and jugs costing £3 6s. 6d. Five years later, Dunkin raced Ebenezer Preston to Rhinebeck to purchase property near Dover Furnace from Frederick DePeyster. Dunkin had the faster horse, bought the land, and built his store near Swamp River. The Dunkin Store area near Dover's town hall is named Dunkin Hill. (TDHS.)

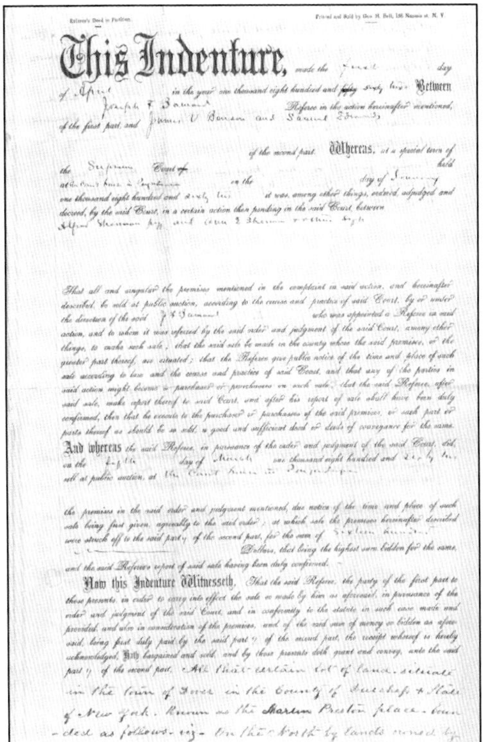

Referee's Deed in Partition. Printed and Sold by Geo. H. Bell, 136 Nassau st. N. Y.

This Indenture, made the day of April in the year one thousand eight hundred and sixty Between Joseph F. Barnard Referee in the action hereinafter mentioned, of the first part, and James V. Benson and Samuel Edmonds, of the second part. Whereas, at a special term of the Supreme Court held at the Court house in Poughkeepsie on the day of January one thousand eight hundred and sixty it was, among other things, ordered, adjudged and decreed, by the said Court, in a certain action then pending in the said Court between

That all and singular the premises mentioned in the complaint in said action, and hereinafter described, be sold at public auction, according to the course and practice of said Court, by or under the direction of the said J. F. Barnard who was appointed a Referee in said action, and to whom it was referred by the said order and judgment of the said Court, among other things, to make such sale; that the said sale be made in the county where the said premises, or the greater part thereof, are situated; that the Referee give public notice of the time and place of such sale according to law and the course and practice of said Court, and that any of the parties in said action might become a purchaser or purchasers on such sale; that the said Referee, after said sale, make report thereof to said Court, and after his report of sale shall have been duly confirmed, then that he execute to the purchaser or purchasers of the said premises, or such part or parts thereof as should be so sold, a good and sufficient deed or deeds of conveyance for the same.

And whereas the said Referee, in pursuance of the order and judgment of the said Court, did, on the day of March one thousand eight hundred and sixty sell at public auction, at the Court house in Poughkeepsie

the premises in the said order and judgment mentioned, due notice of the time and place of such sale being first given, agreeably to the said order; at which sale the premises hereinafter described were struck off to the said party of the second part, for the sum of Sixteen hundred Dollars, that being the highest sum bidden for the same, and the said Referee's report of said sale having been duly confirmed.

Now this Indenture Witnesseth, That the said Referee, the party of the first part to these presents, in order to carry into effect the sale so made by him as aforesaid, in pursuance of the order and judgment of the said Court, and in conformity to the statute in such case made and provided, and also in consideration of the premises, and of the said sum of money so bidden as aforesaid, being first duly paid by the said party of the second part, the receipt whereof is hereby acknowledged, Hath bargained and sold, and by these presents doth grant and convey, unto the said party of the second part, All that certain lot of land situate in the town of Dover in the County of Dutchess & State of New York. Known as the Martin Preston place. bounded as follows viz. On the North by lands owned by

In 1786, Martin Preston and 43 others claimed vacant land in the Oblong in Paulings precinct. Jonathan Akins sought 2,500 acres of Schaghticoke Mountain in 1792. In an 1862 tax sale, land "known as the Martin Preston place" was sold to James V. Benson and Samuel Edmonds. Today stone walls and old deeds narrate the past or remember "the ledge where the bear jumped off." (CDS.)

Two

Dover Township in 1807

As farming, mills, and industry increased, population increased in Pawling Township, which was created in 1788. The town of Dover was erected out of Pawling in 1807. The new town was entitled to half the accumulated taxes and half the debt. The first school in Dover was established on East Mountain in 1820. By 1824, 16 district schools were located in and around Dover Furnace, Webatuck, Deuel Hollow, the Band Box, Chestnut Ridge, Hoag's Corners, Dover Plains, and Wingdale. In 1834, a group of private citizens from Dover, Amenia, and Pawling chartered the Dover Academy, an institution for learning for young men and women. About that time, Ammi Phillips, a traveling artist, came to Dover and painted James and Lois Ketcham. In the valley, farming was the mainstay, but cattle drovers and stagecoach traffic to and from Vermont and New York City provided profits for innkeepers, blacksmiths, millers, and others. As iron demands increased, mountain woodlots disappeared as colliers cut and coaled charcoal for the furnaces. Old-timers told of valley walls that glowed red at night from the charcoal kilns. East Mountain residents who were struggling often sold their land and moved to the valley. The railroad arrived as workers built track beds and laid tracks from Pawling through swamp, arriving in Dover Plains in 1849. The New York Central Railroad, Harlem Division provided a modern transportation route and business for new hotels. Although traffic from the drovers ceased, the farmers and the dairy industry expanded with new markets in the city, a short two hours away. One visitor, Asher Brown Durand, saw a breathtaking pastoral scene and painted it. He also sketched the nearby Dover Stone Church, which became a tourist attraction by 1840.

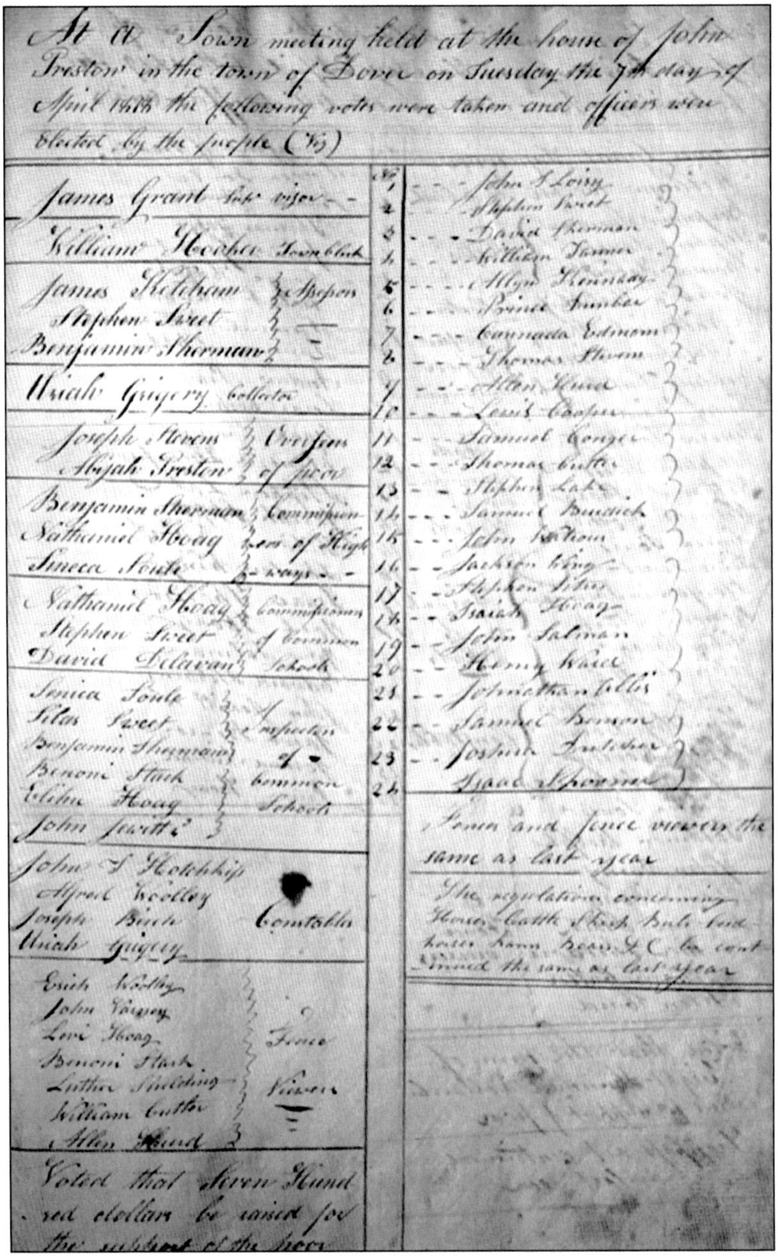

On April 20, 1807, legislation separated Dover from Pawling. New York State mandated the first Dover town meeting be held at the home of John Preston, now known as the Old Drovers Inn. For a century, Old Drovers Inn remained caretaker of the original leather-bound town meeting ledger. Around 1990, the inn had the ledger conserved by experts. Kemper Peacock and Alice Pitcher also had a transcription made. In the Old Drovers Inn library, guests viewed and gently turned the pages, marveling at the feel of the paper, the script, content, job titles, and especially the low costs of doing business in those days. At the 2007 bicentennial opening ceremony, innkeeper David Wilson officially turned the book over to the Town of Dover. The meeting minutes relate yearly town meeting resolutions, elected and appointed officials, oaths of office, road courses, budget information, and even an 1807 list of ear-crop markings. (BR.)

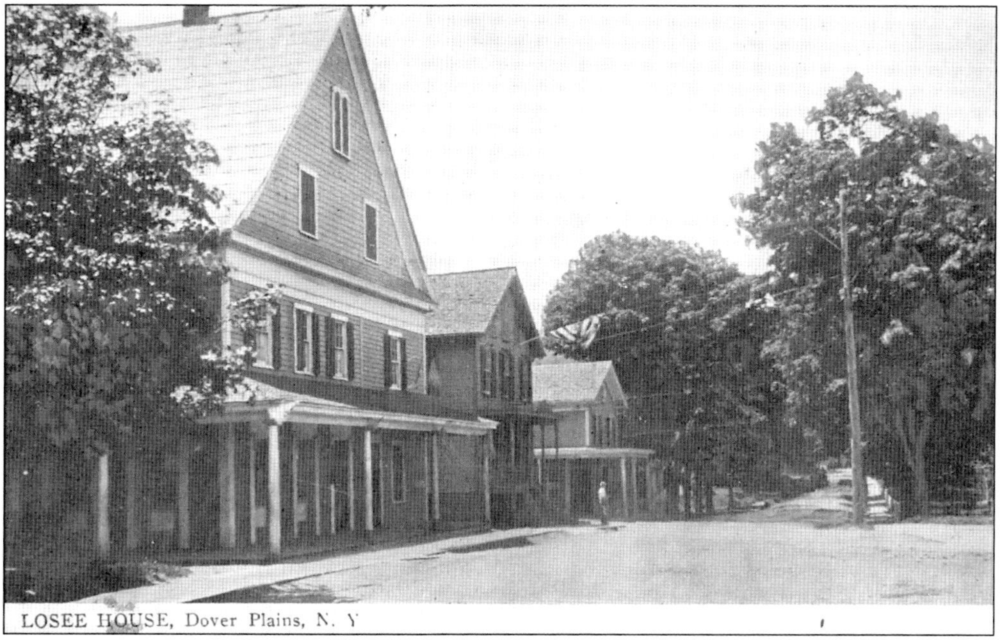

This 1913 postcard shows the Losee House built by George Robson in 1848 for the Preston family. Later George H. Losee purchased and ran the hotel. By 1908, his heirs owned the building. A pizza parlor operated in the building in the 1960s, and in 1972, Tony Robert had his barbershop there when Frank Vinchiarello operated Ye Olde Dover Tavern. Restaurant chef Delfa Nelli's French American menu had a large following. (GH.)

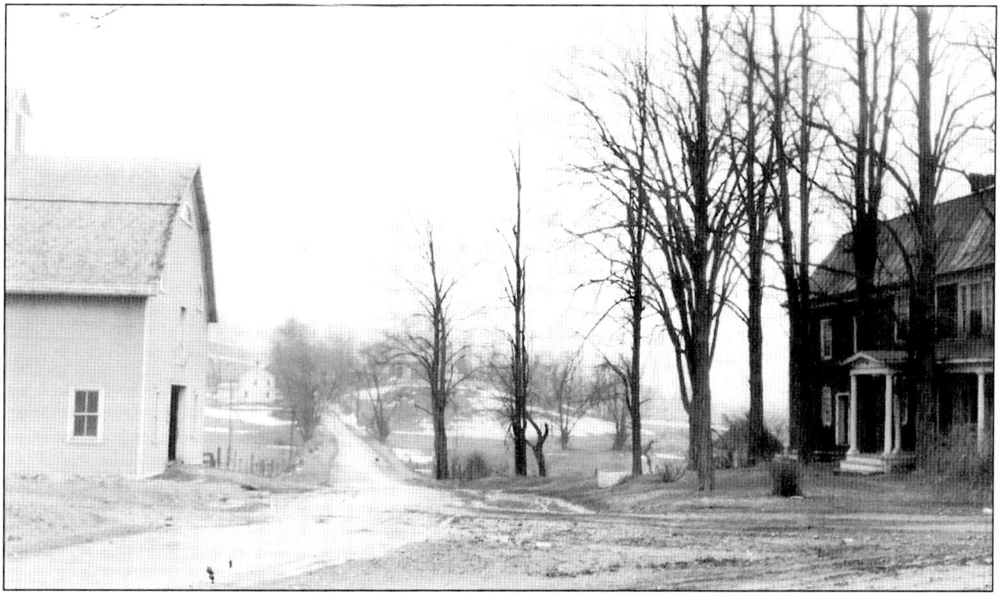

Jackson Wing's inn was built about 1800. "The great road from Albany and Vermont" passed between Wing's inn and his carriage barn and continued south to New York City. The road on the right was part of the Upper Road traveled by George Washington from Hartford to Fishkill. Dutchess County supervisors created the road in 1730 to run from Dover to Poeghquayeck. Richard Sackett Jr. was chosen as the tax collector. (TDHS.)

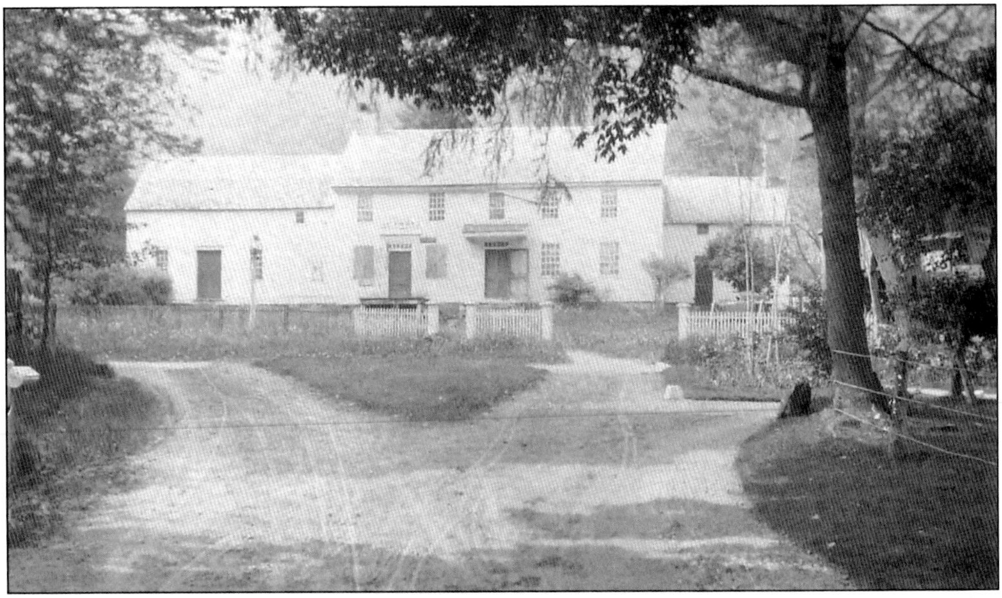

Nellie Townsend's picture shows the Titus house and store, located south of Webatuck Road at Dog Tail Corners. A store operated there from the early 1800s. In 1908, Joseph Titus operated the store and bakery. Ledgers from 1807 show prices and purchases by local residents and occasional Schaghticoke Indians. When business ceased, the building remained stocked with rusting cans, crumbling cloth, and cobwebs. Today it is Mountain View Apartments. (TDHS.)

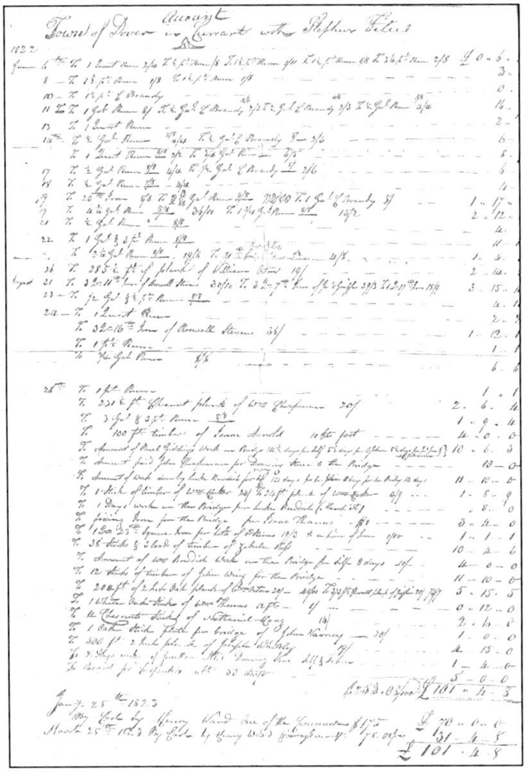

Town of Dover Account Current with Stephen Titus

In 1822, the Town of Dover undertook bridge building over the Ten Mile River at Dog Tail Corners. From June 6 to January 25, 1823, Isaac Thomas, Zebulon Ross, John Wing, William Orton, Nathaniel Hoag, and others drew stone to the riverbank, cut timber, laid planking, and drank rum. On March 23, 1823, Stephen Titus collected $253.08 for the bridge costs from the highway commissioners. (PH, AL.)

According to his 1832 pension deposition, Enoch Crosby recounted his Revolutionary War exploits as America's first spy. He met with Tory sympathizers, including Doctor Prosser of Pawling. Crosby told Col. Andrew Morehouse of South Dover, who captured the Tories. James Fenimore Cooper immortalized Crosby as Harvey Birch in *The Spy*. This sketch, done by H. L. Barnum from life, appears in Benson Lossing's *Field Book of the American Revolution*. (CRR.)

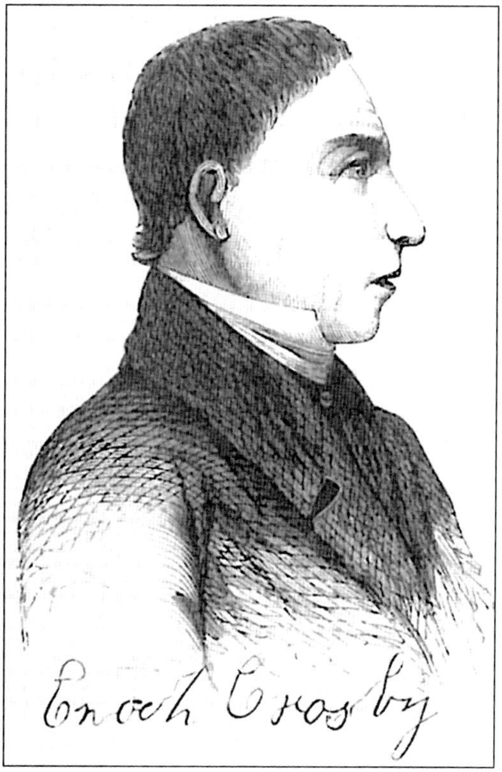

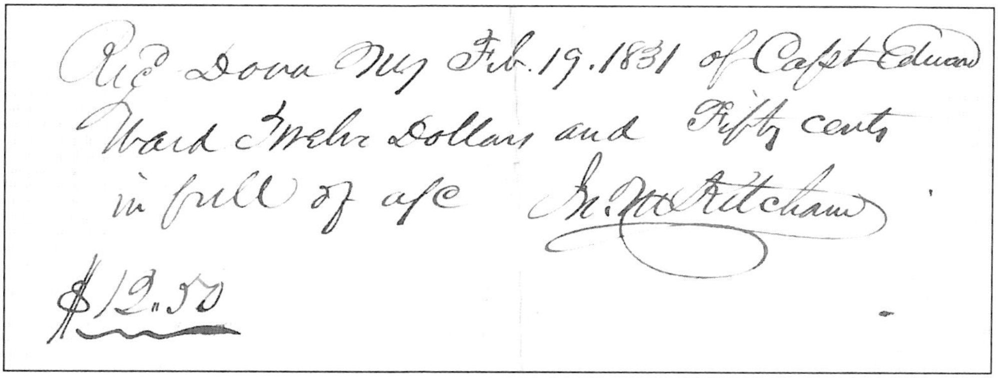

Rec'd Dover NY Feb. 19. 1831 of Capt Edward
Ward Twelve Dollars and Fifty cents
in full of a/c Jn. W. Ketcham

$12.50

James Ketcham clerked in a Dover Plains store previously owned by Lois Belding's father. Ketcham and Belding were married in 1797. He became a member of the Lawrence Belding and Company, which bought Luther Holley's house and store. Ketcham was Dover's first town clerk and later served as supervisor. In 1831, he collected a note from Capt. Edward Ward for $12.50. The Ketchams' grandson was Congressman John Henry Ketcham. (TDHS.)

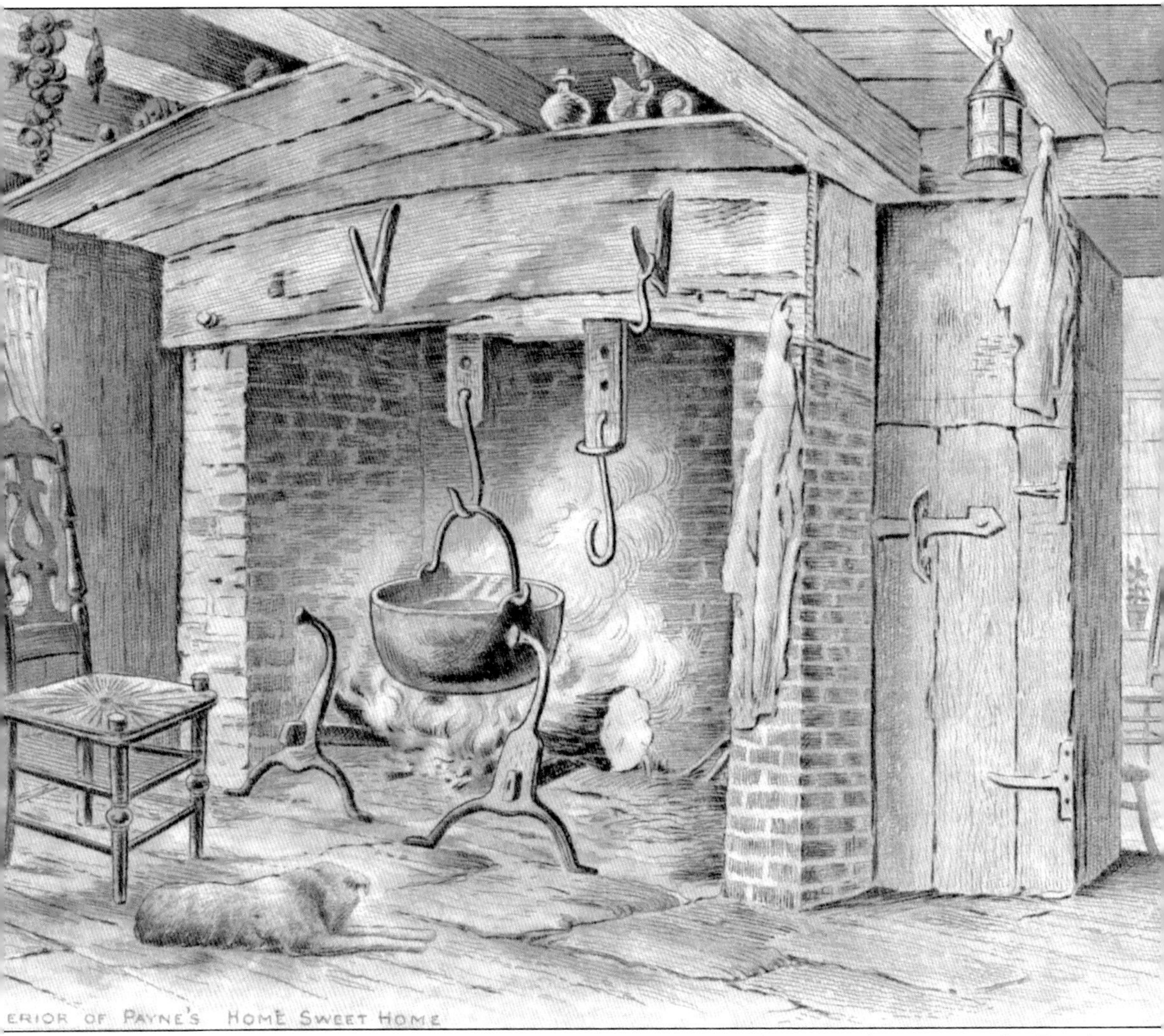

In the 1940s, Robert V. Humeston did carpentry work in Faith Payne's home on Ridge Road in Dover Furnace. Payne created a unique Christmas card for him in return. Today the thick, embossed card has faded to ivory. Payne's firelight scene illustrates rough-hewn rafters, walls, and plank floors. Simple curtains adorn snowy windowpanes. The large, handmade, brick fireplace holds a gently simmering cast-iron pot hung over crackling logs. Dried mushrooms and a lantern hang nearby. The simple closet door hangs from handmade latches and uses an old-fashioned latch. A caned chair before the fire beckons, and the snoozing dog completes the inviting scene from her 1800s home sweet home. (RVH.)

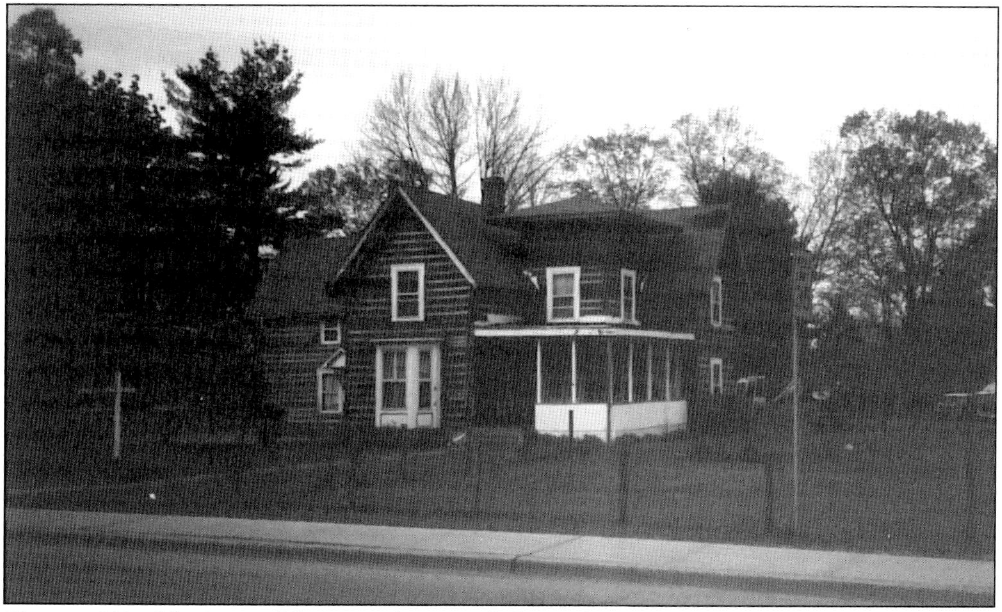

Chapter 263 of the *Laws of the State of New York* shows that on May 9, 1835, the Dover Academy was incorporated for the purpose of establishing, maintaining, and conducting a seminary of learning for the education of both sexes. Trustees from Dover, Amenia, and Pawling were empowered to purchase a school, elect faculty, and prescribe the course of study. The Dover Academy, known as Bangs Academy, was on Main Street in Dover. (WAV.)

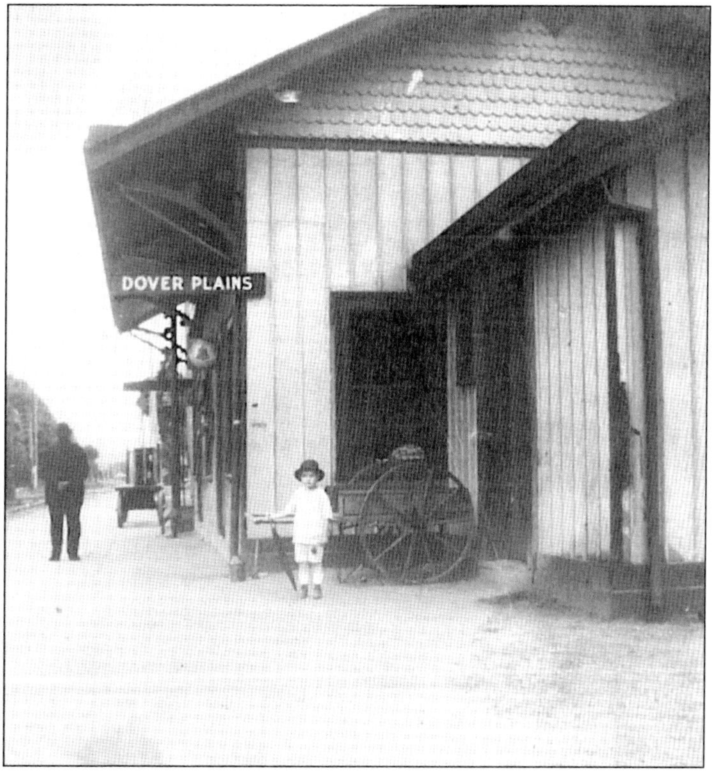

The Dover Plains railroad station was usually a busy place. This image from about 1900 captures a quiet moment at the station as a man in a suit and derby waits for the next train. Near the doors to the waiting room, a solemn little girl stands holding her umbrella against a loaded pushcart from the station, awaiting her train. (MFD.)

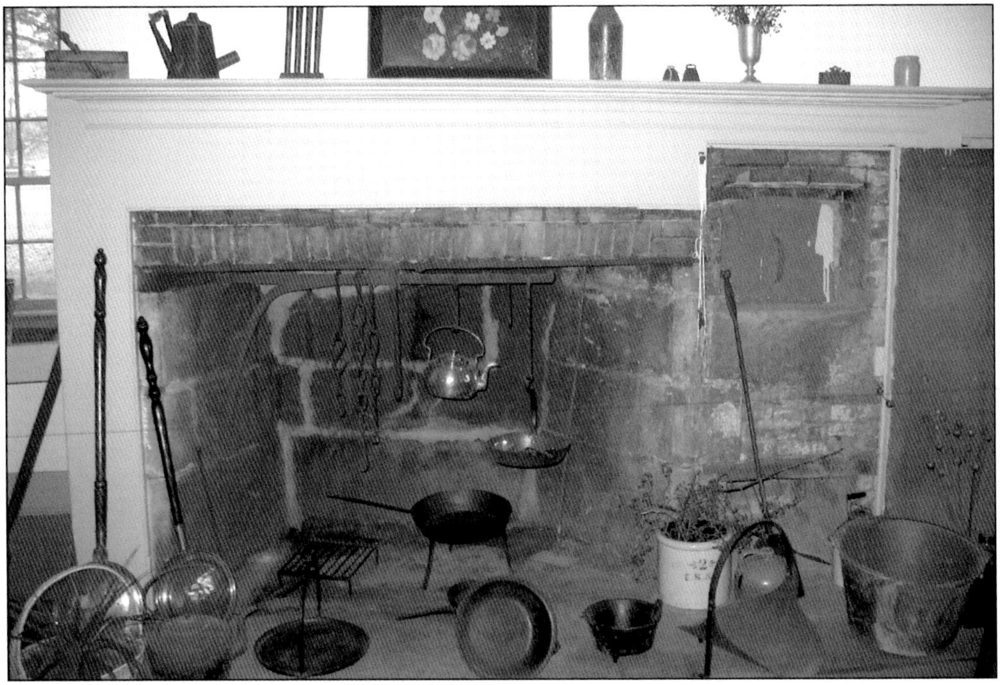

This kitchen is in the Tabor Wing House, built about 1810 for Thomas Tabor by Mahlon Wing. When Mahlon later married Thomas's daughter, Sally, it became their home. Iola Wing Crane sold it to Frank and Mae Connell. The Town of Dover Historical Society purchased the house in 1976. It donated the landmark to the town in 2004. Today the historical society maintains a museum in the kitchen. (DPH.)

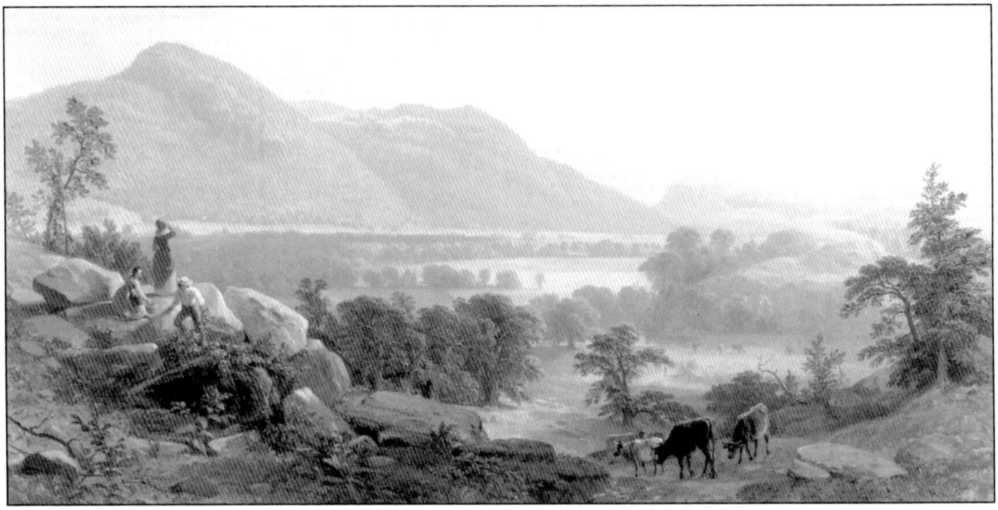

Dover drew artists, tourists, and intellectuals who found inspiration in the natural harmony of the landscape. Asher Brown Durand came to Dover in 1846 and in 1848, painting two landscapes in Dover and sketching the nearby Dover Stone Church. Today *Dover Plains, Dutchess County, NY* is a landmark painting in the Smithsonian American Art Museum. This western view across the valley below Dover Plains looks much the same today. (Smithsonian American Art Museum, gift of Thomas M. Evans and museum purchase through the Smithsonian Institution Collections Acquisition Program.)

Three

The Civil War and Beyond

The area prospered after the railroad went through, continuing eventually to Chatham. Local farms shipped produce and milk to New York City on a daily basis. Farms eventually sent their milk to processing plants like the Borden Condensed Milk Company, which supplied Union troops in the war.

In 1849, Theodore Timby journeyed to New York and saw the circular battlements of Castle William on Governors Island. He thought the cannons would be more effective if the fort rotated on an axis. The 19 year old returned home, drew up a series of plans, and submitted them to the patent office, obtaining a caveat on any patent for a revolving turret until he had finished his design. Timby's Revolving Tower patent was granted in 1862 and was used by John Ericsson on the *Monitor* warship. Timby's concept revolutionized armaments warfare since the ship itself no longer needed to turn to aim the stationary cannons. Inside the ironclad "cheesebox," two men with two cannons could maneuver and aim in any direction, maintaining a constant stream of fire and competing just as effectively.

John Henry Ketcham was a supervisor, legislator, assemblyman, and senator from New York. He organized, outfitted, and commanded the 150th New York State Volunteer Infantry Regiment. He was wounded at Gettysburg and eventually resigned his commission as a major general but attended the return of his men at the railroad station in Poughkeepsie. Nominated and elected to Congress, he served for 17 terms. He only suffered one defeat and spent that time as a commissioner of the District of Columbia, where he helped carry out plans designed by Pierre Charles L'Enfant. Benson Lossing was a friend of Ketcham's. The noted historian lived on Chestnut Ridge and authored over 40 books that chronicled world and national histories, two major wars, and biographies based on personal interviews with and thumbnail sketches of such notables as Abraham Lincoln, various cabinet members, foreign dignitaries, and the actor John Wilkes Booth.

During and after the war, medical knowledge increased and new remedies became advertised and available. Formerly a store owner, Theodore Wing created medicinals from receipts passed down through his family. He manufactured his Wing's Cough and Lung Specific and an ointment.

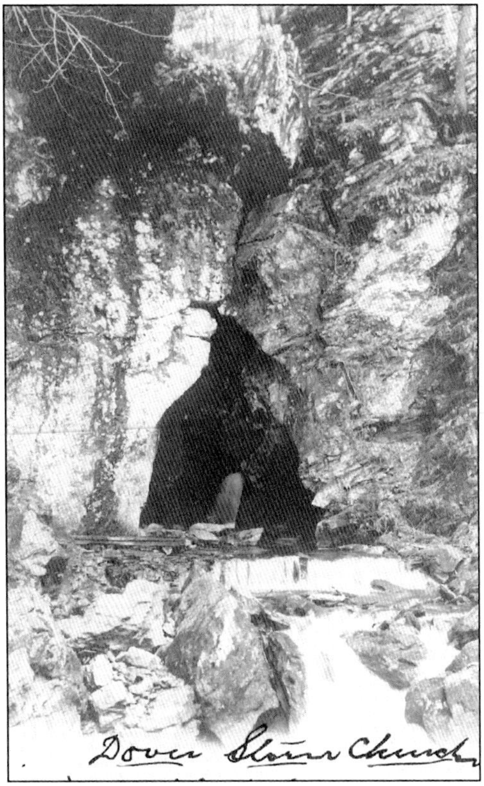

This photograph shows a small wooden boardwalk leading into the cavern. The main laneway, bordered by Norway maples, was destroyed by 1970s soil mining. Today a state-recognized collaboration among Friends of the Dover Stone Church, Town of Dover, Dutchess County, Dutchess Land Conservancy, and a cooperative property owner will use a state grant to re-create the laneway to the Dover Stone Church, the town's newest park. (CD.)

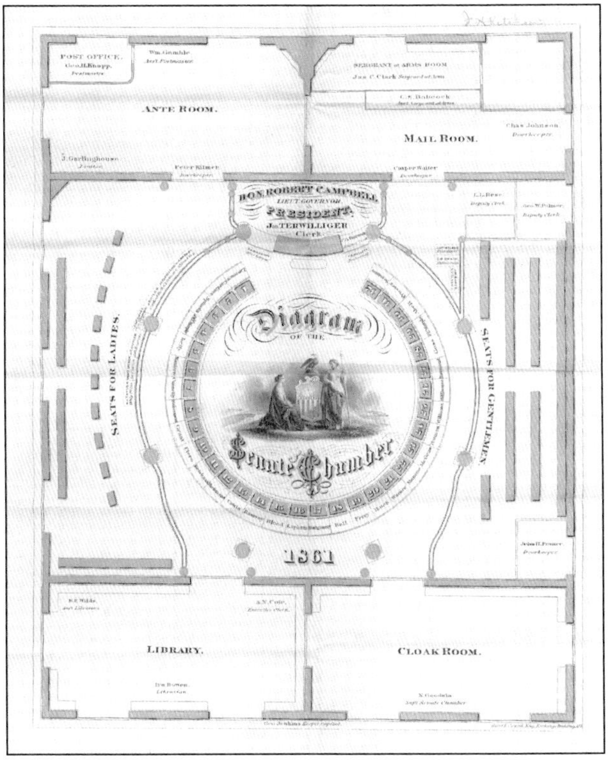

In 1861, John Henry Ketcham was a New York State senator representing the 11th district. The senate chamber diagram shows delegate seating arrangements. From the center of the floor, Ketcham's seat was located toward the lower left in seat 11. This diagram was sent to former town historian Doris Dedrick by the Franklin Delano Roosevelt Library staff with a note saying the document belonged in the Dover archives. (TDHS.)

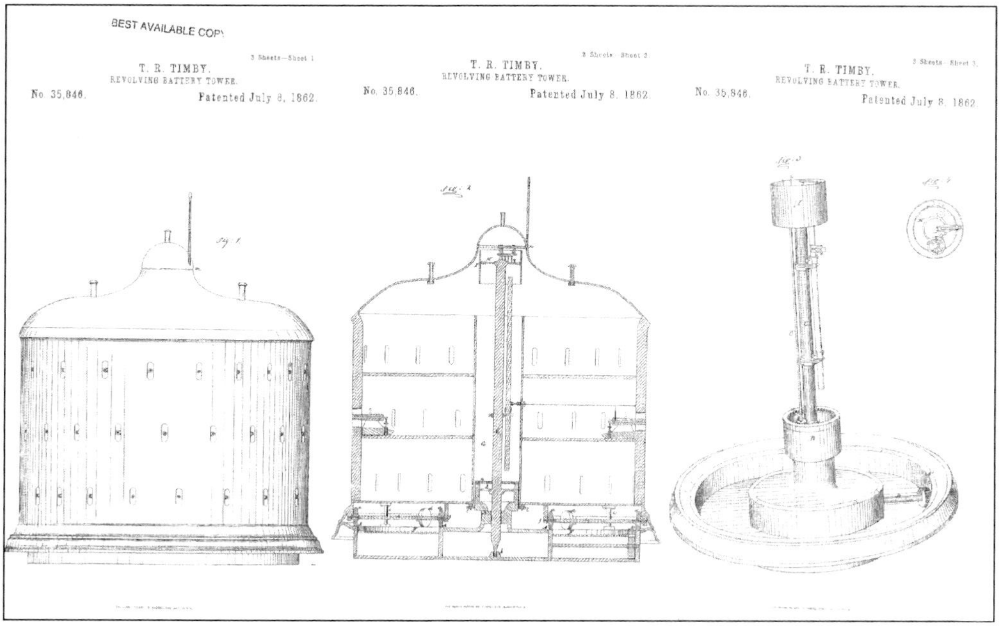

Theodore Timby's Revolving Tower patent No. 35,846 was granted in 1862. It was a commander's platform with two guns revolving within the tower independent of the ship's position. At age 19, Timby had seen Castle William in New York Harbor and thought the round fortress could rotate on an axis. During a time when many guns equaled more power, the two-gun system revolutionized warfare and made wooden ships and navies instantly obsolete. (DPH.)

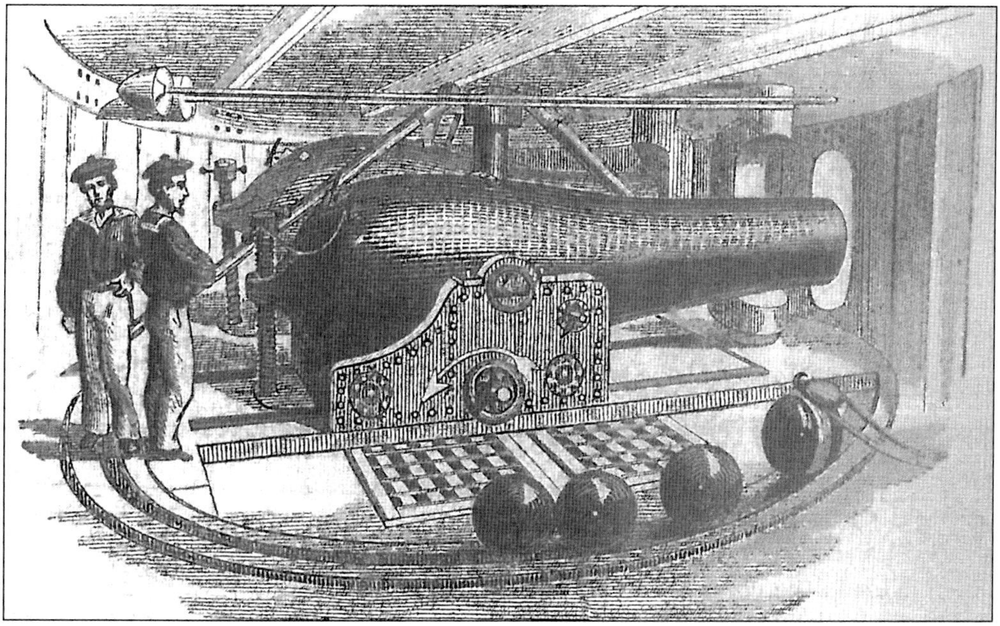

Benson J. Lossing sketched the cannon assembly inside the *Monitor*'s turret. From above, a spotter called distance and direction. Sailors maneuvered the cannon elevations at the fulcrum near the arrow marking. They aimed using compass markings inscribed like molding near the turret top. Cannonballs rolled down a chute for loading. Two sailors could change elevations and rotate the cannon 360 degrees to fire at any enemy vessel with consistent, accurate aim. (DPH.)

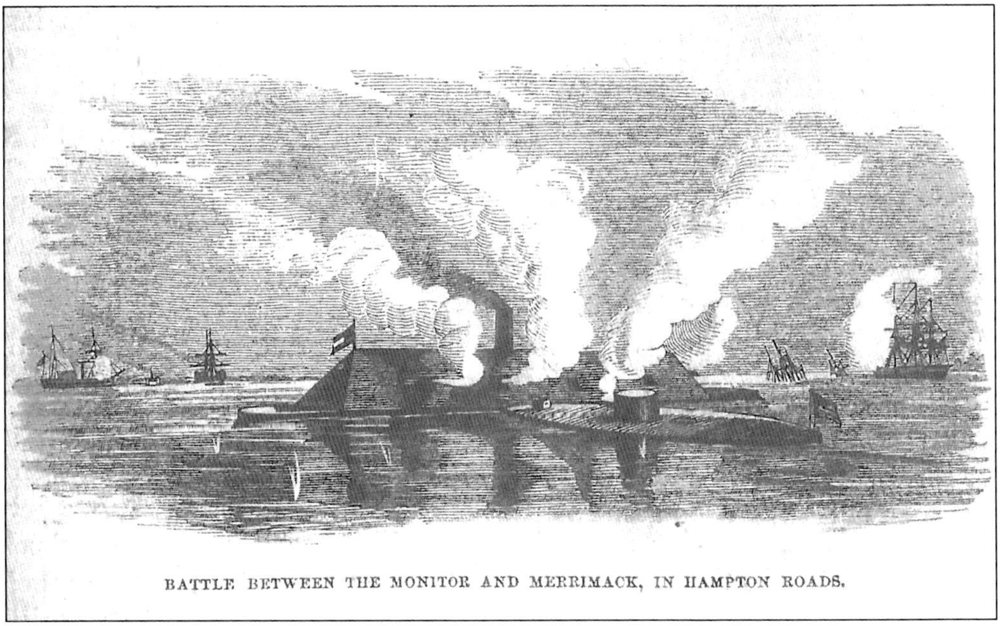

Frank Leslie's etching from the *Famous Leaders and Battle Scenes of the Civil War* shows the battle between the Civil War ironclads the *Monitor* and the *Merrimac* at Hampton Roads in March 1863. The battle was a draw, but cannons in the revolving turret, called the "cheesebox," easily took aim and fired on the *Merrimac* from every angle. (DPH.)

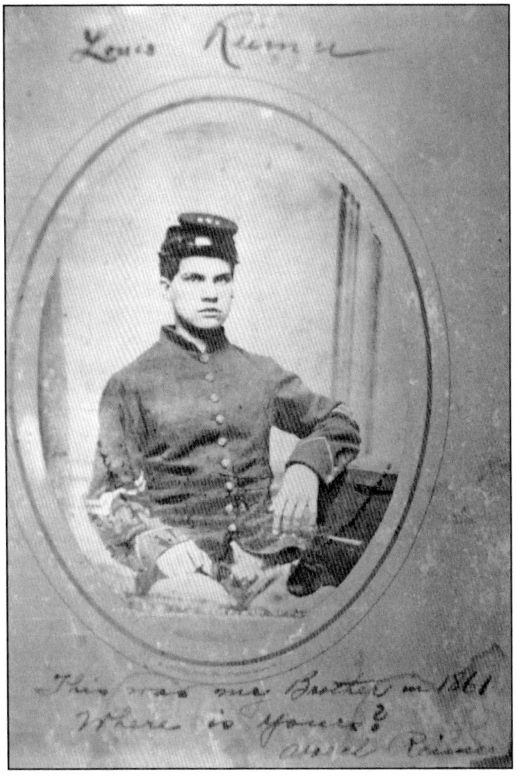

Louis Reimer was born in 1848. Underage when the Civil War began, he enlisted in Company D of the 178th New York Volunteers as August Boris, a drummer boy. This solemn 1861 image shows him in uniform with his drum, forever young at age 13. On February 15, 1864, he was captured at Meridian, Mississippi. Taken to Andersonville Prison, he died on August 21, 1864, and was buried in grave 6371. (WAR, RTR.)

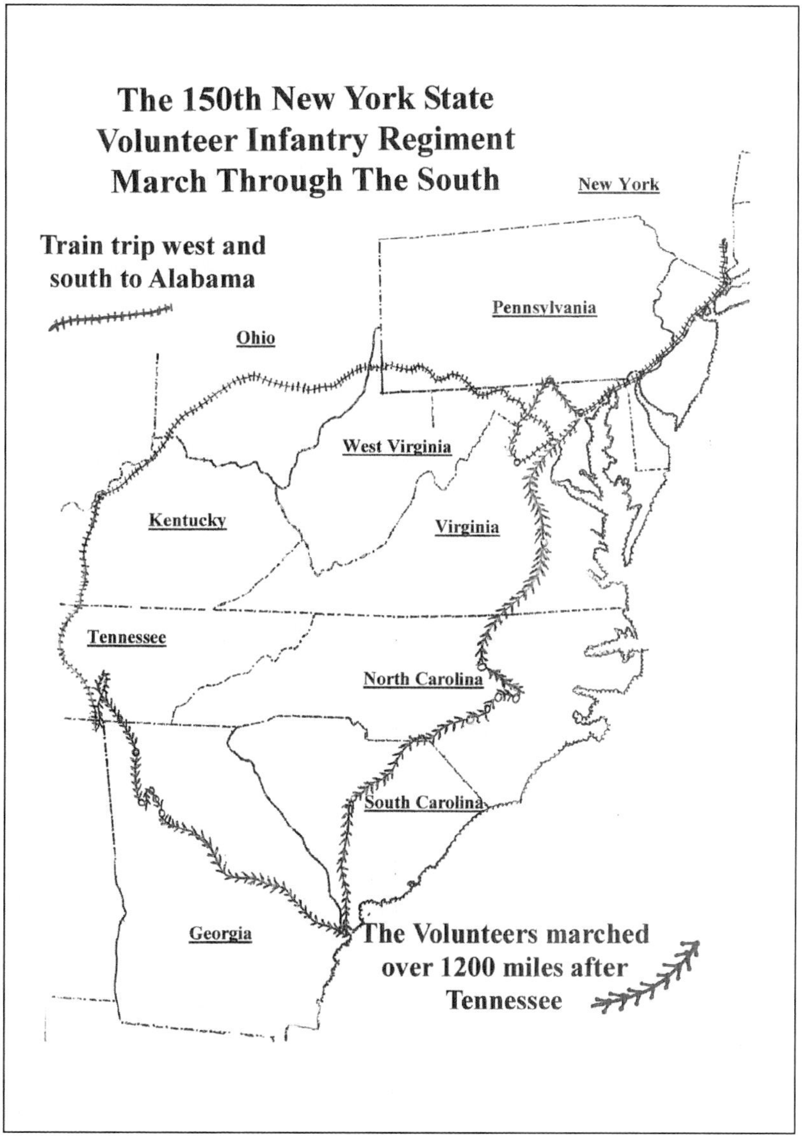

On October 12, 1862, the 150th Volunteers left Poughkeepsie by train for Baltimore, Maryland. War-weary veterans arrived home two and a half years later on June 12, 1865, having fought and marched over 1,200 miles through the South. This map was created using data from William Benson's 1921 article written for the Dutchess County Historical Society. He chronologically lists the following conflicts: In Pennsylvania, there were conflicts at Gettysburg and Cemetery Ridge; a train took the men west then south to Alabama; the conflict continued in Tennessee in Descherd, Wartrace, Normandy, Dutch River, Tullahoma, and Chattanooga; in Georgia William T. Sherman marched through Reseca, New Hope Church, Marietta, Kennesaw Mountain, Culp's Farm, Peach Tree Creek, Atlanta, Madison, Milledgeville, Savannah, Argyle Island, and Robertsville; in South Carolina, there was a conflict in Columbia; in North Carolina, there were conflicts in Fayetteville, Aversboro, Smithfield, Bentonville, and Goldsboro. Marching to Richmond, Virginia, they learned of the war's end. The veterans marched on to Washington, D.C., where they boarded a train home to Poughkeepsie. Gen. John Henry Ketcham was at the station to meet his returning men. (DPH.)

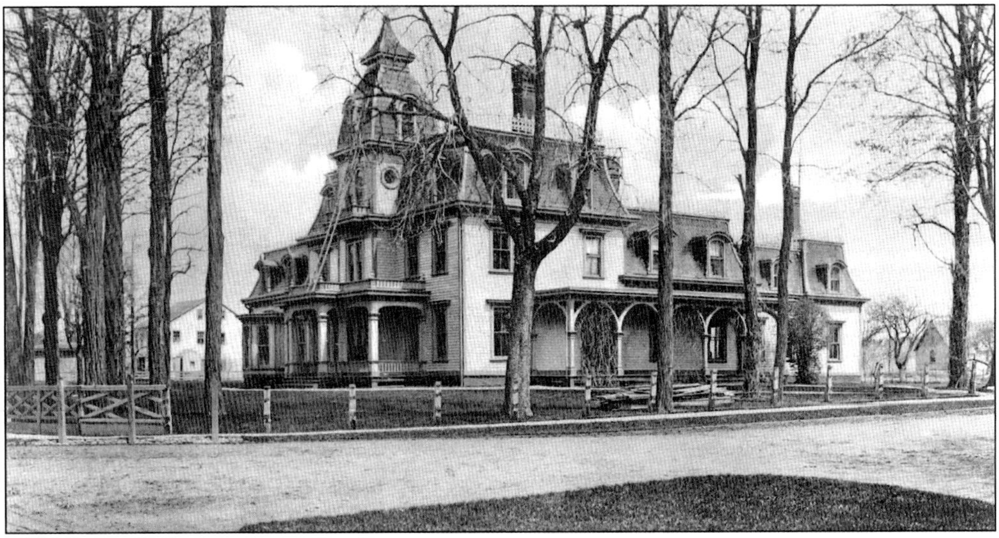

A hometown boy, John Henry Ketcham was Dover's supervisor at the age of 21. By age 23, he was a state assemblyman, and two years later, he was a New York State senator. At the start of the Civil War, he organized, outfitted, and commanded the 150th New York State Volunteer Infantry Regiment and was wounded at Gettysburg. After the Civil War, he served as a United States congressman. Ketcham's home was on Main Street. (TDHS.)

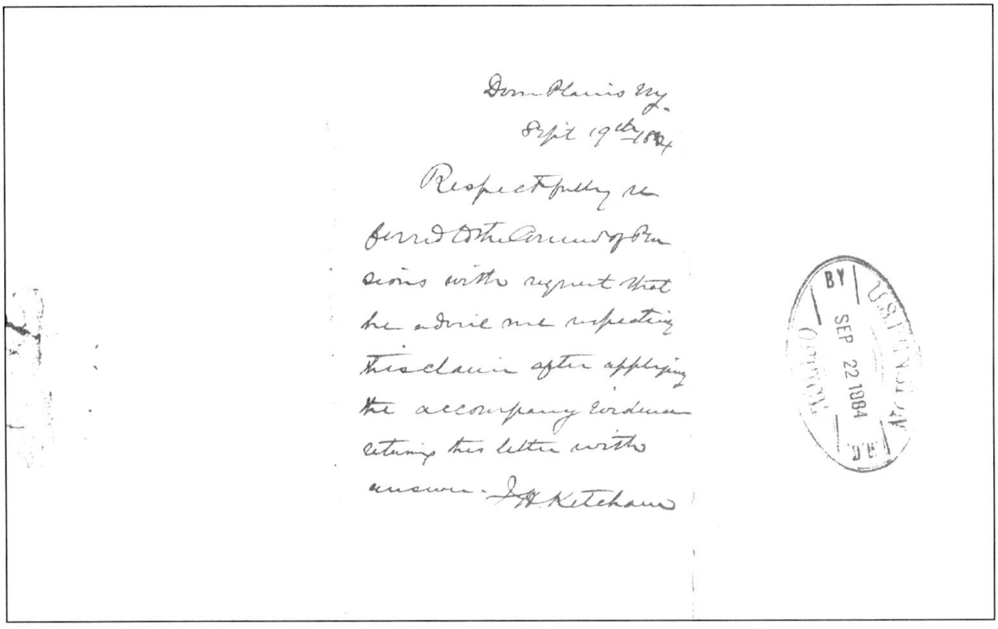

Dover Plains N.Y.
Sept 19th 1884
Respectfully referred to the Commr of Pensions with request that he advise me respecting this claim after applying the accompanying [illegible] returning this letter with answer. J.H. Ketcham

From his Dover Plains residence, Ketcham read the 1884 pension office request by Anton Reimer. Then he turned the document over and wrote, asking for information on pension claim No. 277,806. Sixteen-year-old Louis Reimer, a prisoner known as August Boris, had sickened and died at Andersonville Prison. Anton Reimer, his father, was aged and needed the money his son's pension would supply. (WAR, RTR.)

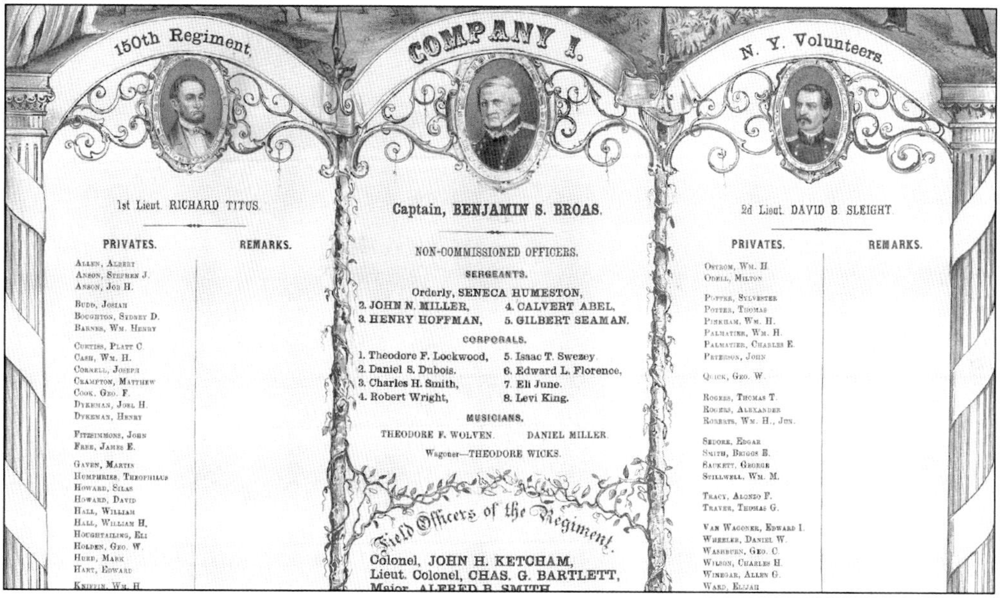

This elaborate commemorative certificate of Company I of the 150th Regiment of New York Volunteers features three adjacent tablets with the names of the noncommissioned officers; the three commissioned officers, who are identified with actual photographs; and field officers. Ketcham is identified as a colonel. Below his name are other officers. This document dates from the post–Civil War era. (TDHS.)

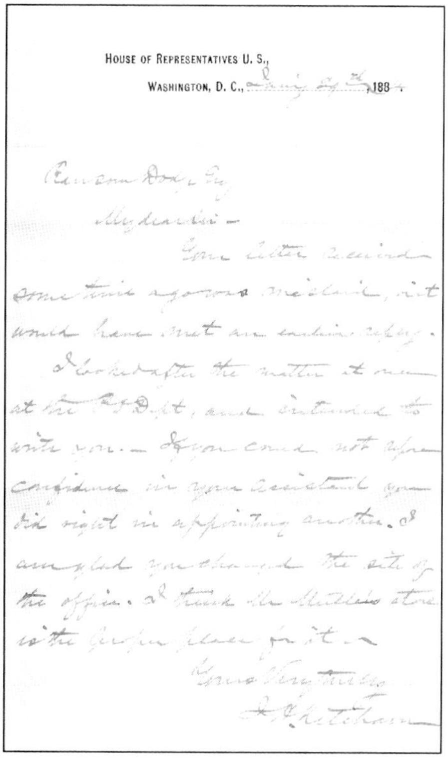
HOUSE OF REPRESENTATIVES U. S.,
WASHINGTON, D. C., 188

In 1884, Ketcham wrote to Ransom Dodge, Esq., of Pawling, who had lost confidence in postal workers. The congressman wrote that he had inquired at the post office department and that Dodge had been correct to appoint another assistant. In addition, he approved of the change in the post office location. According to Emily Benson, her family lived west of Pawling near Dodge Road. (LEB.)

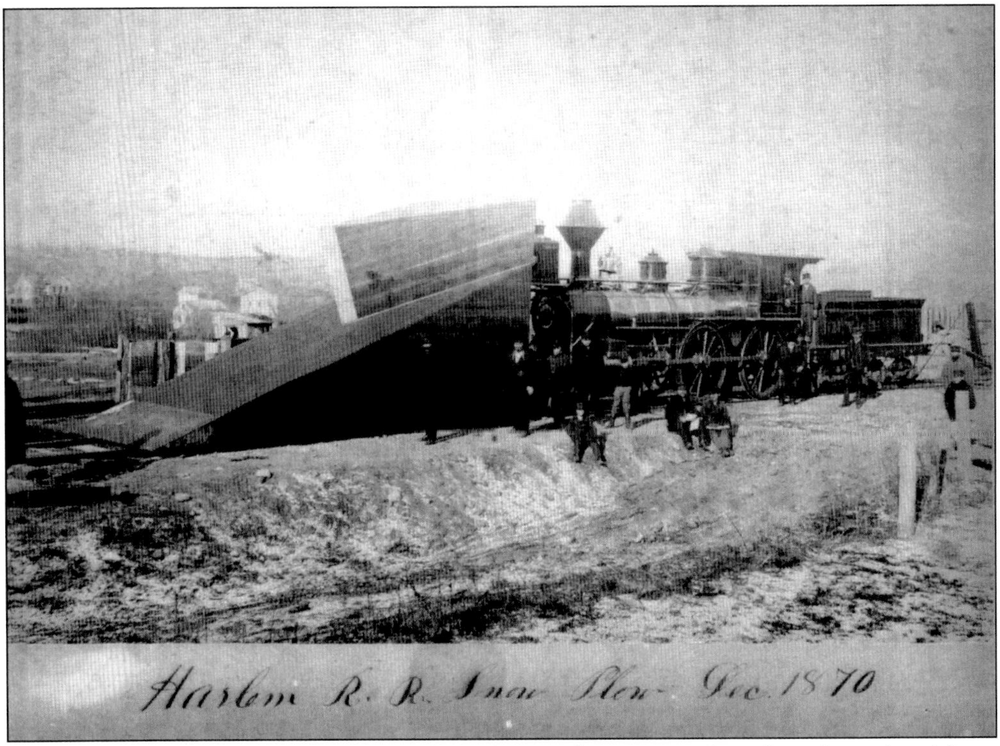

When it snowed in 1870, a Harlem Rail Road snowplow was used to clear the railroad lines through the Harlem Valley towns. Two huge wedges were constructed of thick timbers. The lower rail wedge and the upper engine wedge had metal points to shatter and break through snowdrifts and ice. Depending on the depth of snow, one or more engines pushed the plow. (WAR, RTR.)

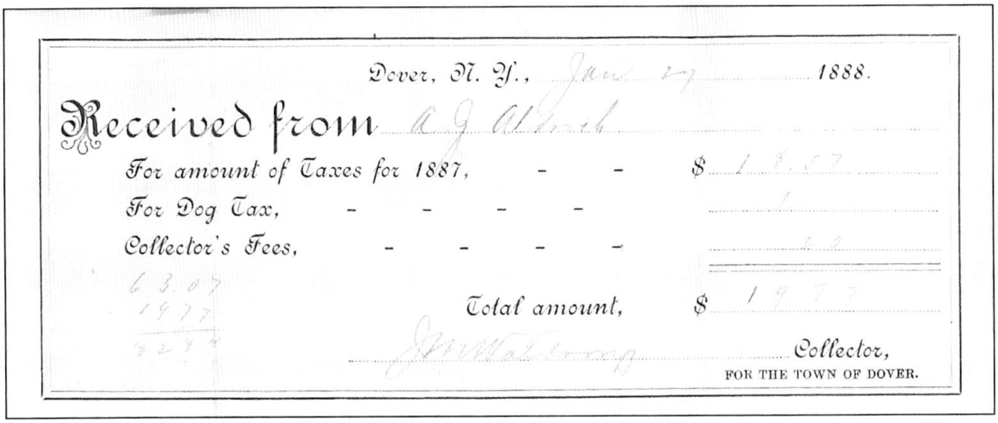

Dover, N. Y., ... 1888.

Received from ....

For amount of Taxes for 1887, - - $ ....

For Dog Tax, - - - - ....

Collector's Fees, - - - - ....

Total amount, $ ....

.... Collector,

FOR THE TOWN OF DOVER.

Andrew Jackson Aldrich of Webatuck paid his taxes on January 29, 1888, to the town of Dover tax collector, J. M. Waldron. Yearly taxes were $18.57. An extra dollar was charged for the dog tax and 20¢ was assessed in collector's fees. The total tax bill was $19.77. During this period, highway taxes were limited since individuals living along the road were assigned jobs that contributed to road upkeep. (JP.)

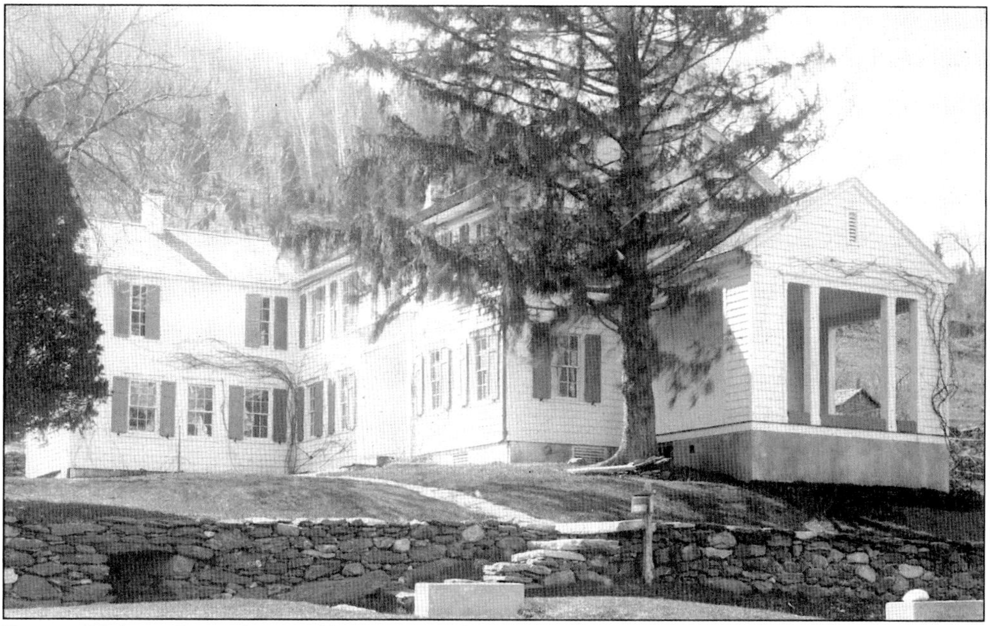

Former Webotuck resident Nellie Townsend noted on the picture that this early-1800s home belonged to the Griffin family. In 1867, the Frederick W. Beers atlas indicated the Aldrich family owned it. Located at the north end of Deuel Hollow, stone walls enclosed a pond, while large slabs of granite topped the fieldstone steps descending along the outside wall adjacent to Deuel Hollow Road. (TDHS.)

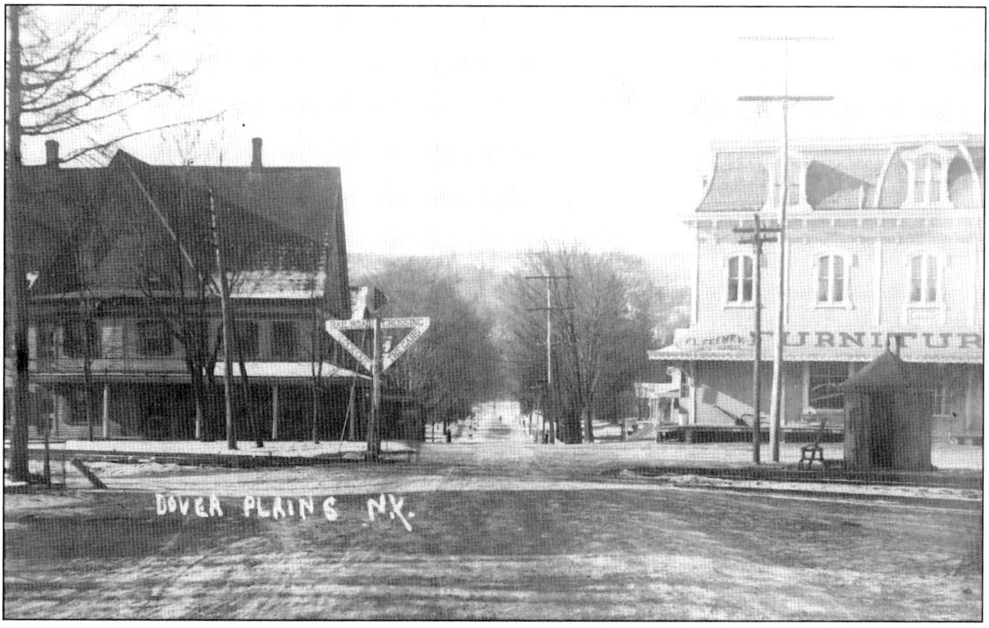

This late-1800s picture of Dover Plains looks westward across the railroad tracks to the hills of Chestnut Ridge. The Preston Hotel (left) and Feeney's Furniture (right) were at the intersection of Market Street. Feeney's porch displays a plow and grindstone. Above Feeney's is the Dover Plains Opera House. Meetings, recitals, and musicals took place regularly for decades beginning in the 1880s. (LEB.)

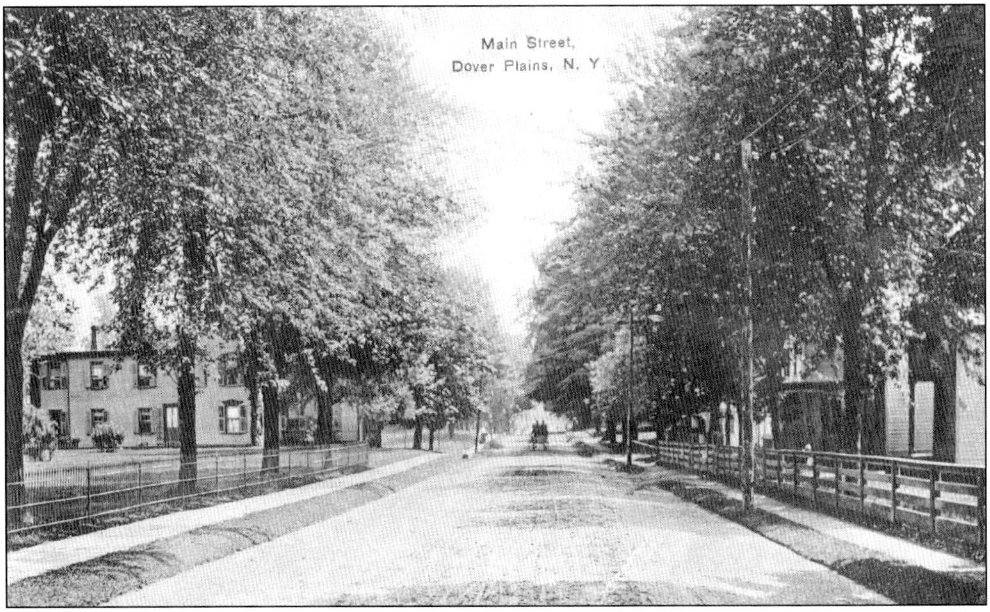

A horse-drawn carriage heads east on Main Street, which runs from Broadway to the New York Central Railroad tracks. Mature trees, slate sidewalks, and power lines border the road. Congressman John Henry Ketcham's home is located on the left. Beyond was James Ketcham Mabbett's house and then Reimer Avenue. Around 1900, Mill Street continued from the railroad tracks to the gristmills and electric mills on the river. Today it runs to Route 22. (TDHS.)

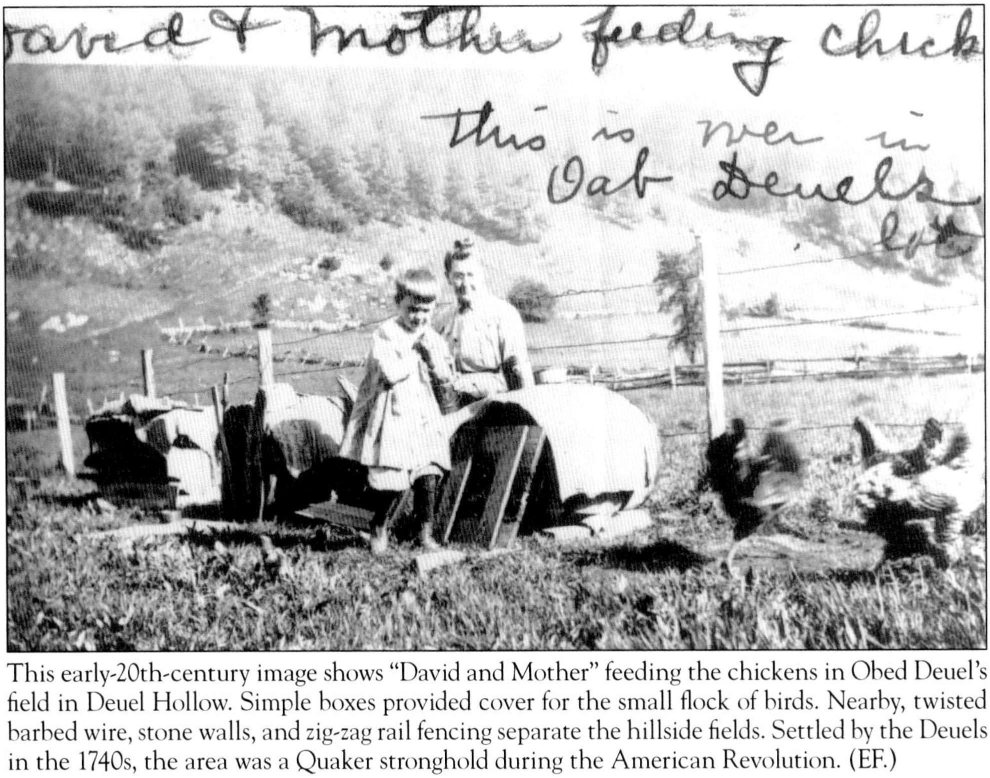

This early-20th-century image shows "David and Mother" feeding the chickens in Obed Deuel's field in Deuel Hollow. Simple boxes provided cover for the small flock of birds. Nearby, twisted barbed wire, stone walls, and zig-zag rail fencing separate the hillside fields. Settled by the Deuels in the 1740s, the area was a Quaker stronghold during the American Revolution. (EF.)

Astute farmers supplemented their incomes with other businesses when possible. Theodore F. Jones operated a sawmill on Deuel Hollow Brook. In the 1890s, his account book entries show neighbor Obed Deuel hauled a log daily during the winter to the mill. Jones's mill turned the trunk into planks for a new building. When the bill was settled, Deuel's horse-drawn sleigh was bartered for $2 as part of the total cost. (DPH.)

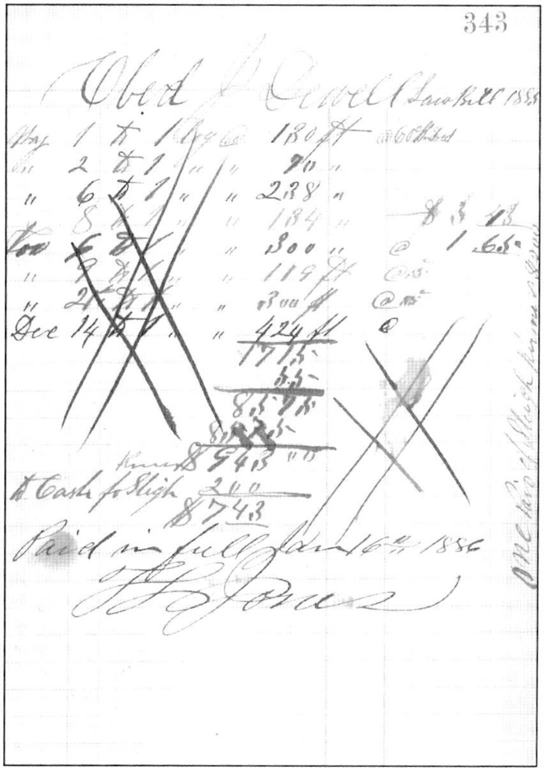

343

Obed J Deuel

To Cash for Sleigh 2 00

$7 43

Paid in full Jan 16th 1886

T F Jones

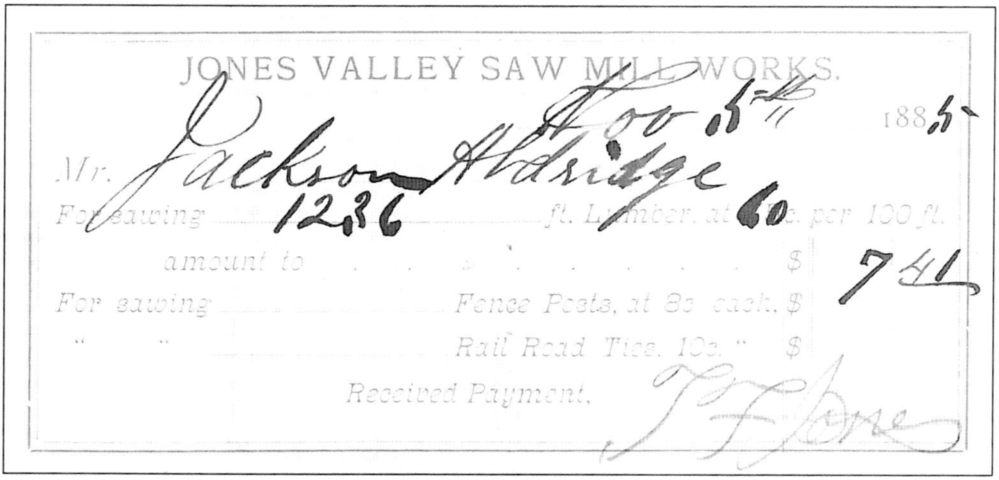

JONES VALLEY SAW MILL WORKS.

Nov 5th 1885

Mr. Jackson Aldridge

For sawing 1236 ft. Lumber, at 60c. per 100 ft.

amount to . . . . $ 7.41

For sawing Fence Posts, at 3c each, $

" " Rail Road Ties, 10c. " $

Received Payment, T F Jones

In November 1885, Jones's sawmill on the Deuel Hollow Brook was called the Jones Valley Saw Mill Works. Jackson Aldridge brought in a 12.36-foot log to be sawn into lumber. It cost $7.41. Jones's sawmill, farm, and milk account ledgers chronicle decades of lumber cutting, timber, shingle making, seed costs, crops per field comparisons, heifer costs, calving dates, milk production information, and city accounts. (JP.)

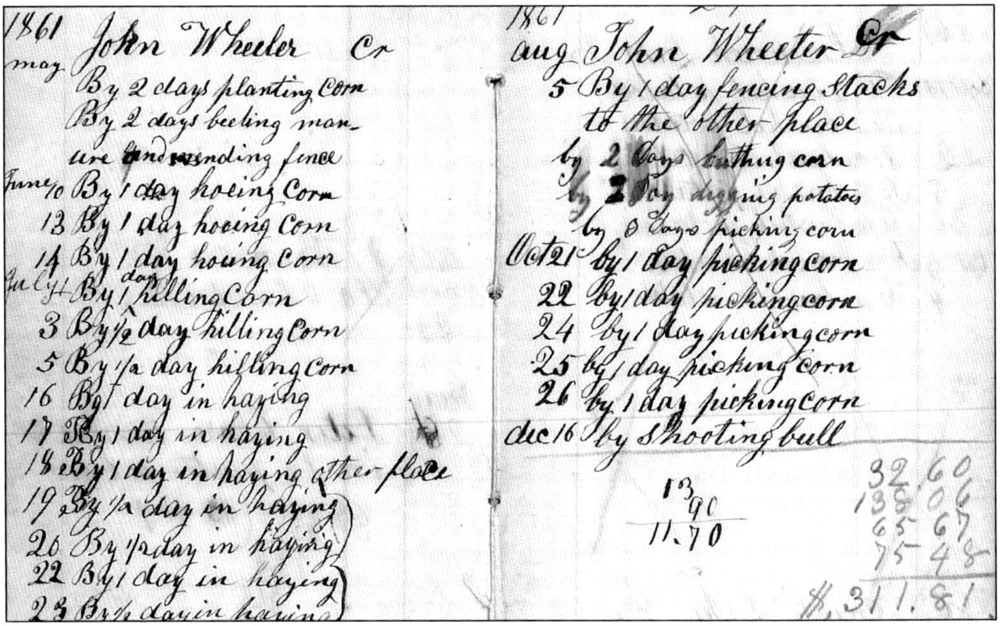

1861 John Wheeler Cr
may By 2 days planting Corn
By 2 days beeling manure and mending fence
June 10 By 1 day hoeing Corn
13 By 1 day hoeing Corn
14 By 1 day hoeing Corn
July 2 By 1 day hilling Corn
3 By 1/2 day hilling Corn
5 By 1/2 day hilling Corn
16 By 1 day in haying
17 By 1 day in haying
18 By 1 day in haying other place
19 By 1/2 day in haying
20 By 1/2 day in haying
22 By 1 day in haying
23 By 1/2 day in haying

1861
aug John Wheeler Dr
5 By 1 day fencing stacks to the other place
by 2 days cutting corn
by 2 day digging potatoes
by 8 days picking corn
Oct 21 by 1 day picking Corn
22 by 1 day picking corn
24 by 1 day picking corn
25 by 1 day picking corn
26 by 1 day picking Corn
dec 16 by shooting bull

13.90
11.70

32.60
138.06
65.67
75.48
$311.81

Caleb Cutler's small, leather-bound journal entries portray slices of life during the early Civil War years. From May to October 1861, John Wheeler bartered his services on the farm for credit at Cutler's in Dover Furnace. Wheeler planted, hoed, hilled, cut corn, hayed, mended fences, and dug potatoes. On December 16, he shot a bull. Daily wages were not recorded, but other pages detailed his account debits. (TDHS.)

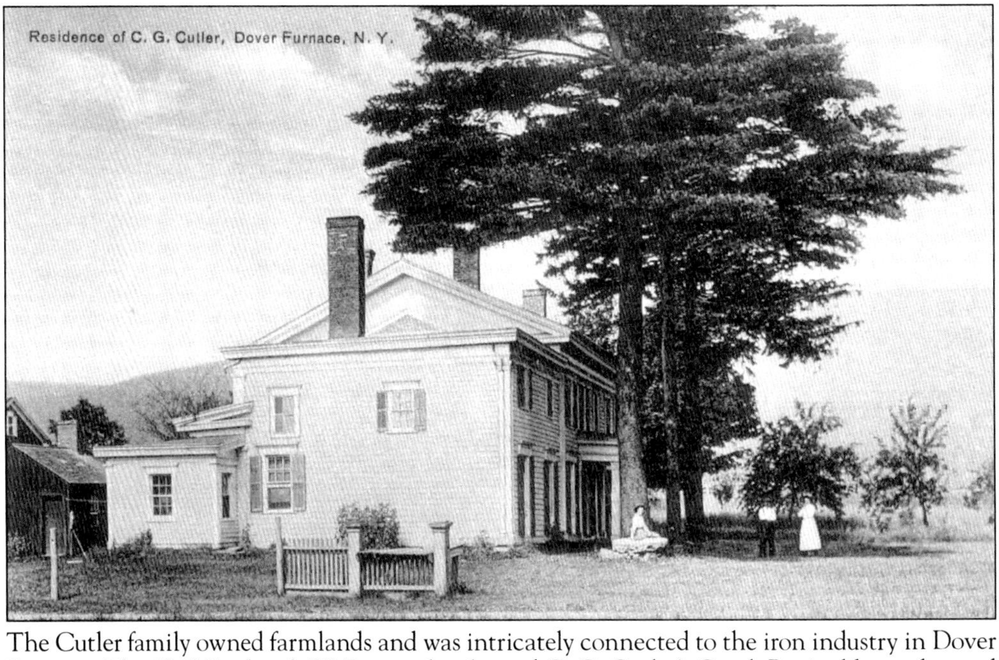

The Cutler family owned farmlands and was intricately connected to the iron industry in Dover Furnace. The 1867 Frederick W. Beers atlas showed C. G. Cutler's Greek Revival home located on the northwest side of Dover Furnace Road. Note the full-length windows in the front of the house and the young woman seated on the millstone on the front lawn. The building no longer exists. (TDHS.)

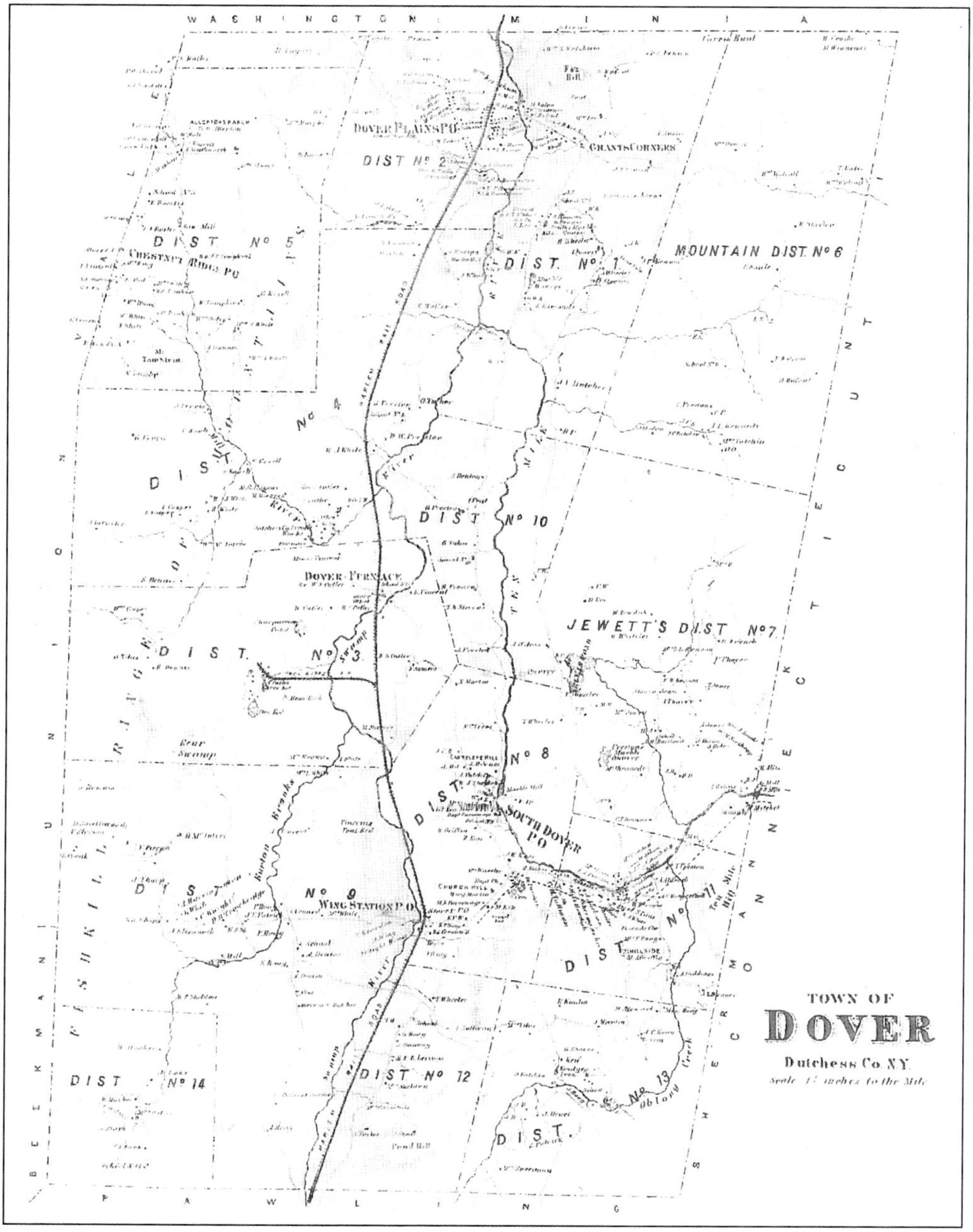

In 1867, the Beers atlas included this map of the town of Dover. The most recognizable feature is the Harlem Rail Road line, traversing the valley. School districts are apparent, bounded by the Ten Mile River, Swamp River, and topography of the steeper hills. The more densely populated hamlets of Dover Plains, Chestnut Ridge, the area by the quarries on Limekiln Road, South Dover, and Webatuck reflect the economics and industry of the day. No houses are noted on most of East Mountain, but a population thrives in Jewett's District near the Bulls Bridge Ironworks at Bulls Bridge in nearby Connecticut. On the southeastern portion of town is Oblong Creek, today known as Deuel Hollow. On the north side of Oblong Creek is the Bridgeport Ironworks. In Dover Furnace, a railroad spur is shown running to the ironworks below Sharparoon Pond. Familiar names appear in all sectors of the town. (TDHS.)

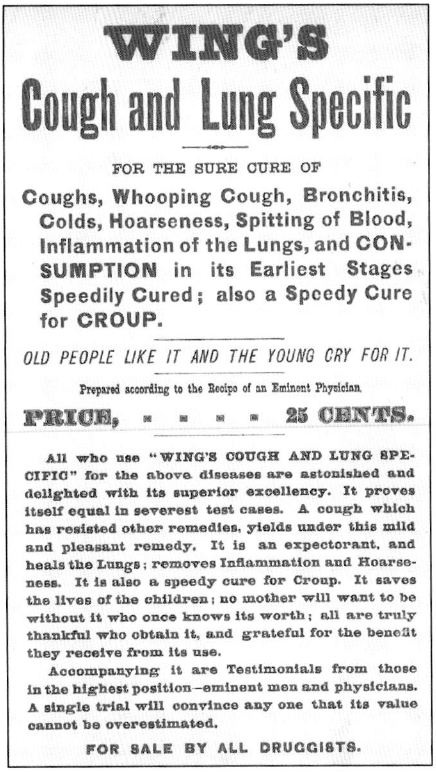

Theodore Wing's advertisement for his cough and lung relief was posted in drugstore windows and run in the weekly newspapers. Lengthy testimonials from grateful parents and healthy adults accompanied the advertisements. Phoebe Wing's formula for the syrup came down through the family to Theodore Wing, who made and bottled it locally. He also sold an ointment packaged in a small, six-sided white jar that cured almost as much as the syrup. (ECL.)

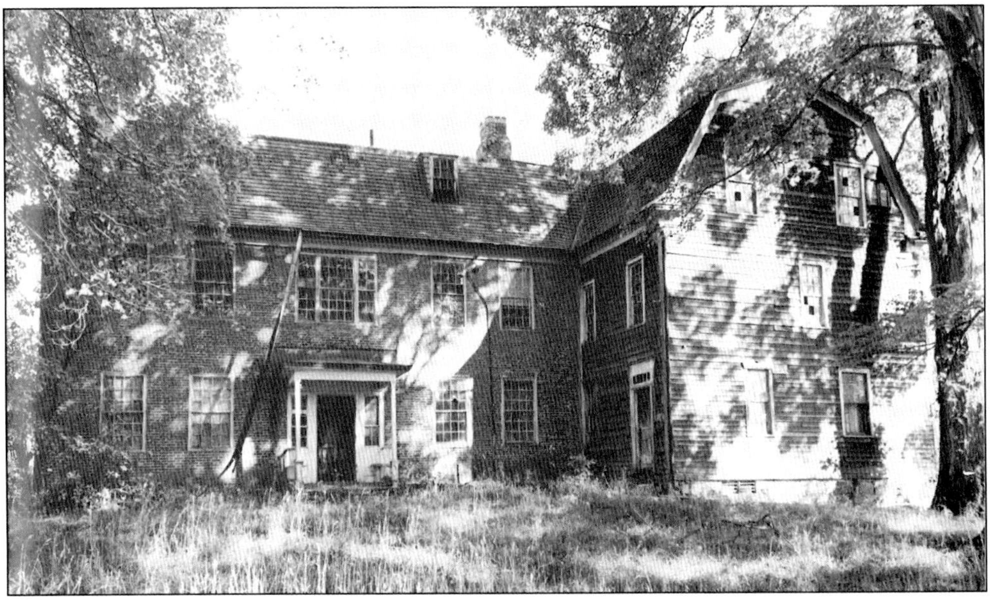

At a Colonial crossroads, Jackson Wing's inn served food, drink, and conversation to drovers and visitors through and beyond the Civil War. The inn hosted meetings before Dover's 1807 separation from Pawling as well as later town meetings. New York State purchased the Wing farm in 1910. Abandoned by 1924, curious visitors such as Priscilla Hunt and her family still saw handmade, original door locks and dusty bottles on the shelves. (Dutchess County Department of Planning.)

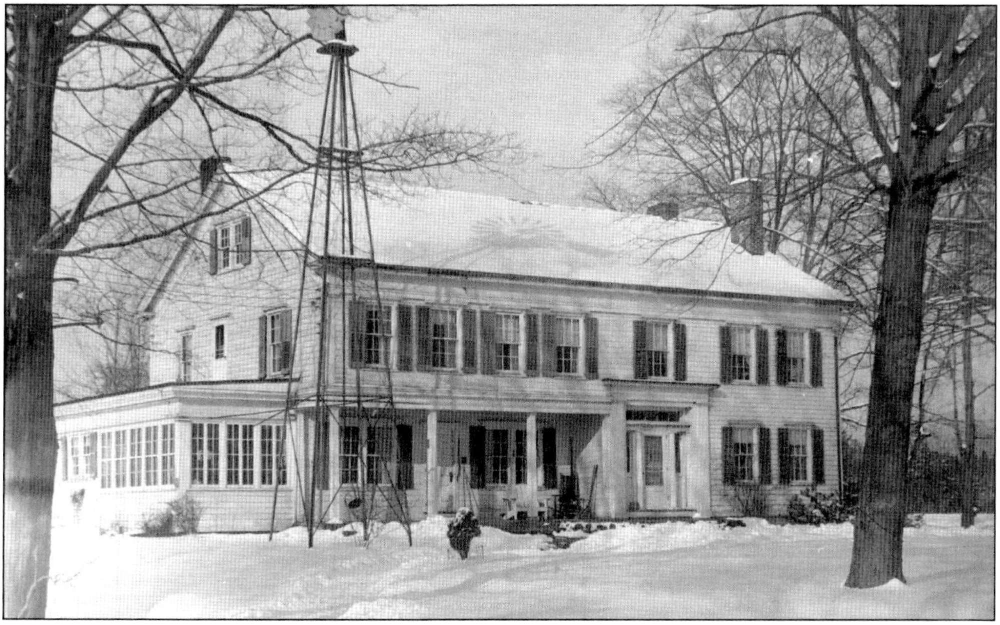

This handsome Greek Revival structure was built in 1840. Old deeds refer to Absalom Vincent's land as the old homestead farm. The first generation built the smallest portion on the left. Five generations of the Vincent family have lived in the home, including Dover lawyer Stanley Vincent. The home remains in the Vincent family. Family farmlands extended from the top of West Mountain across the Swamp River valley. (WAV.)

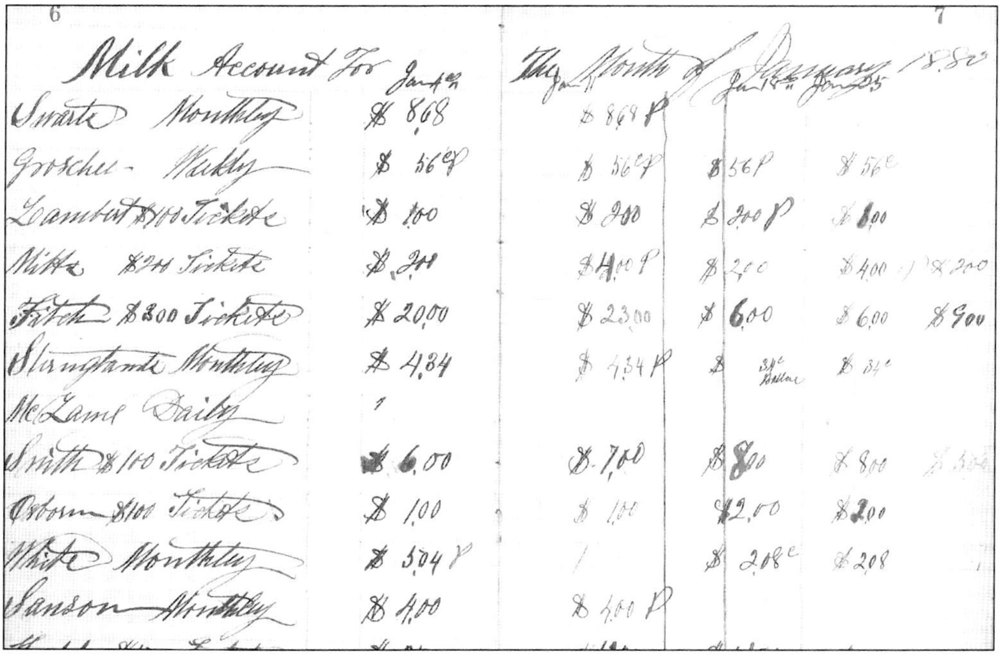

6 7

Milk Account For The Month of January 1880

	Jan 4th	Jan 11th	Jan 18th	Jan 25	
Swartz Monthly	$8.68	$8.68 P			
Gooschee Weekly	$56¢ P	$56¢ P	$56 P	$56¢	
Lambert $100 Tickets	$1.00	$2.00	$2.00 P	$1.00	
Mitts $200 Tickets	$2.00	$4.00 P	$2.00	$4.00	$2.00
Fitch $300 Tickets	$20.00	$23.00	$6.00	$6.00	$9.00
Sturgstands Monthly	$4.34	$4.34 P	$ 34¢ Ballance	$34¢	
McLane Daily	1				
Smith $100 Tickets	$6.00	$7.00	$8.00	$8.00	$5.00
Osborn $100 Tickets	$1.00	$1.00	$2.00	$2.00	
White Monthly	$5.04 P	/	$2.08¢	$2.08	
Sanson Monthly	$4.00	$4.00 P			

In the 1880s, city milk routes were profitable. Theodore F. Jones's milk book accounts show clients paid in a variety of ways based on scheduled milk stops. January 1880 bills were tallied on January 4, 11, 18, and 25. Smith paid $8.68 monthly, Gooschee paid 56¢ weekly, and Fitch bought $2 tickets for his January bill of $55, and $9 remained due at the end. (DPH.)

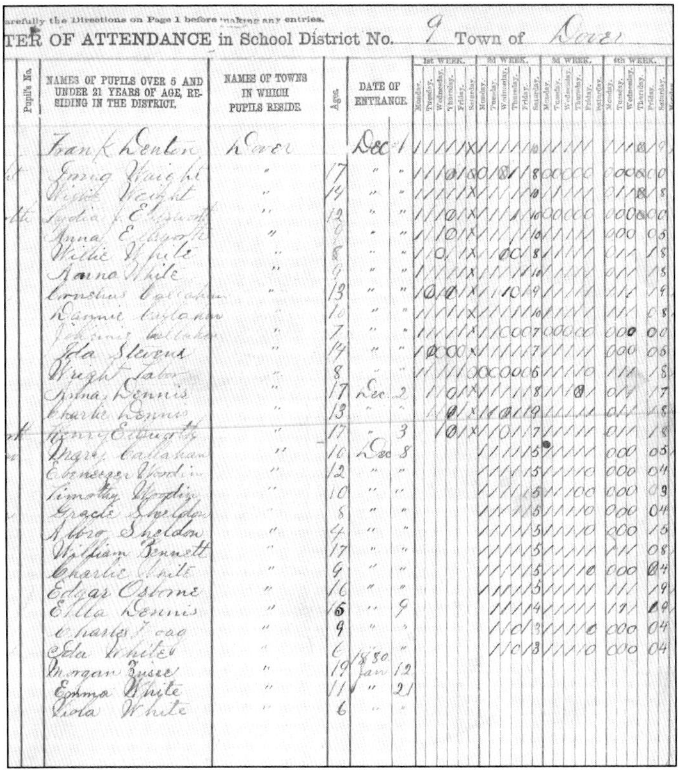

In 1879, Dover School District No. 9 was located around Wing's Station. Children from Chippewalla joined those from West Dover Road. Class attendance for the 1879–1880 school year represented younger generations of old families, new families, farmers, and those who labored at the marble mills, in the iron industry, and on the railroad. Some of the surnames were Denton, White, Callahan, Tabor, Dennis, Woodin, Sheldon, Osborne, and, of course, Hoag. (TDHS.)

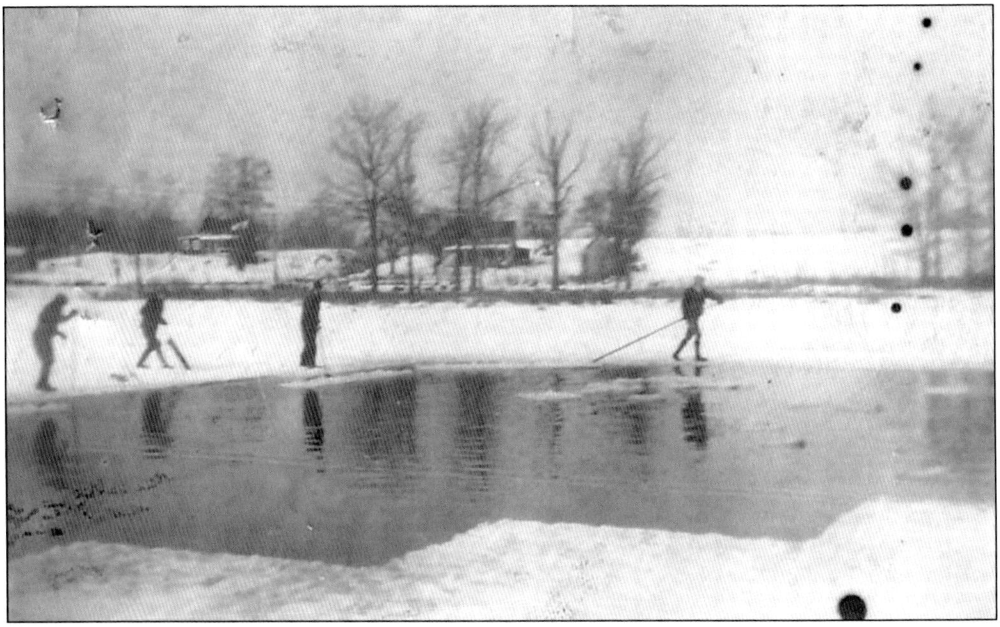

At Wing's Station, Borden Condensed Milk Company's ice pond area was originally a bend in the Swamp River. Ice was important for milk refrigeration and storage until sent for delivery to the city on the morning train. Gathered during the winter, the ice was packed with straw for insulation in the huge ice barn. According to Jackson Wing, the railroad straightened and rerouted the river to the west side when the tracks were laid. (CRR.)

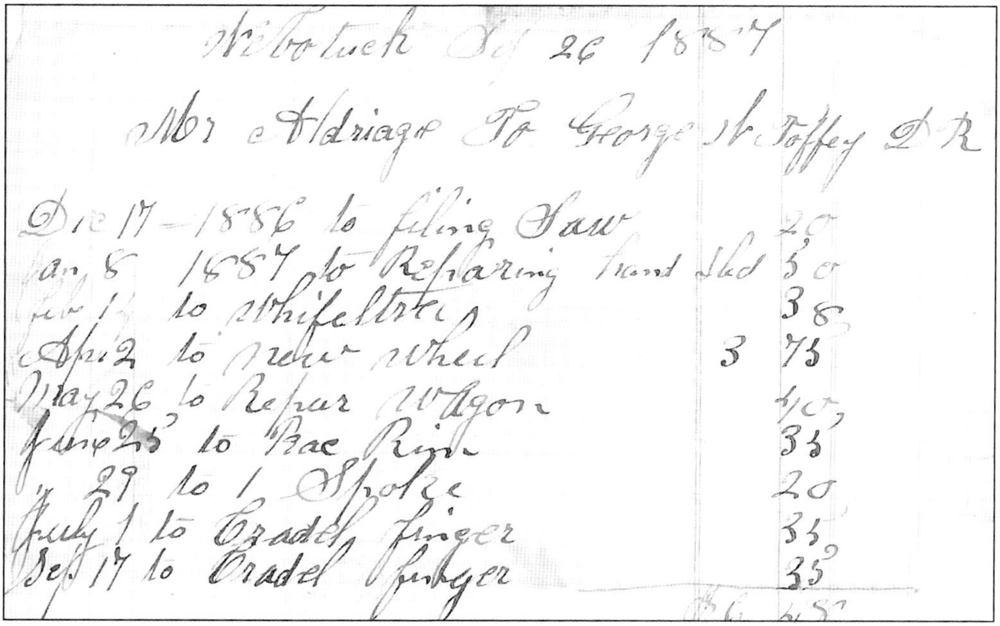

Nebotuck Sep 26 1887

Mr Aldriage To George W Toffey Dr

Dec 17 — 1886 to filing Saw 20
Jan 8 1887 to Repairing hand Sled 50
Feb 1[illegible] to Whifeltree 38
Apr 2 to new Wheel 3 75
May 26 to Repair Wagon 40
June 25 to Rac Rim 35
" 29 to 1 Spoke 20
July 1 to Cradel finger 35
Sep 17 to Cradel finger 35

On September 26, 1887, George Toffey sent a bill to Jackson Aldrich for goods back to December 1886 for filing a saw, repairing a sled and wagon, replacing spokes, and fixing farm equipment. Although $5.70 in credit was bartered for 95 pounds of beef, an unpaid balance of 78¢ remained. Aldrich paid the final bill. Walter Meseck, a later owner of the Aldrich house, collected many documents from it. (JP.)

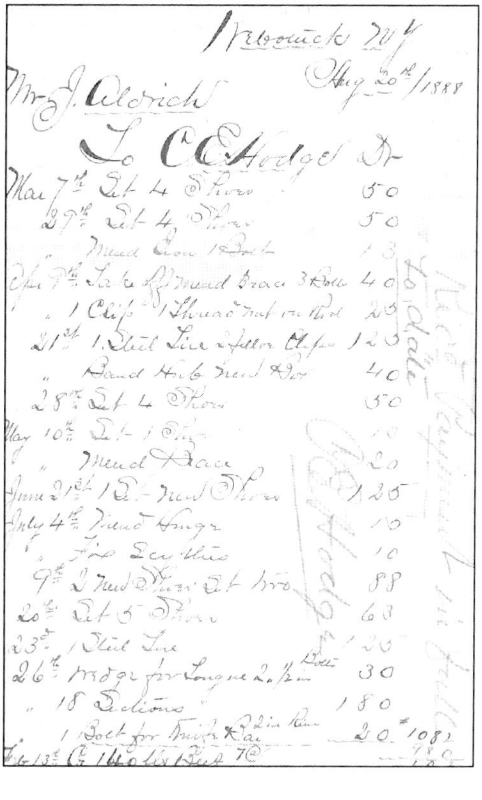

Nebotuck NY
Aug 20th/1888

Mr J. Aldrich
To C E Hodge Dr

C. E. Hodge's blacksmith shop billed his nearby neighbor Jackson Aldrich $1.02 for a balance dating from May 1888. The blacksmith repaired several shoes, threaded nuts, mended a brace, fixed his scythes, and made a steel tire. The bill totaled $10.82. Aldrich bartered 140 pounds of beef for the bill and then paid the small amount remaining. After a barn fire, Meseck salvaged the Aldrich receipts. (JP.)

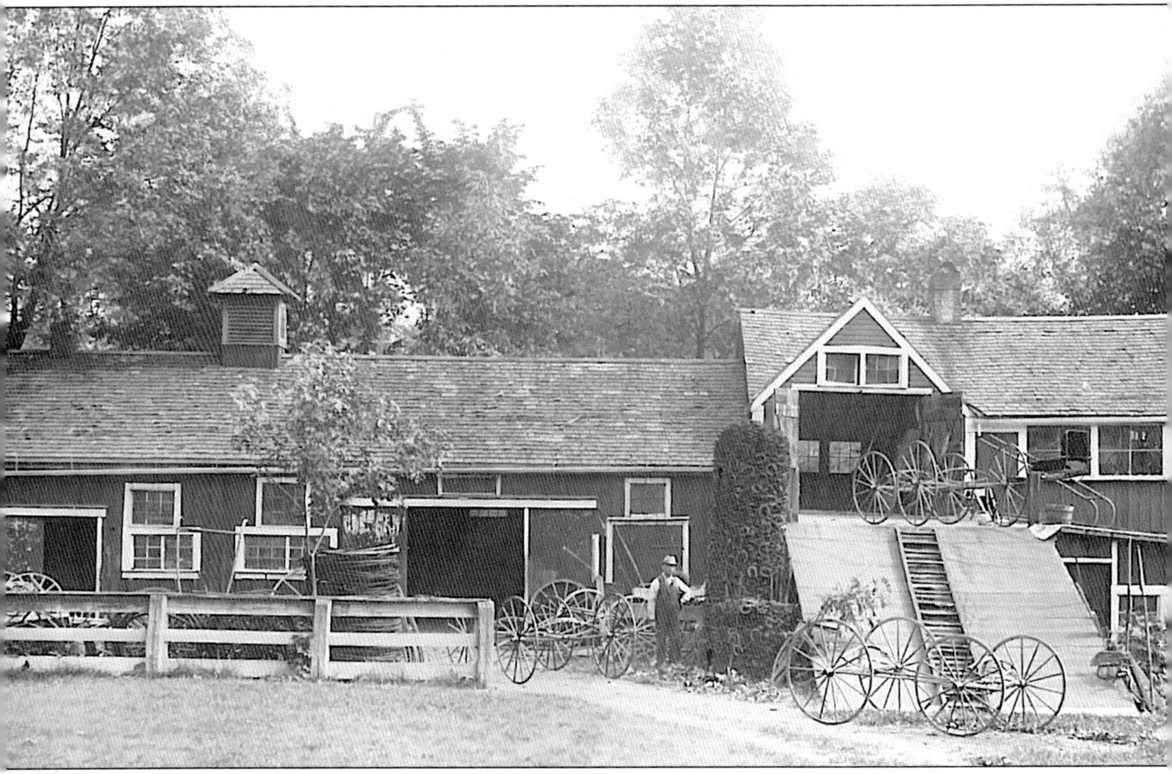

Martha (Hodge) Southworth's collection of photographs included this image of ancestor C. E. Hodge, who ran a blacksmith shop in Webatuck. In the late 1800s, he created a large display of carriages in front of his shop. Many others were stored in the barn attic. Hodge stands in front of the store next to a tower of horseshoes over twice as tall as he is. Another stack appears in the making. Behind the split-rail fence, there is a stack of tire rims. The blacksmith shop was located alongside the Ten Mile River on Dog Tail Corners on the north side of the bridge. The Hodge family had its blacksmith shop for decades, and the historical society has several ledgers from the business that were donated by Southworth. Today passersby would never know that the gift shop, art studio, toy shop, and presently engineering office for the bridge construction were part of the old Hodge blacksmith shop. (TDHS.)

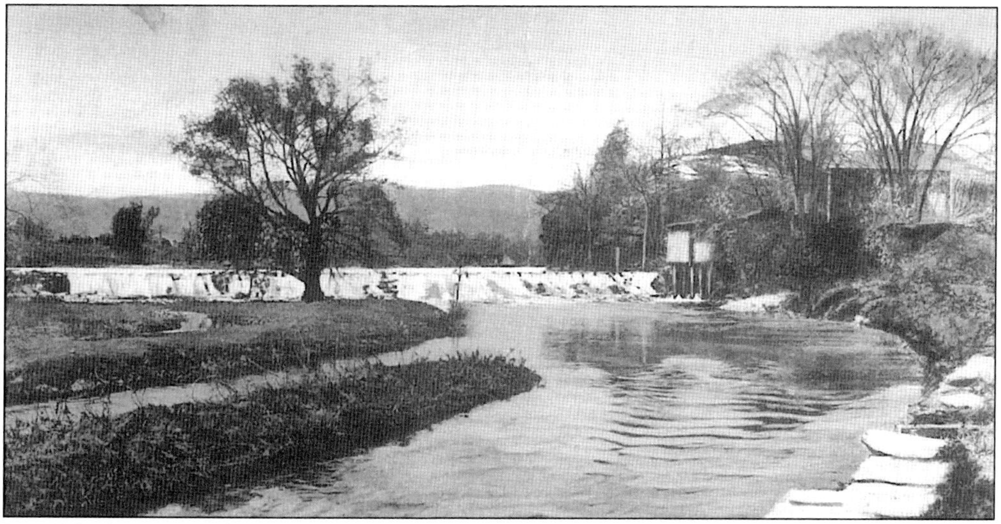

In 1895, the Dover Plains Electric Light and Power Company used a 25-kilowatt generator to produce electricity for its mill, house, and eight customers. By 1918, Dover Plains had electric streetlights before New York City. In 1920, plant owners Charles P. Morgan and Charles S. Wyman, with treasurer Adolph Reimer, purchased power through a right-of-way from Bulls Bridge. The company expanded, providing power from Wingdale to Wassaic. (DD, RTR.)

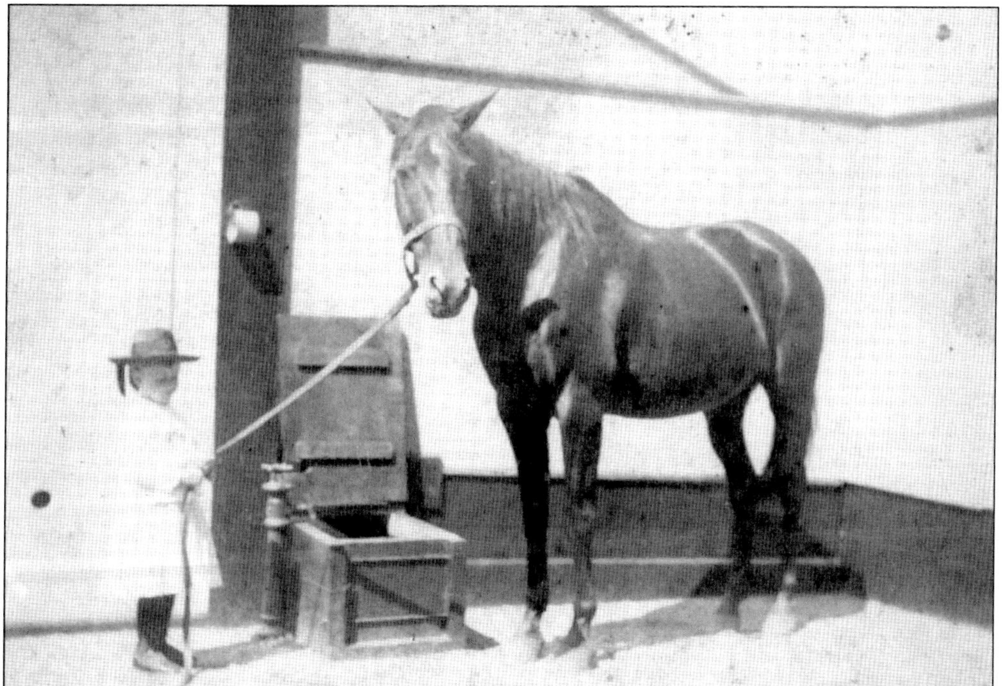

Theodore Crane was photographed in the late 1890s with his horse Billy. Crane's daughter Betty Lawrence remembers him pointing out a stately hemlock on East Mountain, visible against the night sky. At its base was the log making the Wolf Swamp crossing possible on the trip back to Dover. Through the 1930s, children rode horses. Bette (Sedore) Shufelt said children rode horses all over town. Robert Hufcut remembered riding over East Mountain to Kent. (ECL.)

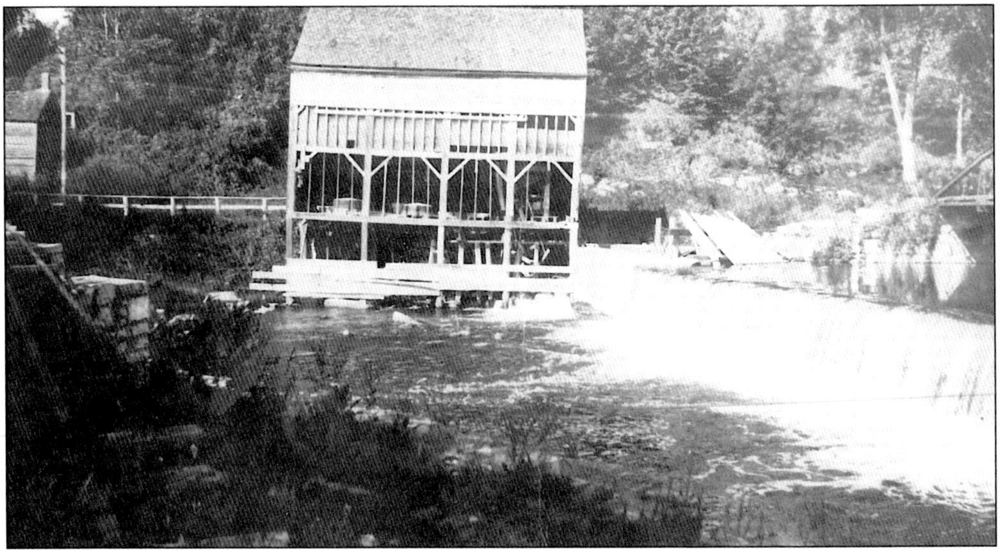

Early grist- and sawmills provided vital services for local residents. This late-1800s image of Ragans Mill under construction was taken from the east bank of the Ten Mile River. In 1908, town clerk Richard F. Maher identified the miller and site as John P. Ragan at Sheldon's Mill. At riverside, the trolley bridge (left) and the 1875 highway bridge (right) flanked the mill. Today the mill site is empty. (IH.)

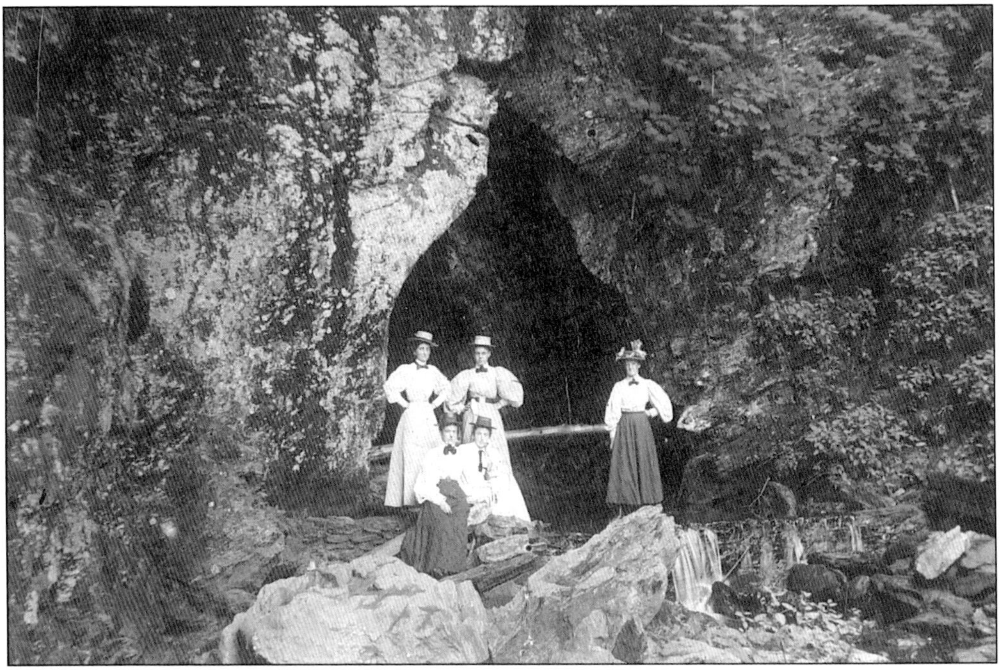

These Dover Stone Church visitors pose in front of the historic cavern around 1897. Soon to be related, the group was photographed by Adolph Reimer. According to the Reimer family, standing from left to right are Katherine Gutelius, Mabel Reimer, and Dora Reimer. Seated are Minnie Reimer and Archie Hamilton. The *New York Times* twice reported in 1897 that Minnie and Hamilton tried to elope three times before they finally succeeded in getting married. (WAR, RTR.)

Four

A Gracious 20th-Century Town

As Dover approached the 20th century, its neighborhoods and hamlets typified a wholesome country life in a beautiful valley. In town, electric streetlights illuminated slate sidewalks and tree-lined streets from one end of town to the other. The town united and built a new high school in 1909, where students from the 16 district schools could continue their education. Town clerk Richard Maher listed many of the local businesses in 1908. Wingdale had two hotels, a coal and cider mill, two general stores, a meat market, a miller, and a barber. The marble company was expanding as New York City planned new buildings and structures. South Dover Marble Company built employee housing and the Marble Hotel in Wingdale. The company employed 100 men and had an office on Fifth Avenue. Increased agriculture kept limestone fertilizer in high demand. Lime Kiln Road was a busy place. In Dover Plains were the bank, two general stores, two groceries, a meat market, coal yards, a cider mill, a feed mill, an electric mill, a druggist, two physicians, a plumber, three hotels, and a jeweler. Even as the automobile proclaimed a time-saving era of travel, convenience, and leisure, mechanization of local industries increased production even further.

The Dover Plains Library moved to the Baptist Band Box in 1929 where it remained until 1966. Churches of all major denominations flourished between Dover Plains and Wingdale. The Masons and other civic organizations held dances and socials and worked to beautify the community. Milk companies like Borden Condensed Milk Company and the McDermott Milk Company had refocused local farm programs from the family's sustenance farm to the dairy business. At Midfield Dairy, Slawson Brothers Company produced and distributed New York's first certified milk. During Prohibition, it has been told that Wingdale and Dover Plains became wild and woolly places. Extra large crops of corn and potatoes were put to good use as well. Members of the older generation still talk about the stills hidden in the woods. Others laugh about seeing the millpond on the Ten Mile River in Dover Plains covered with potato peels, discards from vodka making.

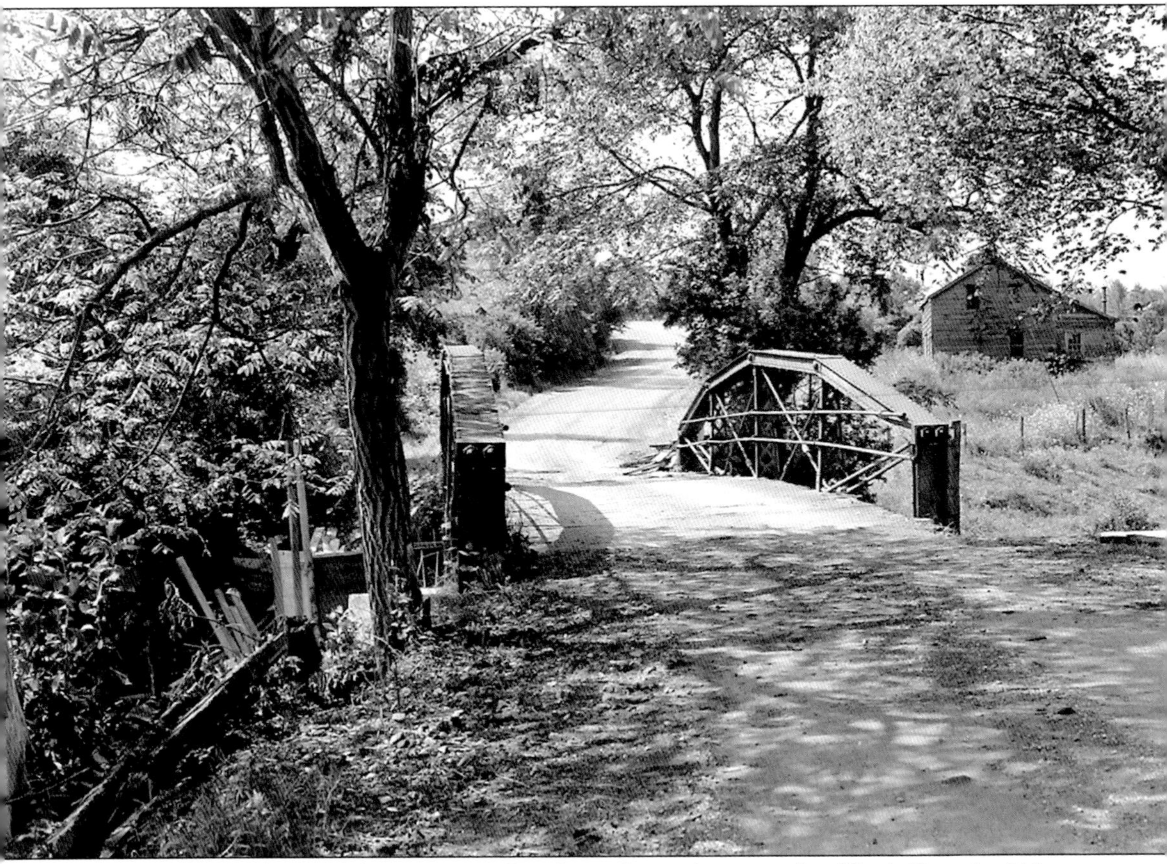

This 1920s bridge over the Mountain Brook was located just south of Faith Payne's old house where Ridge Road intersects with Dover Furnace Road. Looking south beyond the bridge through the barbed wire fence and over field grasses, a weathered saltbox house can be seen. Shade trees and thick bushes crowd the dusty roadside. Up the dirt road at the top of the hill on the left, the second Dover Furnace Schoolhouse held classes. The first schoolhouse was at the south end of Dover Furnace Road closer to the iron furnace housing. From this bridge, back in a field to the right stand the remains of White's Dover Furnace. It was the last furnace built at the end of the iron heyday in Dover and was never put into blast. Both the saltbox building and the schoolhouse at the top of the hill have been carefully renovated into homes. (TDHS.)

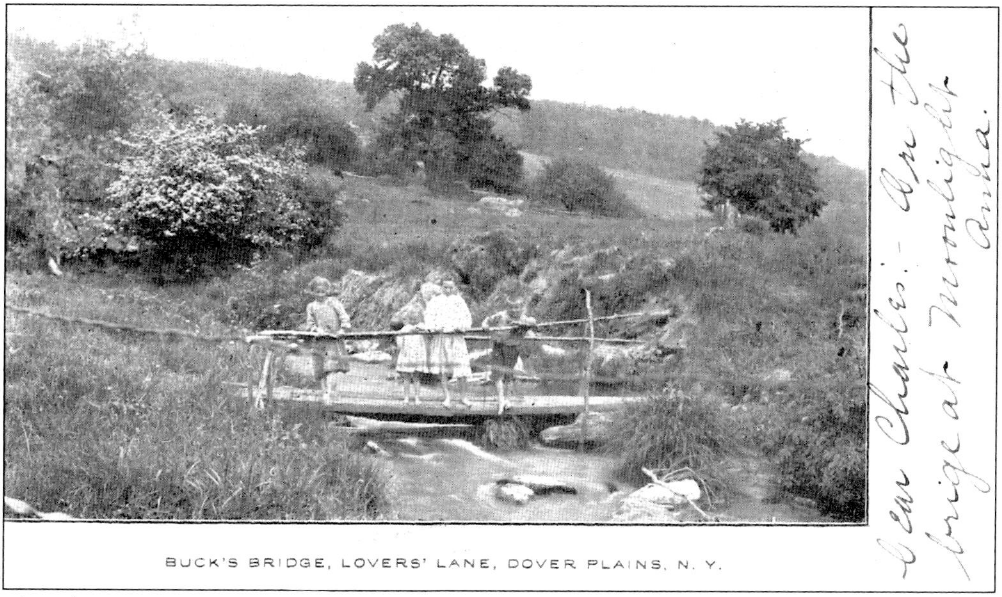

This photograph of Buck's Bridge, taken in 1907, shows four children crossing a simple, wooden bridge over a rippling brook. The postcard image typifies that wholesome country life experienced by children of all ages in Dover in the late 19th and early 20th century. A cryptic note from Anna to Charles mentions moonlight on the bridge. Many older people remember a boarded crossing with a similar streamside look at the Dover Stone Church, but the location remains unknown. (KD.)

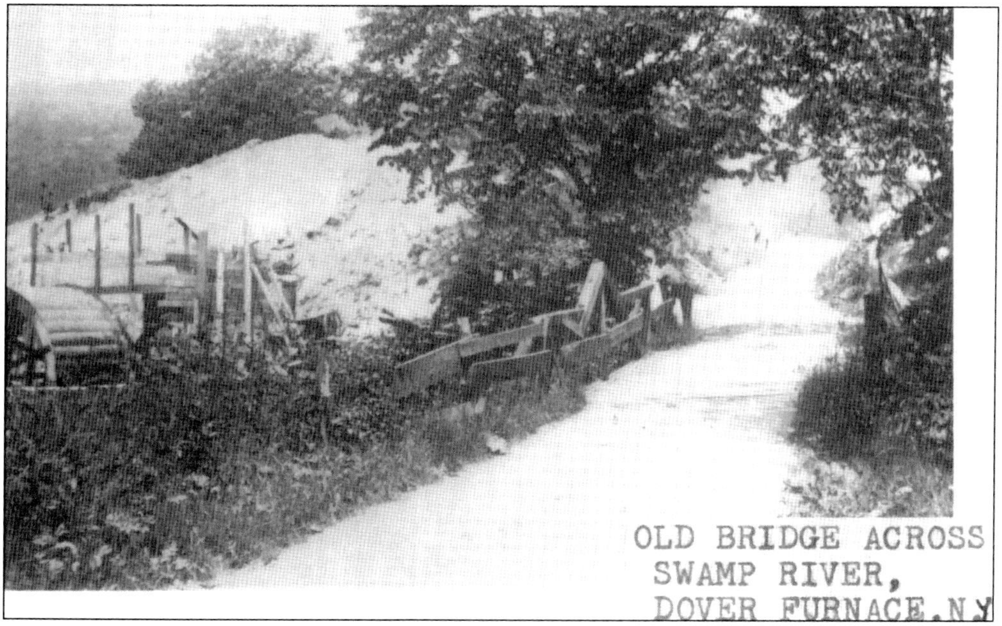

Around 1900, Dover Furnace was intended to have electrical power generated by the Swamp River. The W. S. Sterling Company, which had a business nearby, built the mechanism for the power wheel and its buckets in the early part of the 1900s. The rusting remains of the power wheel and mechanism can still be seen on the western side of the present Swamp River Dam. (WAV.)

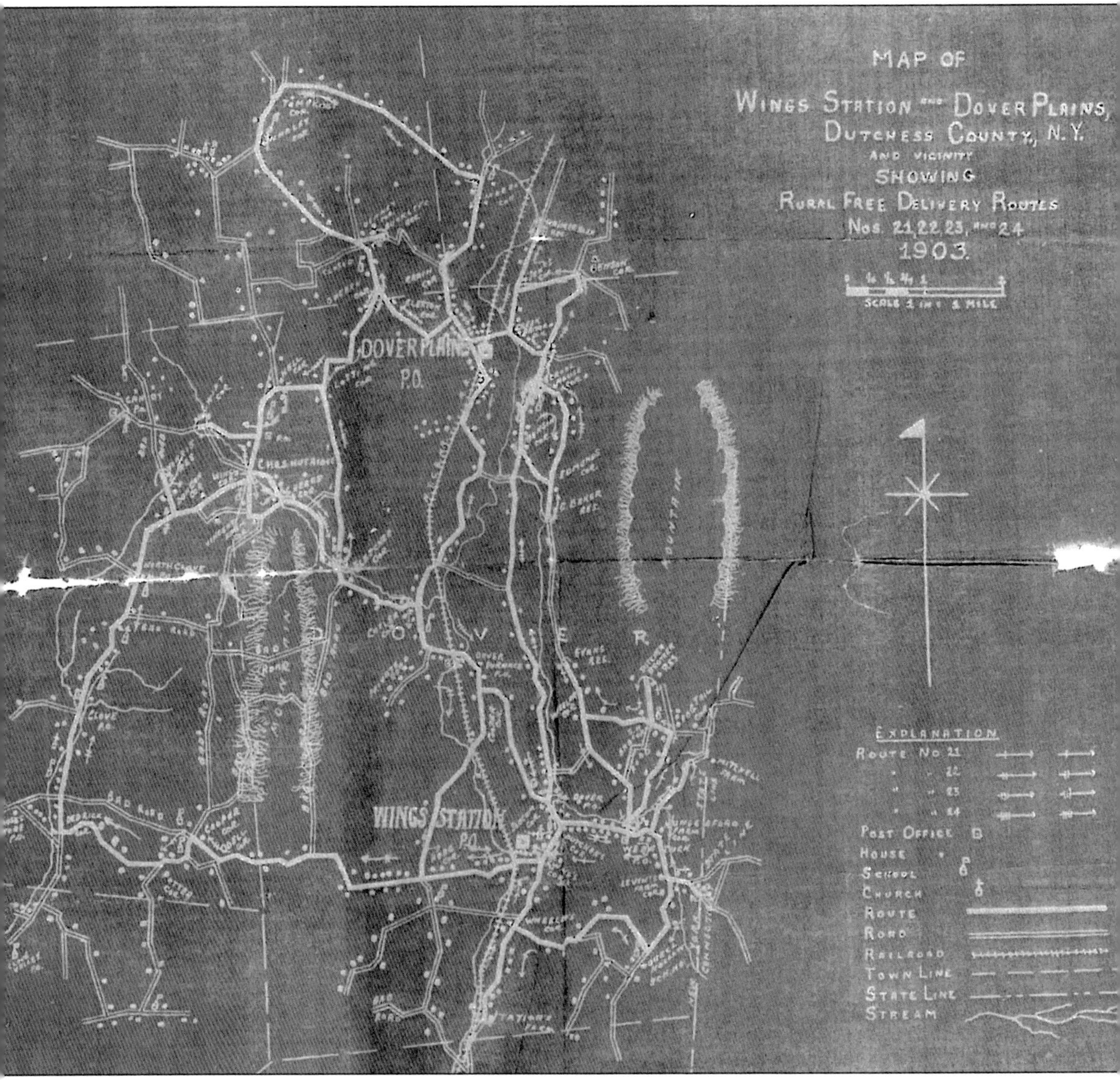

The rural free delivery routes in 1903 provided postal service to those living on the outskirts of the community. Where roads intersect and settlements built up, the neighborhoods were often denoted by corners. Wing's Station neighborhoods included Hoag's and Slocum's Corners. Wingdale's neighborhoods included Levings Farm and Dutcher's Corners. Post offices were identified at Wingdale, Webatuck, Dover Furnace, and Dover Plains. Where Deuel Hollow crossed over the mountain on Leather Hill, the road met Wheeler's Corners on today's state hospital property. Dover Furnace included Cutler's Corners. Dover's neighborhoods included Lossing's Corner and Benson's Corner. Chestnut Ridge was crossed by two roads. One road was a "bad road." West Dover Road had a bad section where Pawling Lake Estates is today. On East Mountain, the population was sparse with none on the top. Outlying routes included parts of the towns of Amenia, Washington, and Union Vale. (WAR, RTR.)

In 1903, Henry A. Hufcut was appointed a regular letter carrier, and Henry J. Hufcut was appointed a substitute letter carrier on Route 23, beginning with the establishment of the routes in October. Their route ran down old Route 22, through Dover Furnace, across to the bottom of Crickett Hill, and then up along the river to town. Henry A. retired in October 1933 and received a $1,200 annual retirement from the post office. (DRH.)

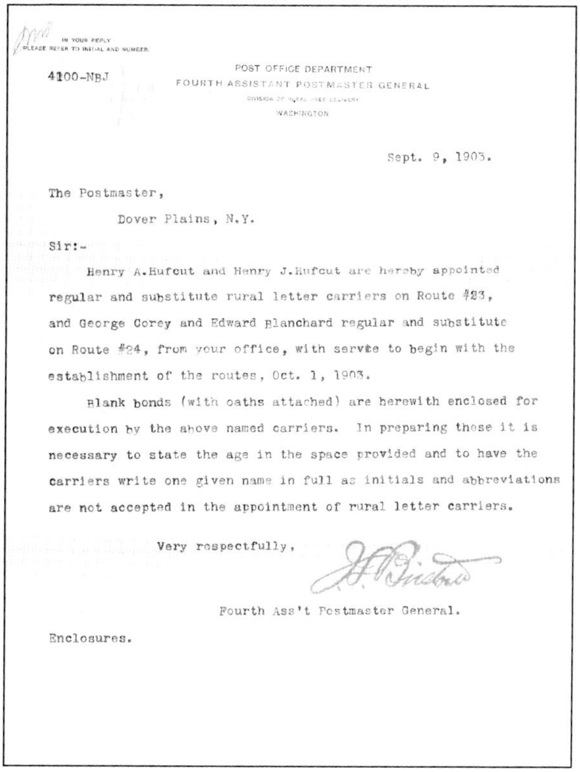

IN YOUR REPLY PLEASE REFER TO INITIAL AND NUMBER.

4100-NBJ

POST OFFICE DEPARTMENT
FOURTH ASSISTANT POSTMASTER GENERAL
DIVISION OF RURAL FREE DELIVERY
WASHINGTON

Sept. 9, 1903.

The Postmaster,

Dover Plains, N.Y.

Sir:-

Henry A.Hufcut and Henry J.Hufcut are hereby appointed regular and substitute rural letter carriers on Route #23, and George Corey and Edward Blanchard regular and substitute on Route #24, from your office, with service to begin with the establishment of the routes, Oct. 1, 1903.

Blank bonds (with oaths attached) are herewith enclosed for execution by the above named carriers. In preparing those it is necessary to state the age in the space provided and to have the carriers write one given name in full as initials and abbreviations are not accepted in the appointment of rural letter carriers.

Very respectfully,

Fourth Ass't Postmaster General.

Enclosures.

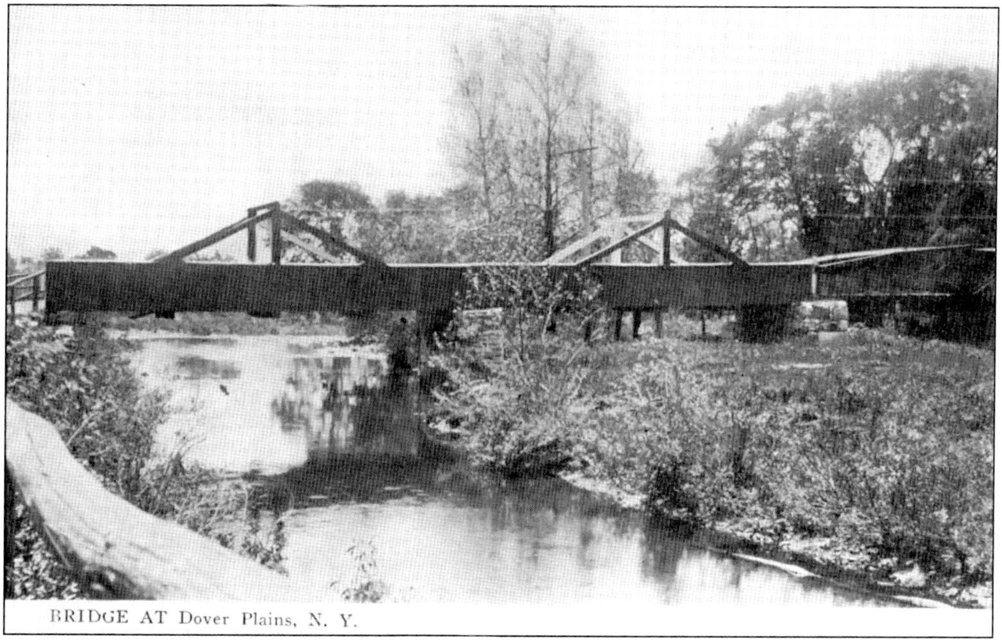

This two-part bridge of the early 1900s spanned the Ten Mile River (left), an island, and a stream (right). North of the bridge, the Ten Mile River dam powered the Dover Plains Light and Power Company. On the river's west bank, the small stream was dammed for a mill. The river and stream joined south of the bridge. The bridge was destroyed by a flood in the 1930s. (WAR, RTR.)

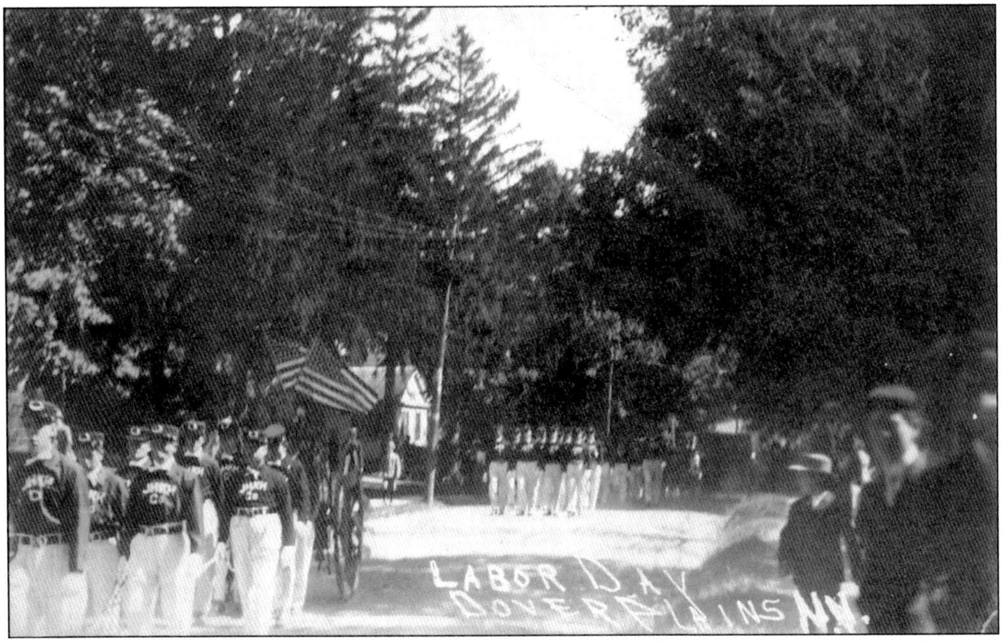

J. H. Ketcham Hose Company, Inc., was incorporated on July 20, 1903. The first voluntary contribution was $25 from M. C. Hall on August 2, 1909. The *Amenia Times* praised the volunteers for their grit, public spirit, and "sticking together" against adverse criticism and public indifference. Today the fire company, rescue squad, fire, police, and ladies' auxiliary volunteers proudly reflect their century of donated service. (TDHS.)

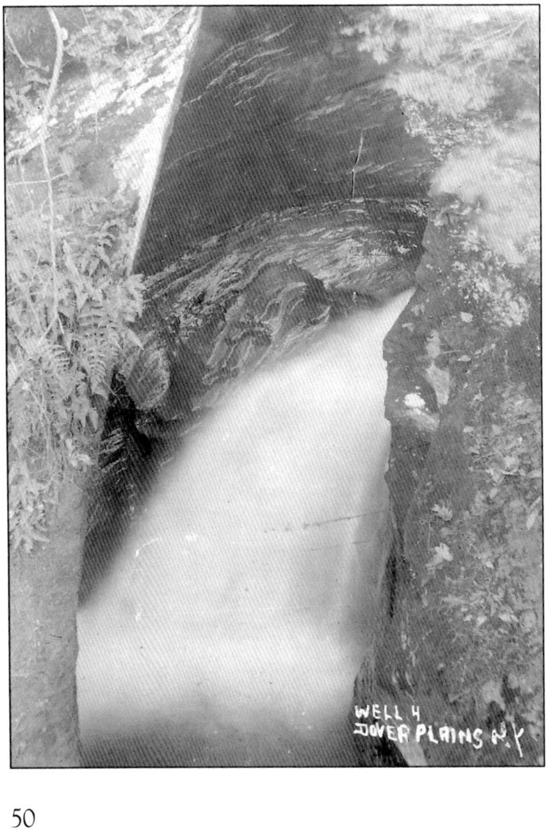

Dover's first water source was gravity fed by cascading water. Seven deep pools worn in the limestone of Seven Wells Brook collected the water. The Dover Plains Water Company was organized in 1900. One founding member was Frank Feeney. Walter Crane married Feeney's daughter Helen and eventually took over the business. As Dover Plains grew, the company changed from a gravity-fed system to artesian wells in 1960. (KD.)

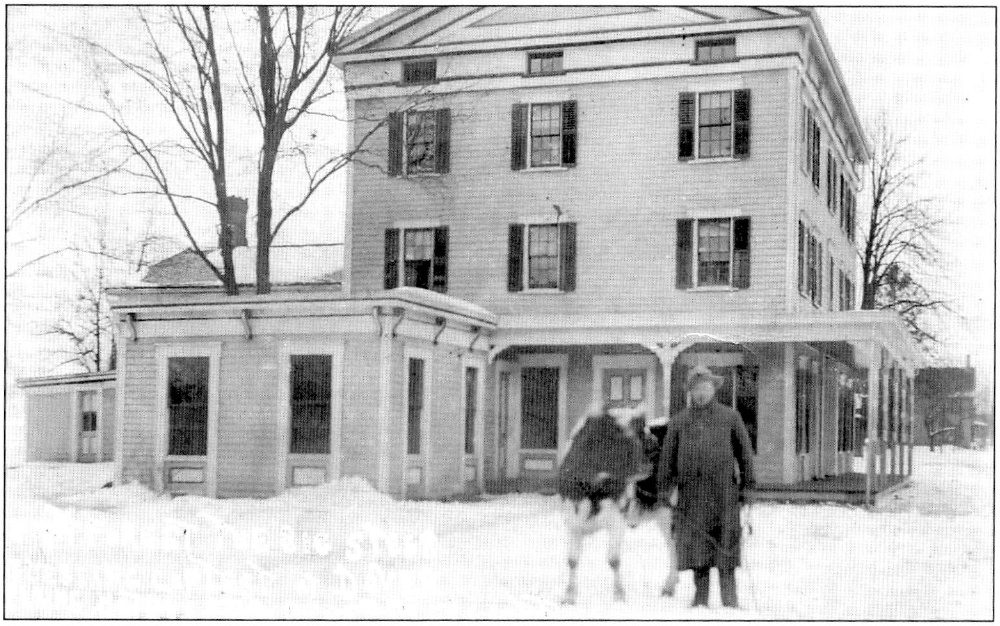

William T. Elliott's Dover Plains Hotel was located on Market Street across from the New York Central Railroad, Harlem Division station. Guests rode the train from New York City for a week or weekend in the country. "Diamond Jim" Brady and Lillian Russell were among the rumored guests. In the early 1900s, Elliott's postcard bore the advertising note "Don't Forget the Big Steer Guessing Contest at Dover Plains Hotel Feb. 11." (TDHS.)

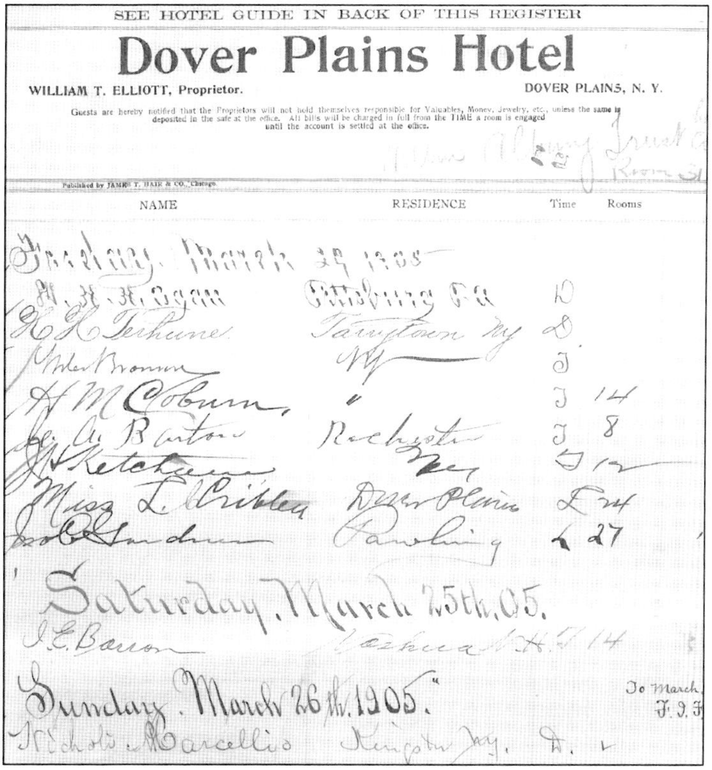

SEE HOTEL GUIDE IN BACK OF THIS REGISTER

Dover Plains Hotel

WILLIAM T. ELLIOTT, Proprietor. DOVER PLAINS, N. Y.

Guests are hereby notified that the Proprietors will not hold themselves responsible for Valuables, Money, Jewelry, etc., unless the same is deposited in the safe at the office. All bills will be charged in full from the TIME a room is engaged until the account is settled at the office.

Published by JAMES T. HAIR & CO., Chicago

NAME	RESIDENCE	Time	Rooms
Friday, March 24 1905			
H. M. Coburn		T	14
G. A. Barton	Rochester	T	8
Miss L. Cribben	Dover Plains	L	24
	Pawling	L	27
Saturday, March 25th, 05.			
I. E. Baron	Nashua N. H.	T	14
Sunday, March 26th, 1905.			
Nichols Marcellis	Kingston N. Y.	D	

On March 24, 1905, Elliott was the proprietor of the Dover Plains Hotel. The log was updated daily, and guests signed upon renting a room. Guests were from Pittsburg, Tarrytown, Rochester, and nearby Pawling. Ketcham also signed for his room at the hotel where his additional visitors and guests could stay. A note was made for Wilbur of the Albany Trust Company, room 31. (TDHS.)

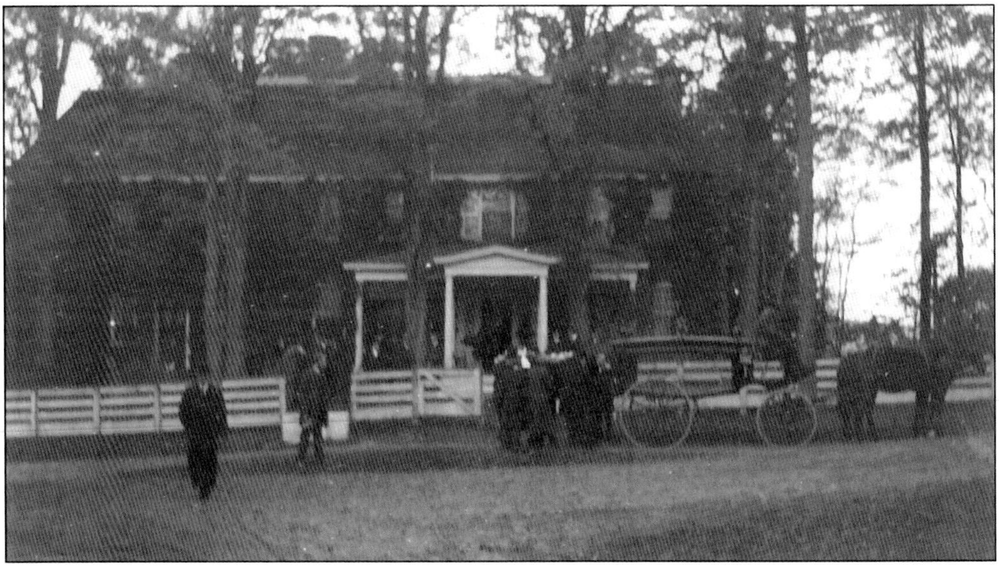

Congressman John Henry Ketcham died on November 6, 1906, in New York City. Dignitaries from the White House, Congress, New York State, and other political entities attended his funeral in Dover Plains. Some mourners stayed at the former Jackson Wing's inn, run by his grandson Sheldon. The image shows solemn dignitaries gathered at the rear of a horse-drawn carriage and at the inn. (TDHS.)

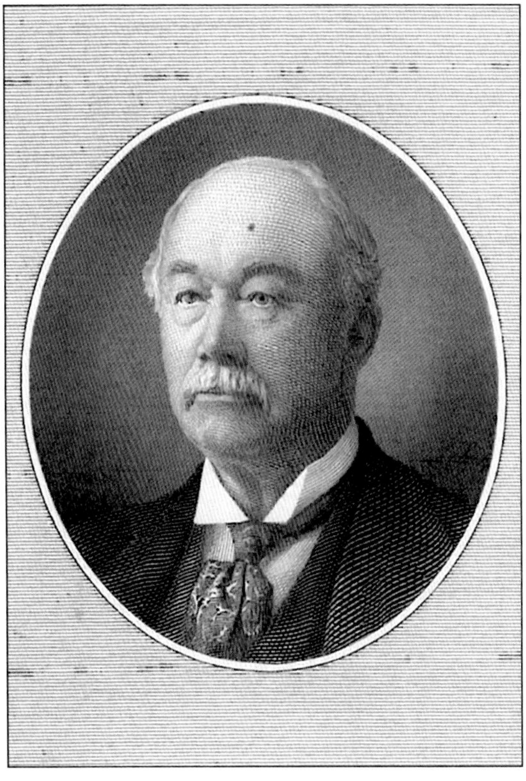

On the day of Ketcham's death, resolutions were set forth, voted on, and adopted in both houses of Congress to adjourn as a mark of respect for his passing. Memorial addresses to the House took place in February 1907 and the Senate in March 1907. Ketcham believed in people, and they believed in him. He was remembered as a sympathetic and understanding man who led best by example. (TDHS.)

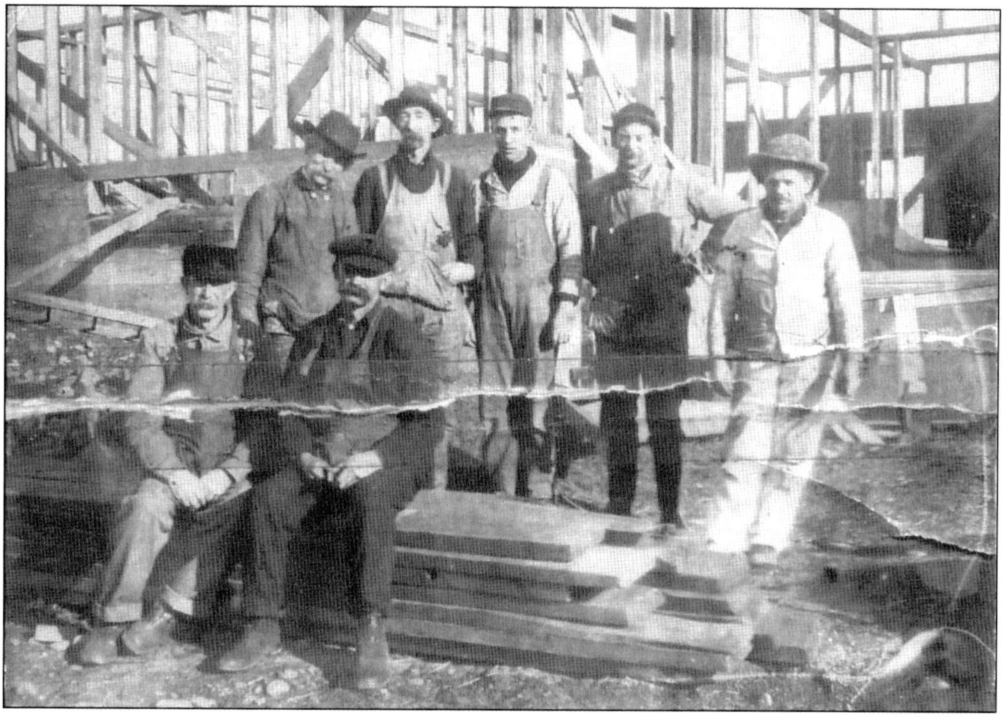

Among the construction workers building the school in Dover were Mike Shermerhorn, George "Muggy" Vincent, and Allie B. Murphy. Dover High School was completed by September 1909. For the first time, 127 pupils from Dover Plains and Wingdale joined in classes. Horatio S. Benson was principal. Some students in classes were James Miller, Jessie Benson, Mildred Benson, DeWitt Benson, Darwin Benson, Byron Benson, Helen O'Brien, and Eunice Boyce. (MLW.)

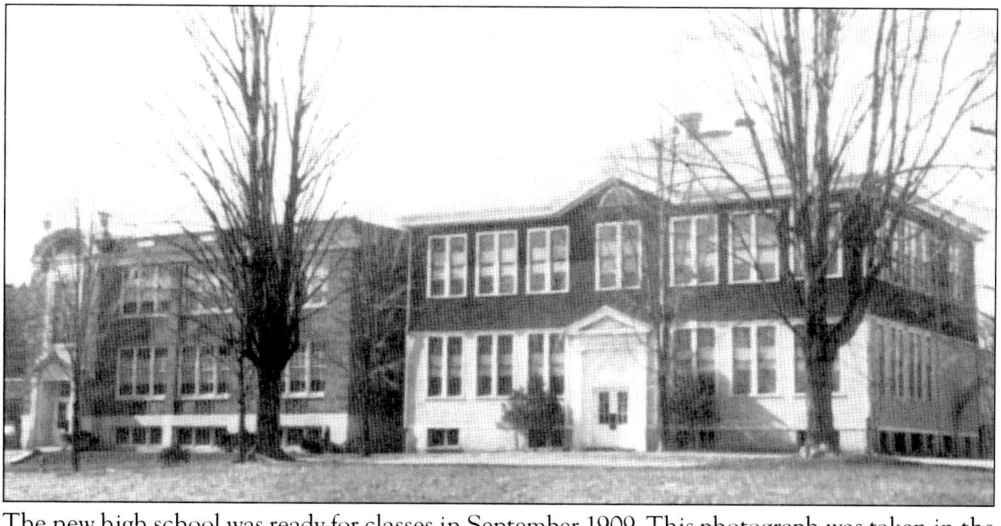

The new high school was ready for classes in September 1909. This photograph was taken in the early 1950s. It shows the addition put on the school in 1939. A later addition was added in 1951, and by 1964, the Dover Union Free School District purchased land midway between Wingdale and Dover, built the new Dover Junior-Senior High School, and graduated the first class from the school. (DRH.)

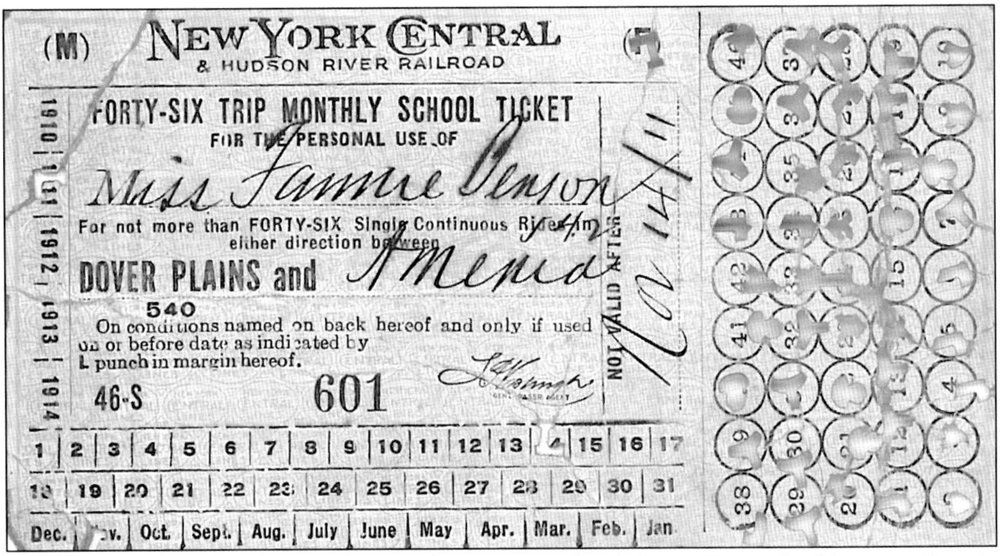

(M) NEW YORK CENTRAL
& HUDSON RIVER RAILROAD

FORTY-SIX TRIP MONTHLY SCHOOL TICKET
FOR THE PERSONAL USE OF
Miss Fannie Benson
For not more than FORTY-SIX Single Continuous Rides in either direction between
DOVER PLAINS and Amenia
540
On conditions named on back hereof and only if used on or before date as indicated by punch in margin hereof.
46-S 601
NOT VALID AFTER

In the early 1900s, students often rode the train to school. Louie Benson's older sister Fannie used this 46-trip monthly school ticket commuter pass on the New York Central and Hudson River Railroad to attend high school in Amenia. Her senior class commencement was held at the Dover Opera House on June 23, 1914. The opera house later became Chertock's Department Store and then Electronic Technologies Corporation. (LEB.)

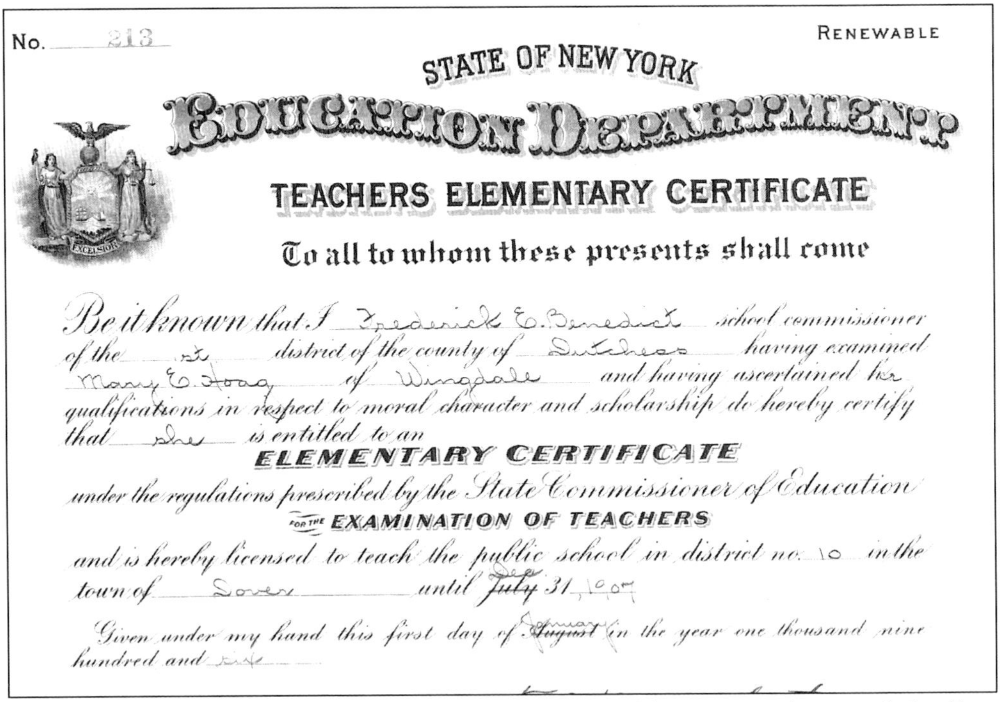

No. 213 RENEWABLE

STATE OF NEW YORK
EDUCATION DEPARTMENT
TEACHERS ELEMENTARY CERTIFICATE
To all to whom these presents shall come

Be it known that I Frederick E. Benedict school commissioner of the 1st district of the county of Dutchess having examined Mary E. Hoag of Wingdale and having ascertained her qualifications in respect to moral character and scholarship do hereby certify that she is entitled to an
ELEMENTARY CERTIFICATE
under the regulations prescribed by the State Commissioner of Education for the EXAMINATION OF TEACHERS
and is hereby licensed to teach the public school in district no. 10 in the town of Dover until Dec 31, 1907

Given under my hand this first day of January in the year one thousand nine hundred and five

Mary Elizabeth Hoag grew up on Hoag's Corners in Wingdale. In 1902, she attended college in New Paltz, and in 1905, she received her temporary elementary teaching license for Dover District No. 10, an elementary school in Wingdale, at $9 a month. In 1908, she received a raise to $10 a month. Almost a century later, her nephew Charles Hoag was president of the Dover District School Board. (PH, AL.)

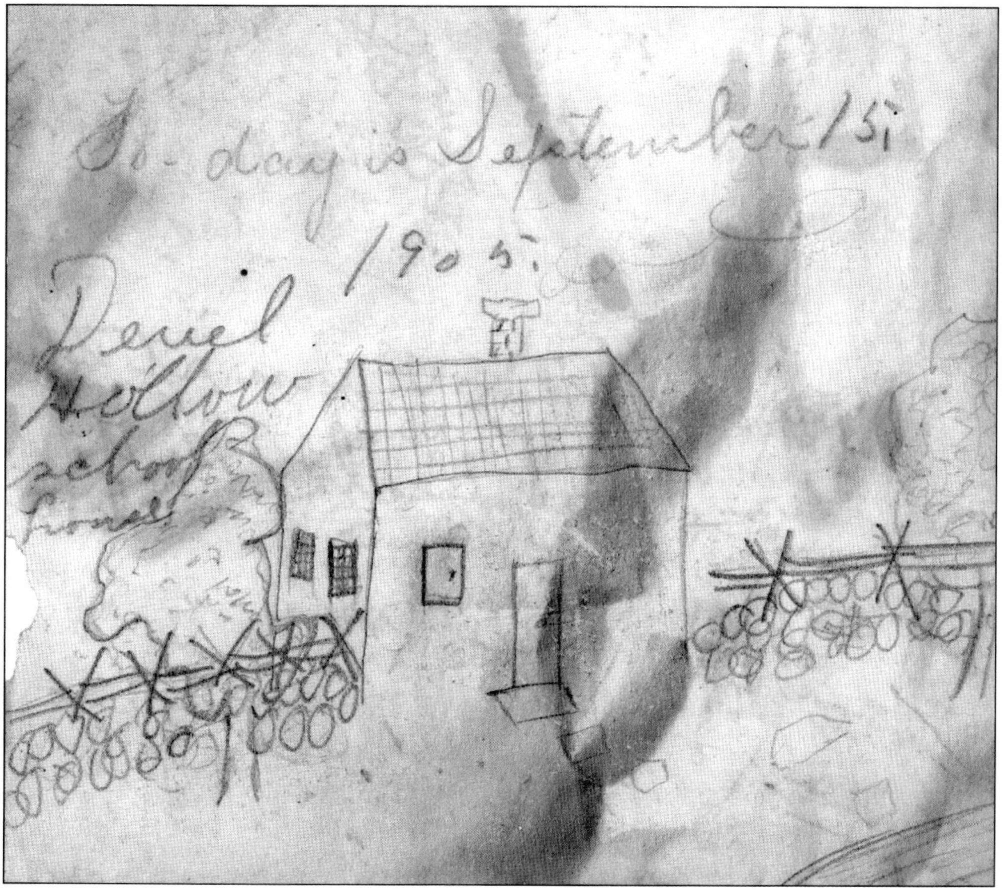

Young Lucy Aldrich prepared several drawings for a class assignment on August 15, 1905. This picture shows the Deuel Hollow School, located at the intersection with Leather Hill Road. A shingled roof covers the small school. A single chimney and three windows are shown. Stone slabs line the schoolhouse path while stone walls and fences border the lot. Other assignment pictures showed the nearby Aldrich barn and wildflowers. (JP.)

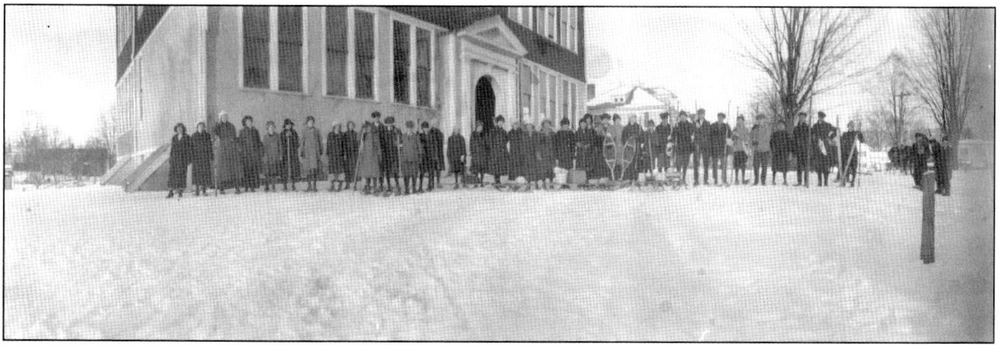

The old-timers say, "When we were kids we walked to school." This incredible picture shows students at Dover High School in the 1920s. After a snow, 41 students posed in front of the high school to show off their snow gear. Some wore boots and pulled sleds. Others used walking sticks, snowshoes, and skis. To their right is a horse-drawn sleigh. (RAR.)

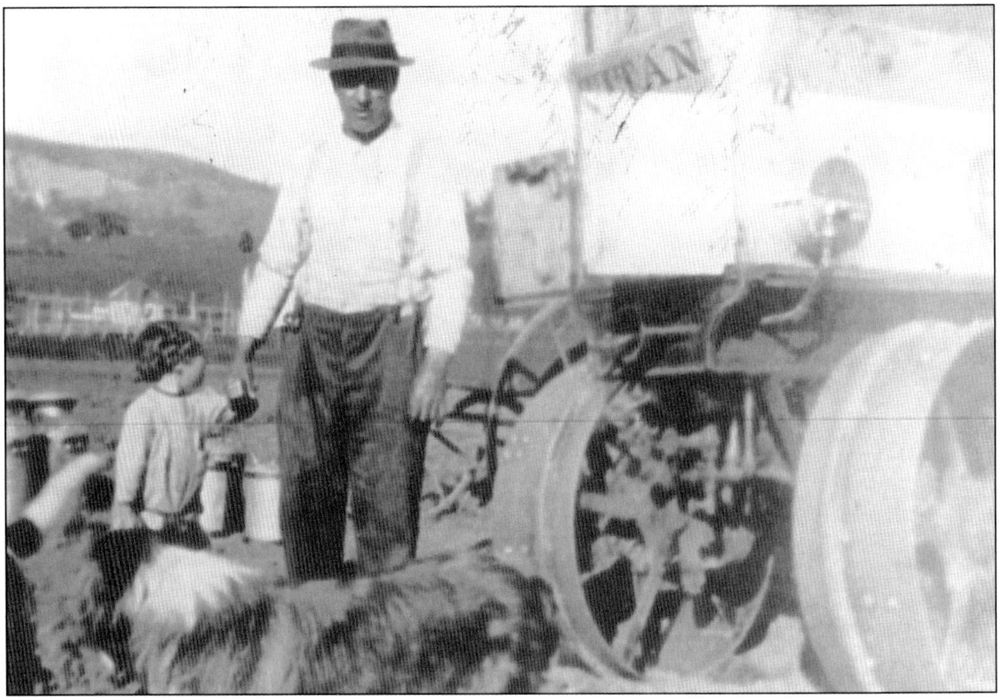

Around 1912, Ben Duncan Sr. worked close to home at the Midfield farm on Route 22 in Dover Plains. With him is Ben Duncan Jr. To the child's left are two large milk cans used for the dairy, which had a modern, on-site milk-testing facility. Note the wide metal tires on the Titan steam-driven tractor. (PDP.)

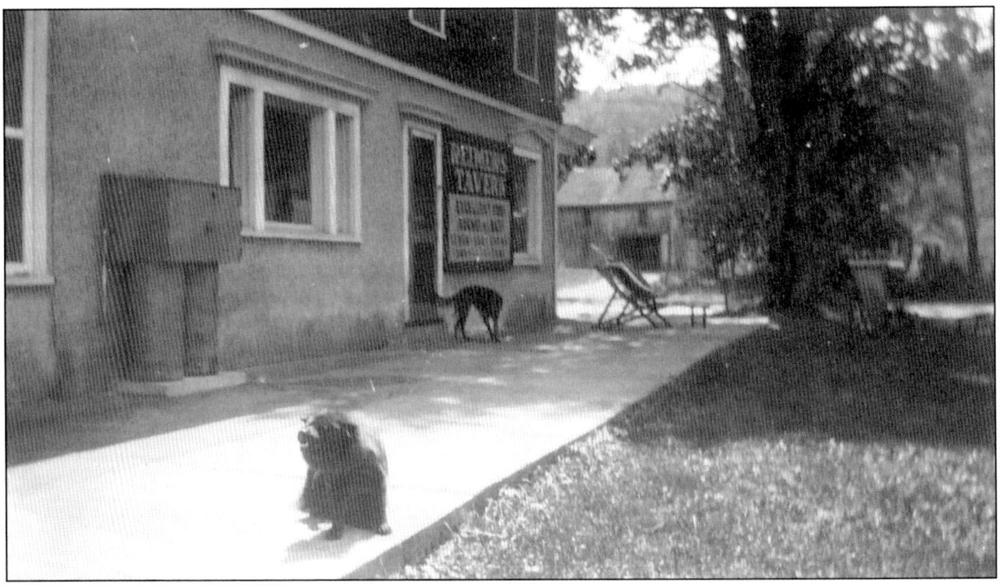

Adolph Reimer was industrious and built this cold-storage plant when few existed. The huge barn doubled as both a prosperous store and a tavern on Main Street, now Route 22. This south-facing view of Reimer's Tavern shows gas tanks for cooking. Nearby were the pets, a dog and pot-bellied pig. Later owner Frank Vinchiarello added bowling alleys. Across the street was Duncan's barn. (WAR, RTR.)

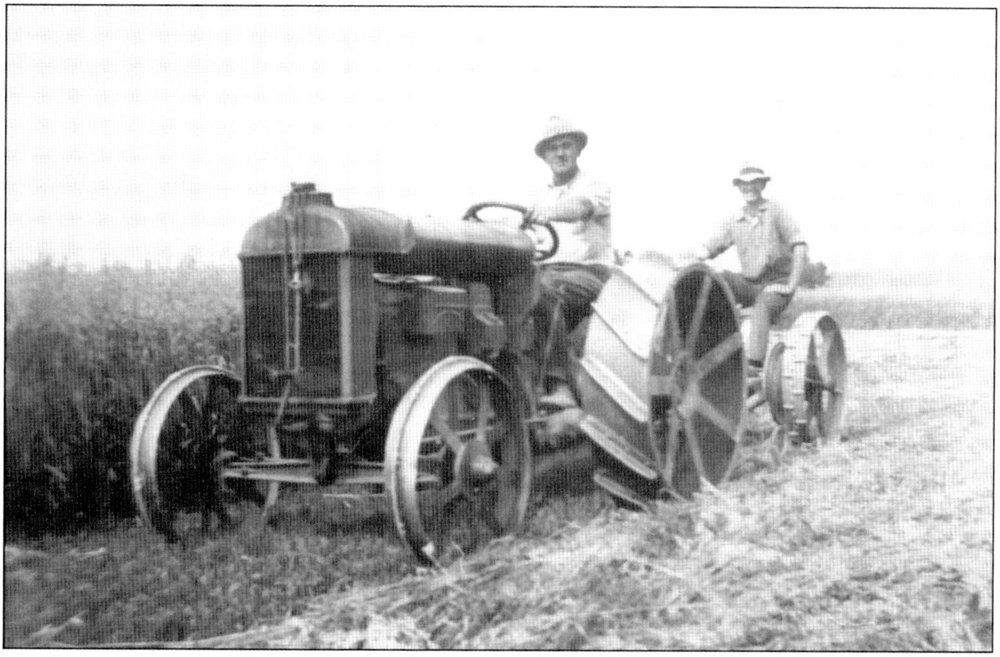

Adolph Reimer (center) and his son Thomas worked their farm on the valley floor just east of the Ten Mile River in Dover Plains. This image captures them on their tractor about 1915, as they crossed a summer field. The steel wheels have three different traction treads. Eventually the Keller family purchased the farm. It continues to be run as a working farm. (RDR.)

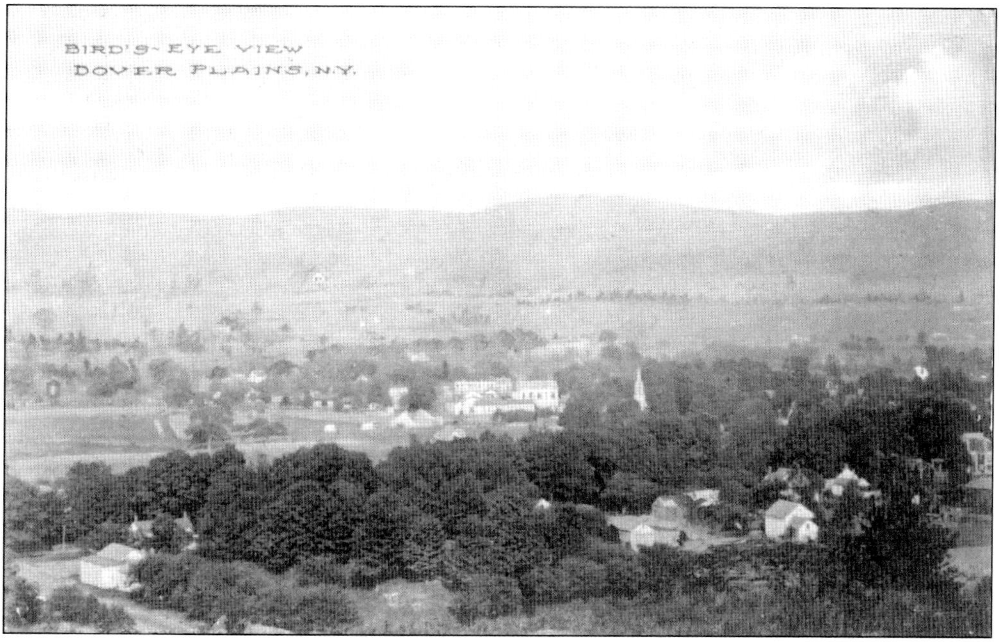

This bird's-eye view of Dover Plains from the heights of a western ridgeline shows the hamlet in 1912. The Dover Second Baptist Church steeple on today's Mill Street can be seen right of center. Today's Route 22 is at the lower left. The large buildings (center) are Reed Block and the opera house near the railroad tracks. A railroad water tower is at the extreme left. (KD.)

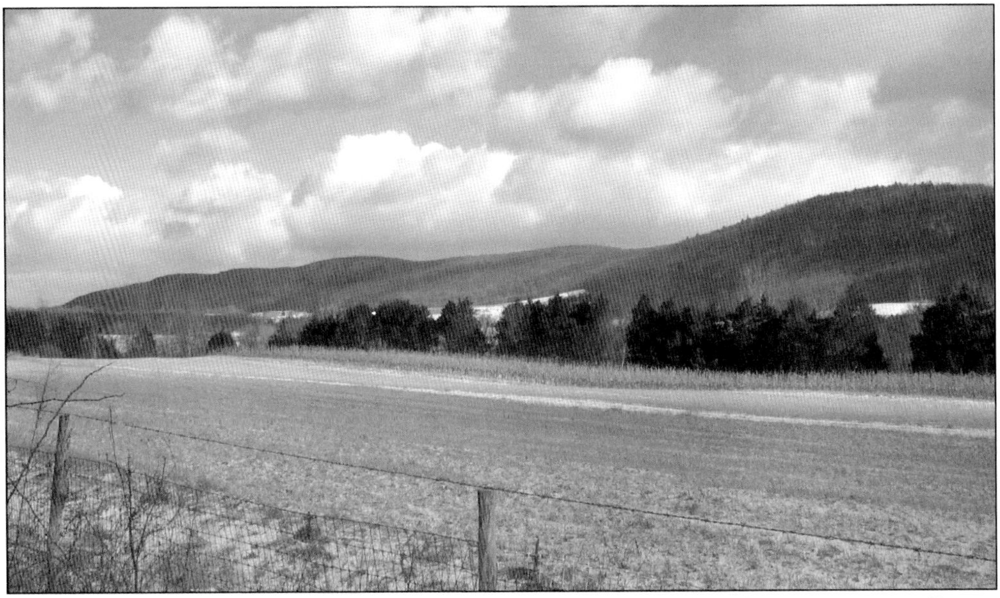

Soaring, mountainlike hills, such as East Mountain and Schaghticoke Mountain in Dover, enclose the Harlem Valley. Photographed from old Route 22 looking north, rolling land spreads eastward to the steep limestone ridges. East Mountain folks made their way down the mountainside via steep, winding trails to the valley below. According to the 1857 Boundary Commissioners Report, the New York and Connecticut boundary line bisects the Schaghticoke Mountains. (DPH.)

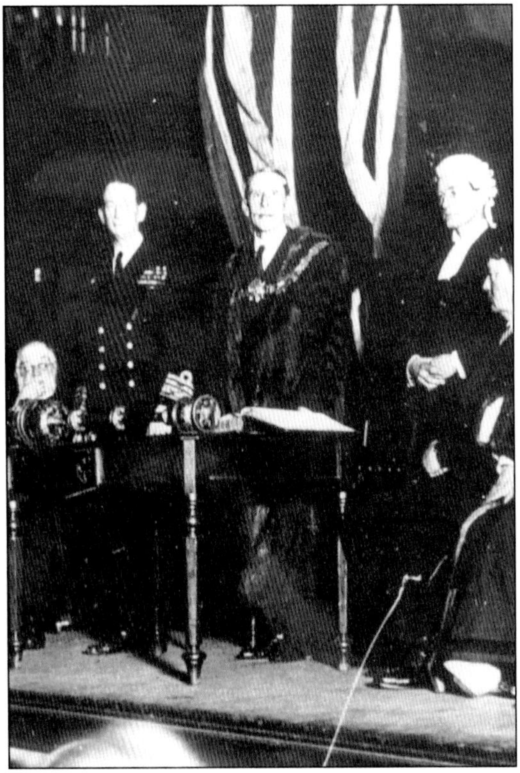

In May 1916, Dover teacher Arthur T. Benson sent a letter to Mayor Edward T. Farley of Dover, England, asking about his town being the "Mother Dover." The mayor answered that he had no doubt that Dover, England, was the mother town of many other Dover towns. Shown in this 1918 image is Farley of Dover, England. Farley was knighted after World War II for his governmental assistance. (Dover Museum, Dover, England, LS.)

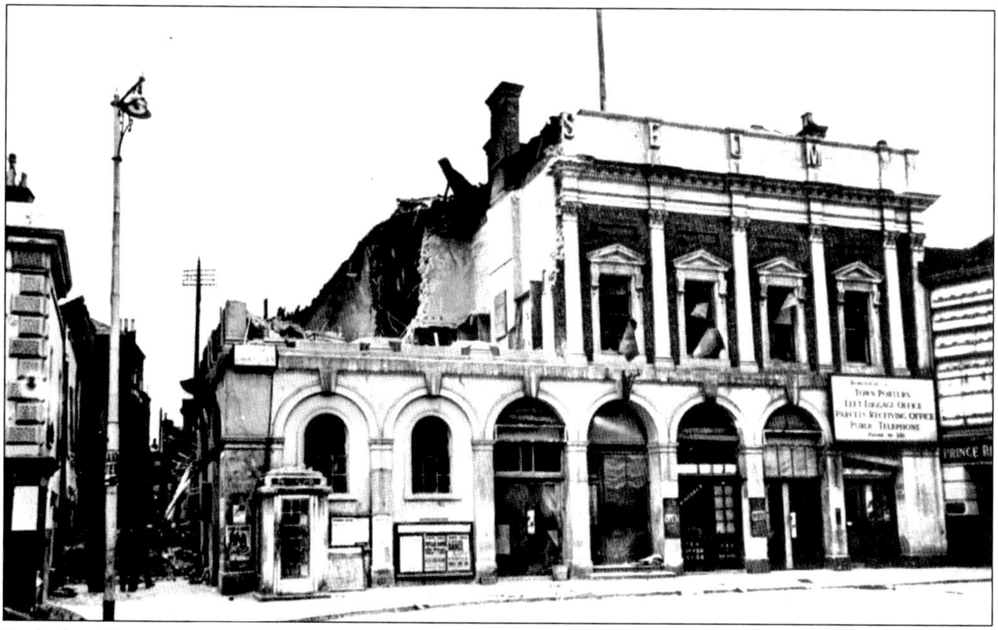

Farley's office in Dover, England, was the repository for Benson's letter. During the blitzkrieg bombing of England during World War II, his office and repository was extensively damaged. A request was made to Dover, England, correspondent Lorraine Sencicle for information on the mayor's office. She responded that during document recovery, the oldest papers got priority. Her extensive research and generosity provided these pictures. (Dover Museum, Dover, England, LS.)

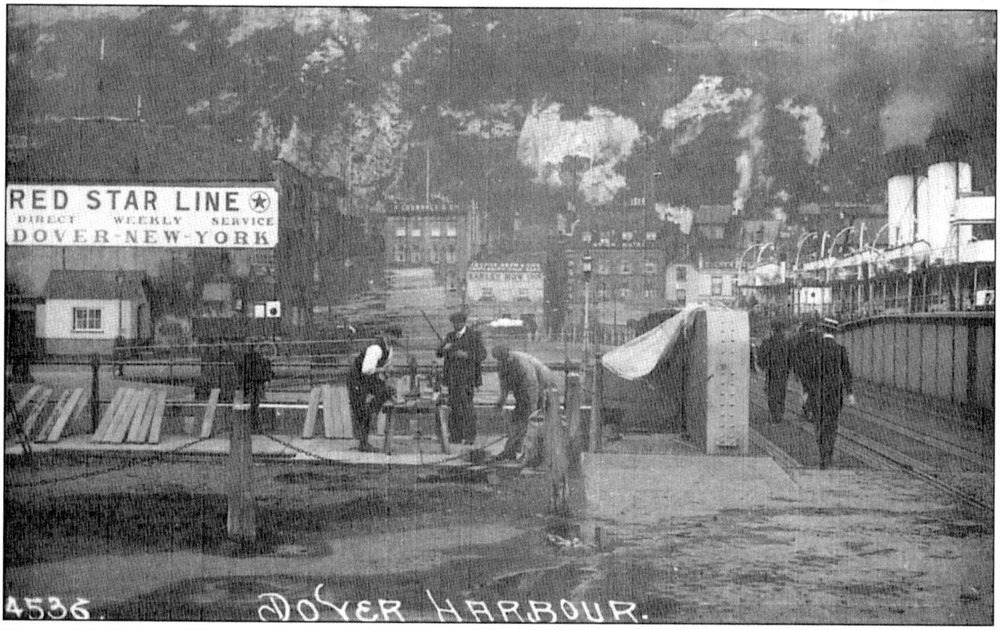

Dover Harbor in Dover, England, is situated at the base of the massive cliffs of Dover. This view shows the immense size of the cliffs as they overshadow the community below. While in New York, perhaps the view of Dover reminded founder, Richard Sackett, of Dover, England. Cruise ships left Dover, England, for New York City. In this 1913 picture, a quick glimpse at the destination looks like Dover, New York. (Dover Museum, Dover, England, LS.)

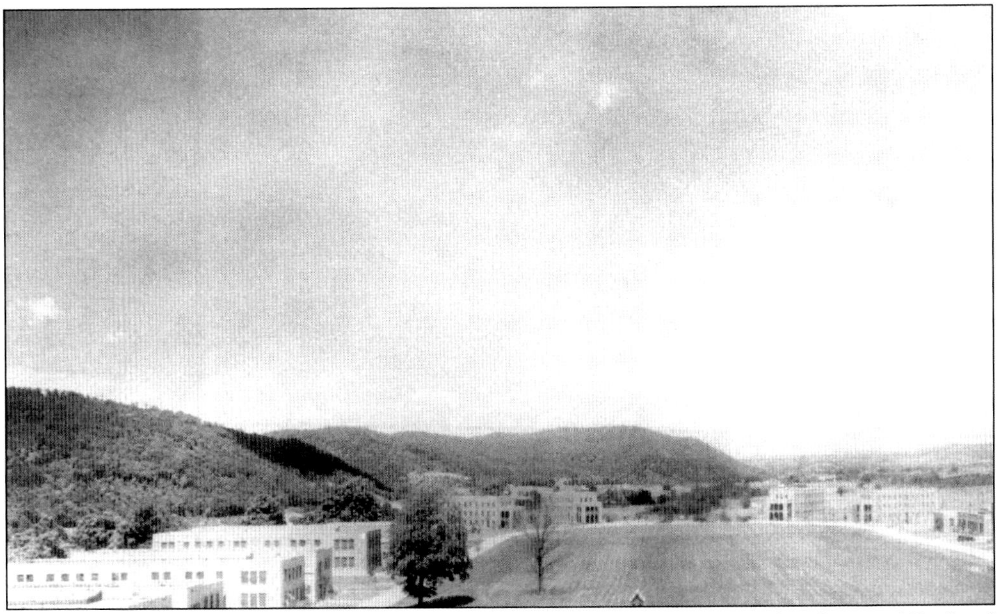

This 1930s aerial view looks south over the newly built Wassaic State School toward Richard Sackett's original 7,500-acre patent in Dover. The view is similar to that from the Englishman's hilltop farm in Wassaic. Dover's East Mountain (left) dominates and looms over the valley of the Ten Mile River. The view also resembles the cliffs of Dover as they dominate the harbor town of Dover, England. (DPH.)

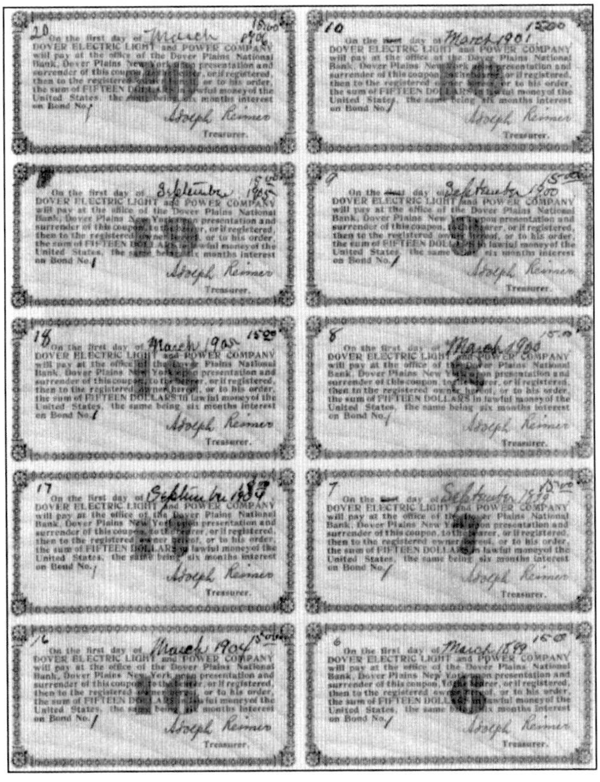

The Dover Plains Electric Light and Power Company was incorporated in 1895 by Charles P. Morgan and Charles S. Wyman, who expanded the business in 1909. When presented at the Dover Plains National Bank, the Dover Plains Electric Light and Power Company paid dividends on March and September 15 to the bearer of the coupons. When the registered owner surrendered the coupon for bond 1, treasurer Adolph Reimer paid a $15 dividend. (RTR.)

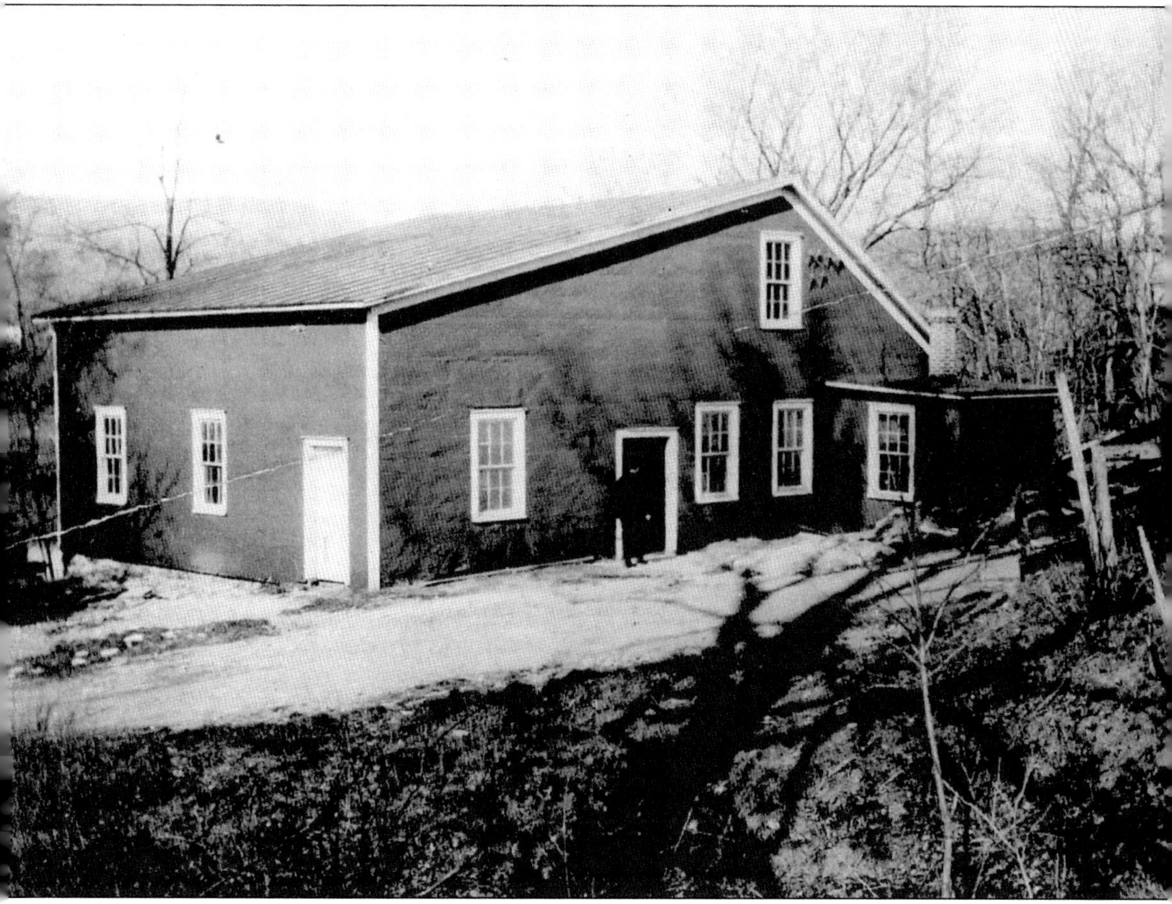

According to a presentation written by Bill Roach around 1964 titled *The History of the Harlem Valley Electric Utility Industry*, Morgan's gristmill on the Ten Mile River became the "grand-daddy" of New York State electric and gas companies in the Harlem Valley. This photograph shows the original powerhouse along the river around 1906. The Reverend Walter Allyn Rogers donated the picture series to the Town of Dover Historical Society. (DD.)

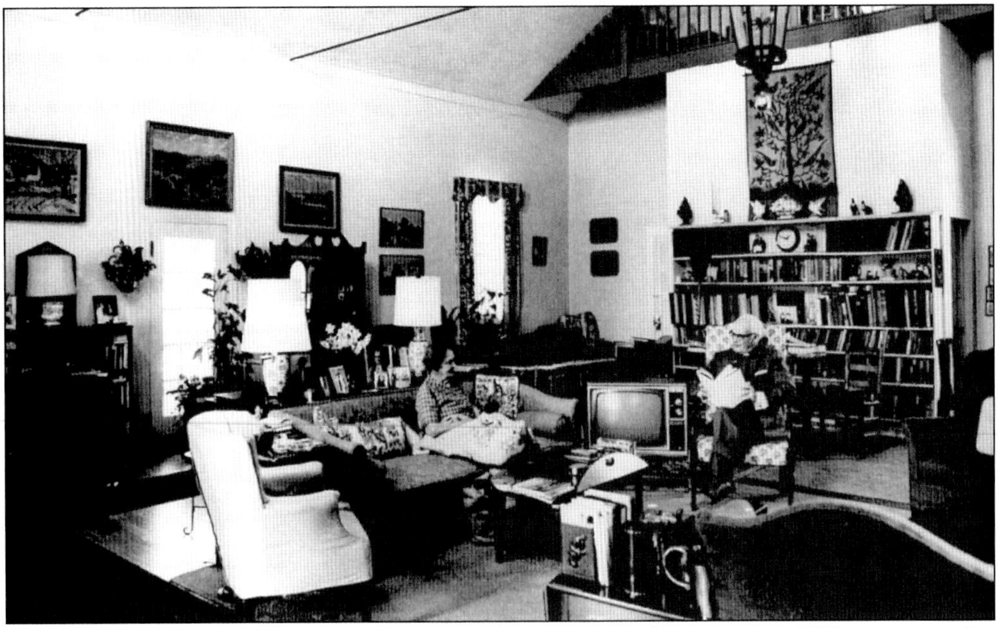

The existing structure was remodeled in the late 1920s. Local artist Harry Waltman turned it into a studio. Upon his death in 1951, Dorothea Hayward purchased the property for a summer home. She eventually donated the house to St. James Episcopal Church for the vicarage. This photograph, donated by the Reverend Walter Allyn Rogers in 1975, shows the ultimate transformation from powerhouse and studio into a home. (TDHS.)

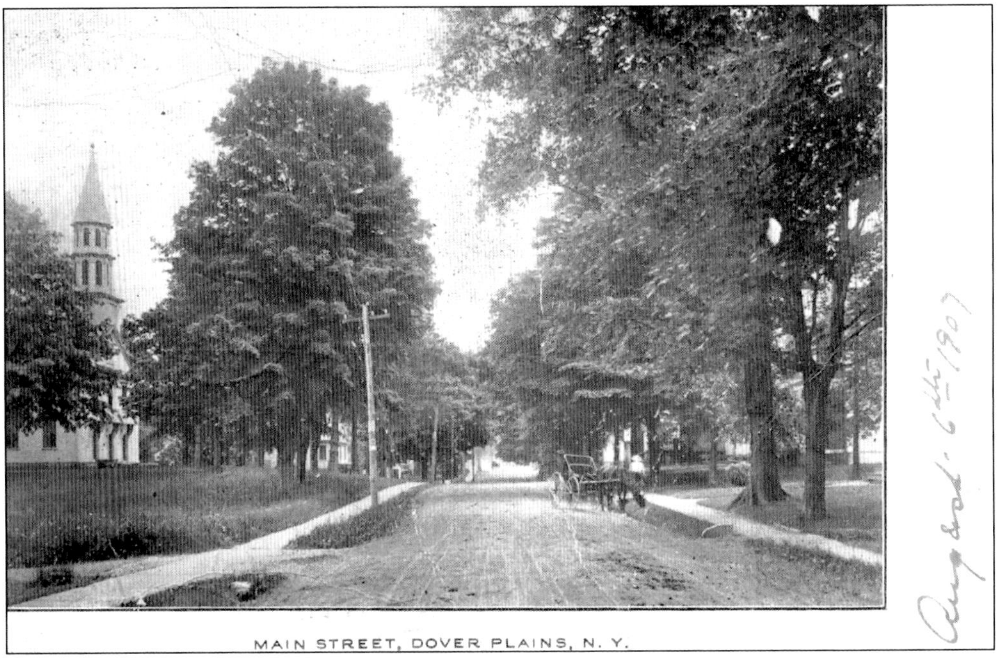

In 1907, Main Street in Dover Plains led to the market area of the hamlet. Carriage wheel tracks can be seen in the road bordered by slate sidewalks. On the left is the Dover Second Baptist Church. The adjacent lot of hay was ready to be cut. A horse-drawn carriage sits across the street in front of the Methodist church. Today this road is Mill Street. (KD.)

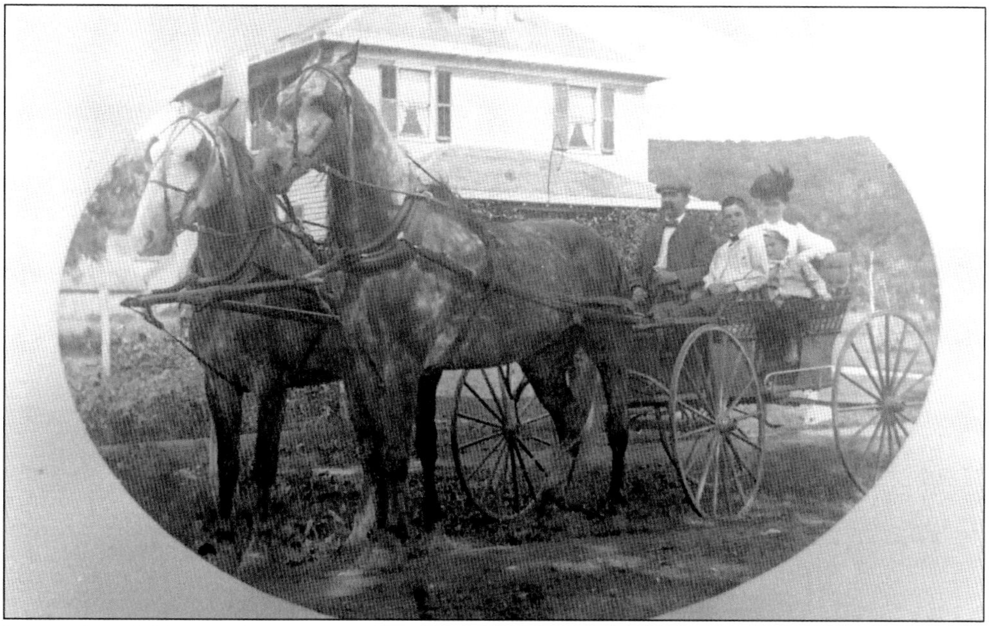

Pictured in 1907 near their Reimer Avenue home in Dover Plains are Laurence Lloyd Colligan and his 12-year-old son Raymond. They sit in the front seat of a horse-drawn carriage. Ellen (Doyle) Colligan sits in the back seat with her five-year-old cousin Arthur. Laurence and Raymond owned Colligan's Market on Market Street. Raymond's children were Laurence "Butch" Colligan and Janet Colligan. (CSC.)

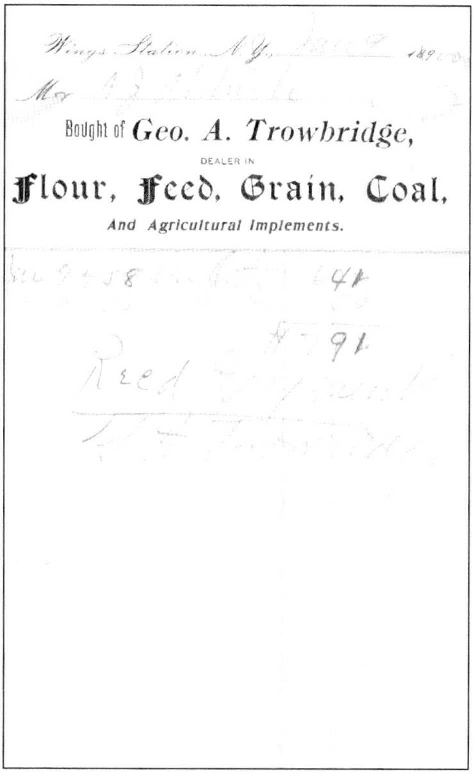

Wings Station, N.Y., 189

Mr

Bought of Geo. A. Trowbridge,

DEALER IN

Flour, Feed, Grain, Coal,

And Agricultural Implements.

In 1908, George W. Trowbridge had a general store that sold agricultural implements and products, such as feed, grain, flour, and coal at Wings Station. The Trowbridge receipt shows that on January 9, 1900, A. J. Aldrich purchased 458 pounds of oats for $6.41 and 150 pounds of rice for $1.50. His total bill of $7.91 was paid that day. (TDHS.)

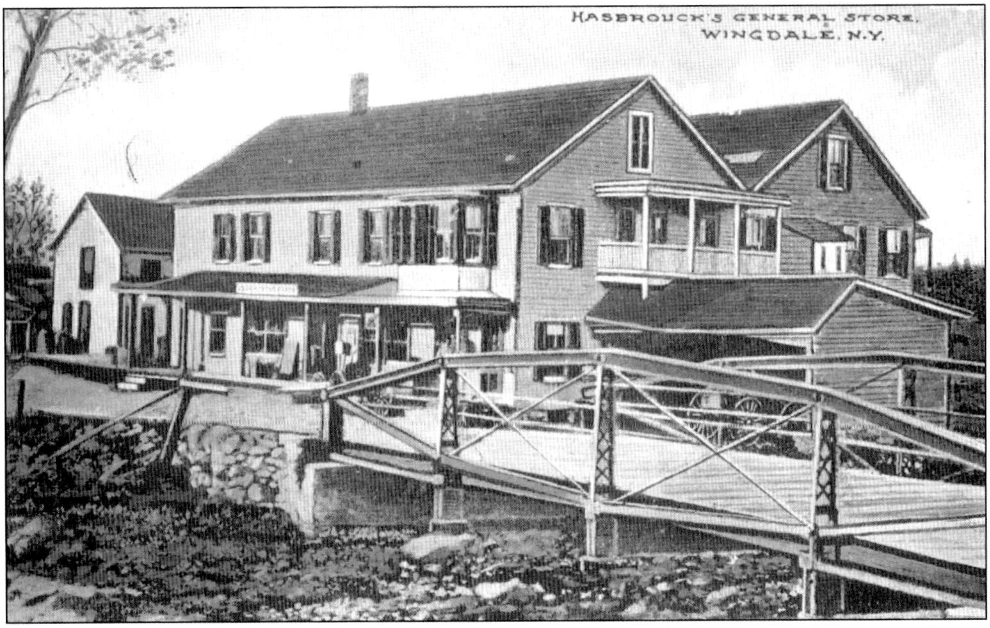

Oscar Hasbrouck's General Store in Wingdale was west of and adjacent to the Swamp River bridge and railroad tracks. The store sold dry goods, tools, and products to area folk, farmers, laborers, and the nearby Borden Condensed Milk Company factory. His store doubled as the post office in 1908. The store advertised via postcard. By 1920, the store name was Garrisons. Converted to apartments in 1938, the building burned about 1980. (RA.)

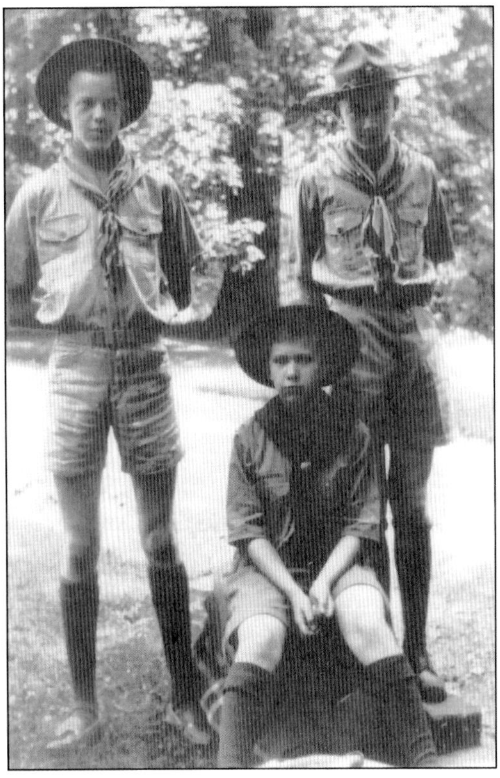

According to Robert Crane Sr., he and his brothers, Duncan and Philippe Crane, spent several summers at the Camp Siwanoy on Deuel Hollow Road in Wingdale during the 1930s. Beginning in February 2000, Robert was interviewed about his memories and summer years in Dover. Robert, an engineer, remembered times spent at the farm and cabins on Cranes Pond as some of the most wonderful in his life. (RC.)

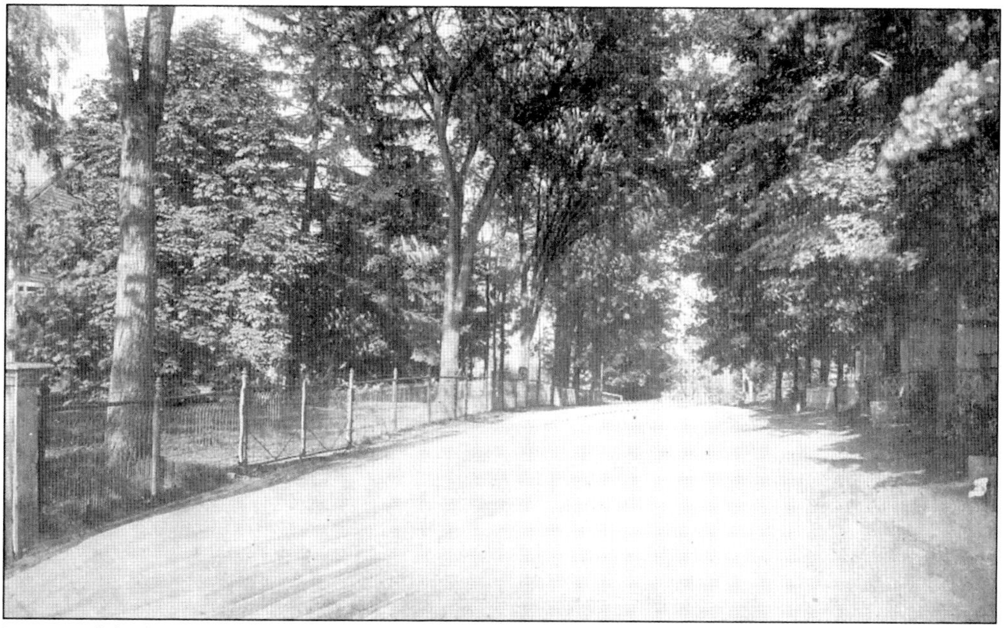

In Wingdale, homes peek from behind shady trees that line the road. Neat lawns border gateposts with wire fences. Across the street, white clapboard fencing encloses the houses and yards. This quaint image of a residential section in Wingdale was taken in the early 1900s. Based on the steep hill in front of the viewer, it is thought to be the Cottage Avenue area. (KD.)

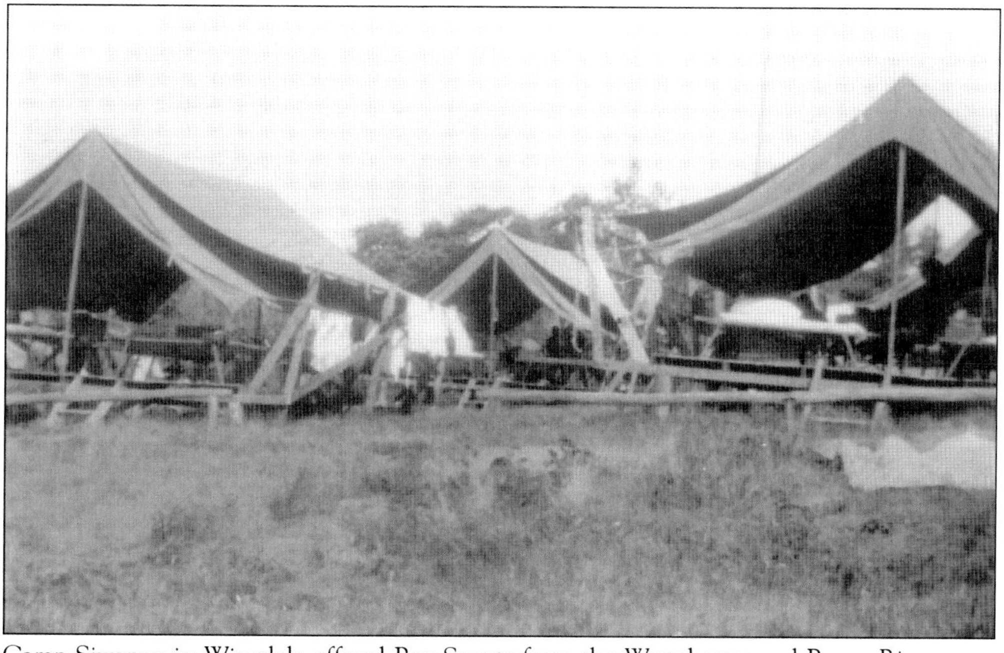

Camp Siwanoy in Wingdale offered Boy Scouts from the Westchester and Bronx River areas the opportunity to camp in and learn from the great outdoors. The tent and sleeping area was on platforms, surrounded by the camp area. Tents had two layers for rain protection and air circulation. Scouts were responsible for their own laundry, and wet clothes were hung on the rope lines outside the tents. (RC.)

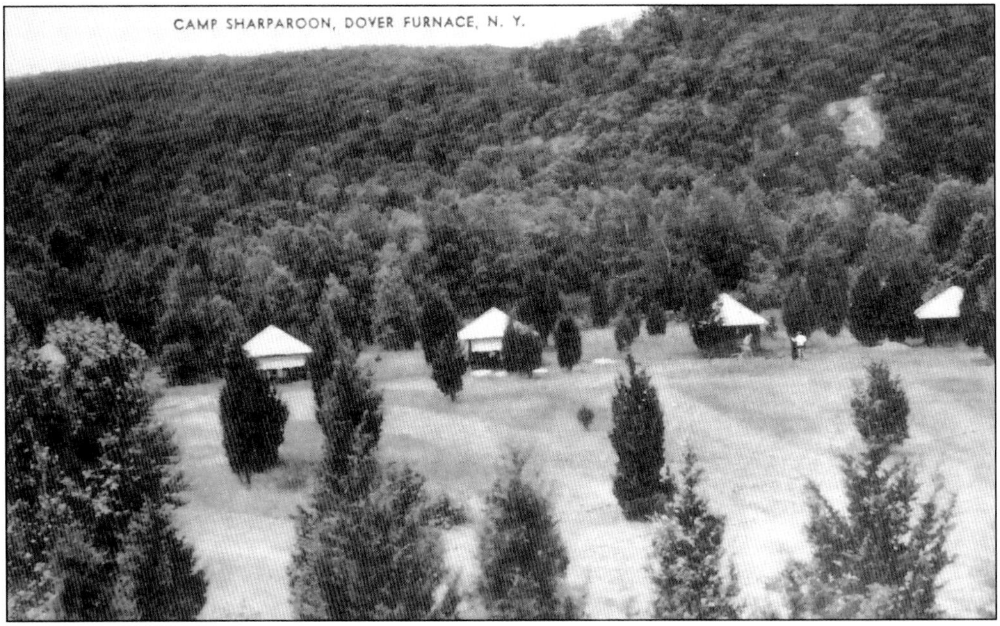

Camp Sharparoon was named for witch Goody Sharparoon, who flew over the pond. Purchased in 1921 by the New York City Mission Society, the Dover Furnace area became a summer camp for underprivileged young men from Harlem. Tents, lean-to campsites, and dormitories housed campers and staff. Four decades later, the camp program went coed and added families. Eventually summer enrollment declined, and around 2000, the facility closed. (KD.)

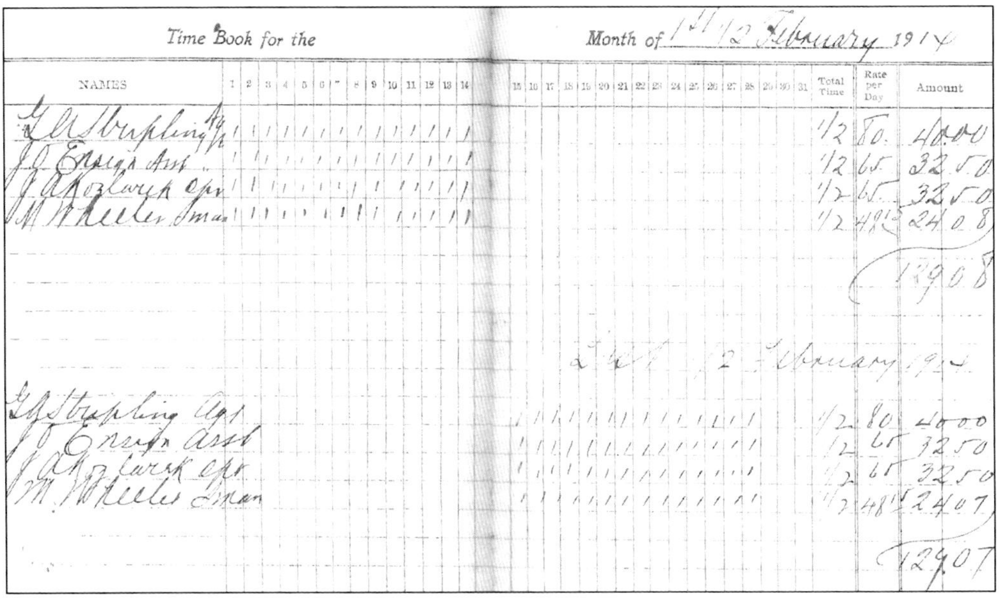
Time Book for the Month of 1st 1/2 February 1914

NAMES	Total Time	Rate per Day	Amount
G A Stripling Agt	1/2	80.	40 00
J O Ensign Asst	1/2	65	32 50
J A Kozlarek Opr	1/2	65	32 50
M Wheeler Fman	1/2	48 15	24 08
			129 08

2nd 1/2 February 1914

NAMES	Total Time	Rate per Day	Amount
G A Stripling Agt	1/2	80	40 00
J O Ensign Asst	1/2	65	32 50
J A Kozlarek Opr	1/2	65	32 50
M Wheeler Fman	1/2	48 15	24 07
			129 07

During February 1914, the New York Central Railroad, Harlem Division time log recorded four men working at the Dover Plains depot, operating switches and turntables and doing whatever was required. They worked a half-day seven days a week for the entire month. Employees were station agent Augustus (Gus) Stripling, assistant agent John O. Ensign, operator John A. Kozlarek, and fireman M. Wheeler. The agent earned $80, and the fireman earned $48.15 per month. (CRR.)

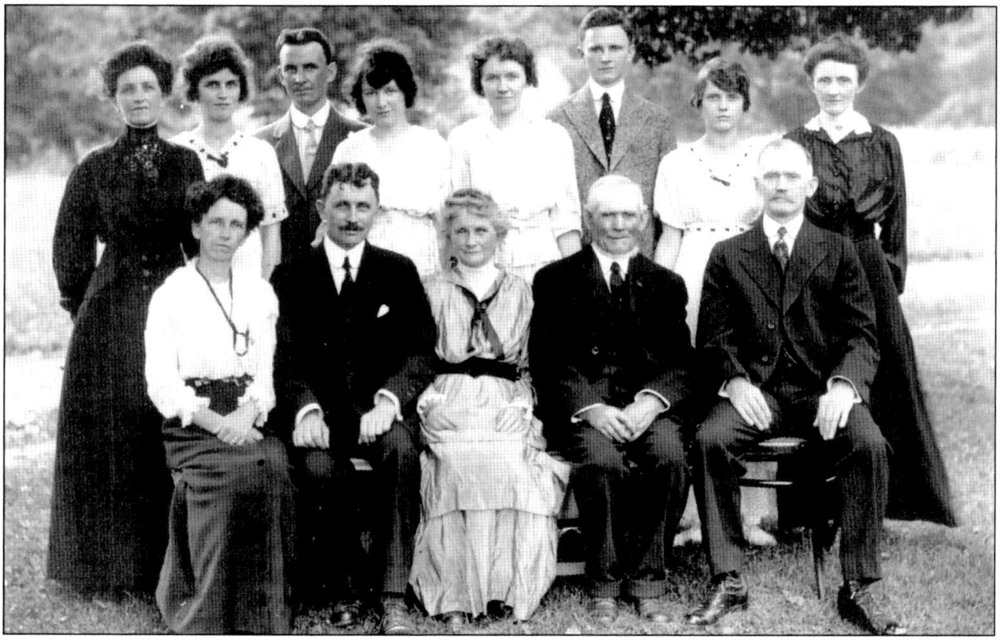

In 1915, Roger Callahan's grandparents Mary Ellen (Donahue) and Andrew Carey celebrated their 50th wedding anniversary with all their children. Pictured from left to right are (first row) Elizabeth, John, Mary Ellen (mother), Andrew (father), and William; (second row) Margaret, Alice, Andrew, Emma, Sarah, Frank, Loretta, and Mary Ellen. Their eldest was William at age 50, and Loretta was the youngest at age 17. Loretta married James Callahan, and they also had 11 children. (RMC.)

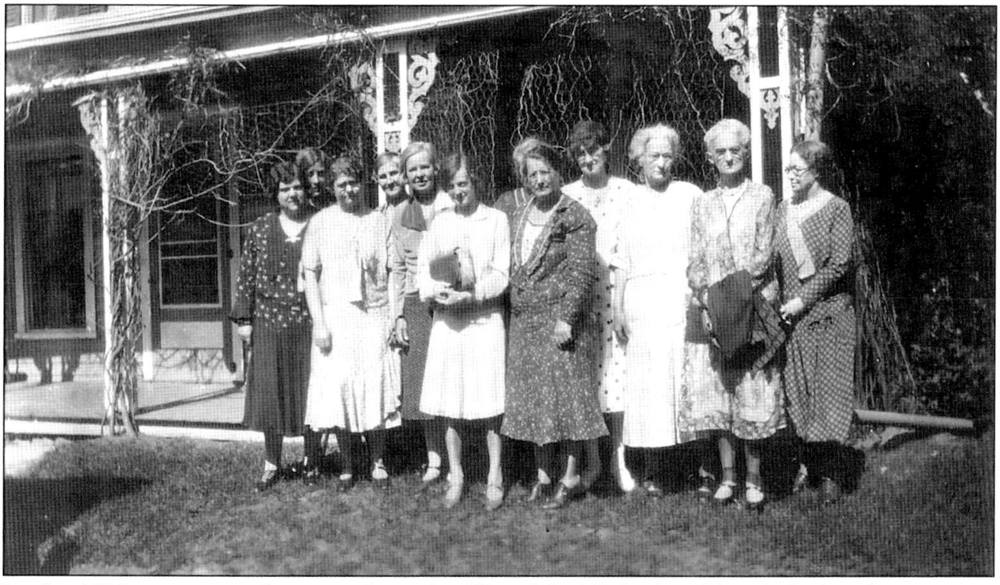

In the 1920s, a group of women from the Wingdale Methodist Church Ladies Society pose in front of the vine-covered porch of Melvin Benson's house. Members, from left to right, are Gertrude (Trowbridge) Havener; Hattie Parsons; Louise Lewis; unidentified; unidentified; the minister's wife; Alice Hodge; Cora Gardner; Ada Trowbridge; unidentified; and Annie Herrings. Ada was the central operator for the telephone system in Wingdale. (TDHS.)

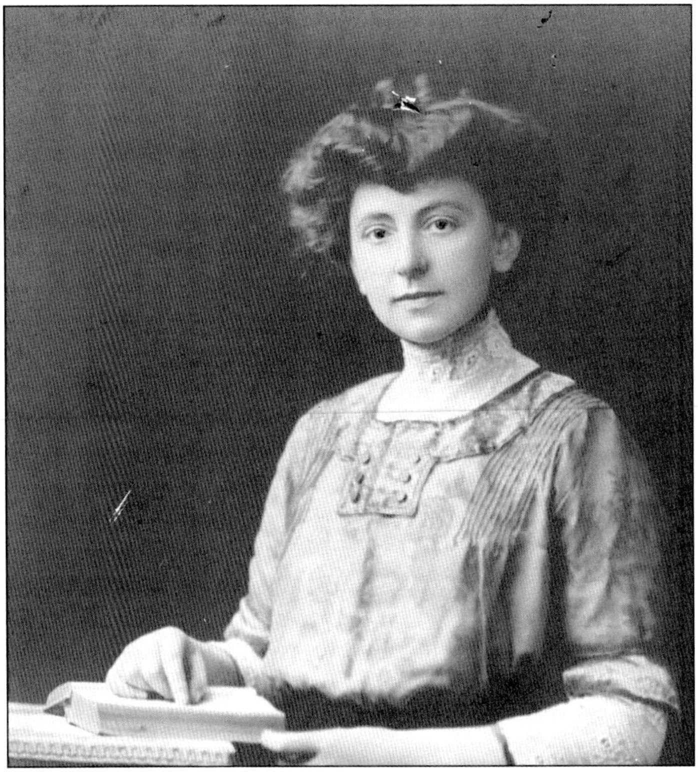

Helen Wachter was extremely independent and fluent in German, French, and Italian. She operated the boardinghouse at Dover White Marble Company. When the boardinghouse burned, she barely escaped with her life. She purchased the farmhouse across the road in 1915, cleaning and renovating one room at a time. Soon Elsie (Wachter) Puglisi and her father emigrated from Germany and came to live with Helen on the farm. (EP.)

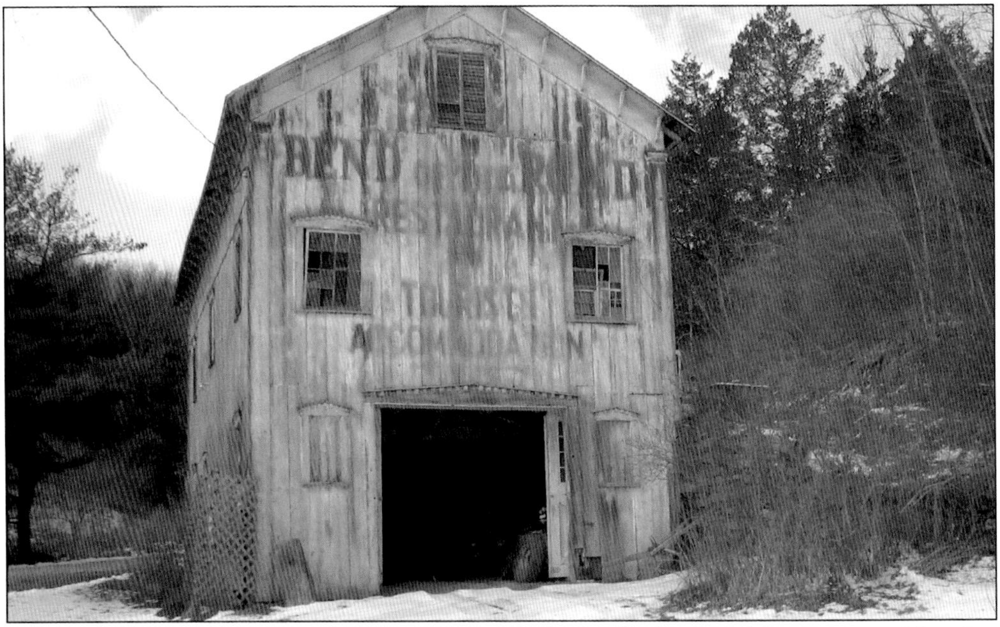

The barn advertised Wachter's "Bend-in-the-Road" farm, which catered to tourists and families who escaped the heat of New York City. To Puglisi, summer in the country meant picnics, gardens, and happy children at her house. On Friday evenings, her father took the horse and fringed-roof carriage to the train station to pick up the husbands and fathers of the women and children who boarded during on the week. (EP.)

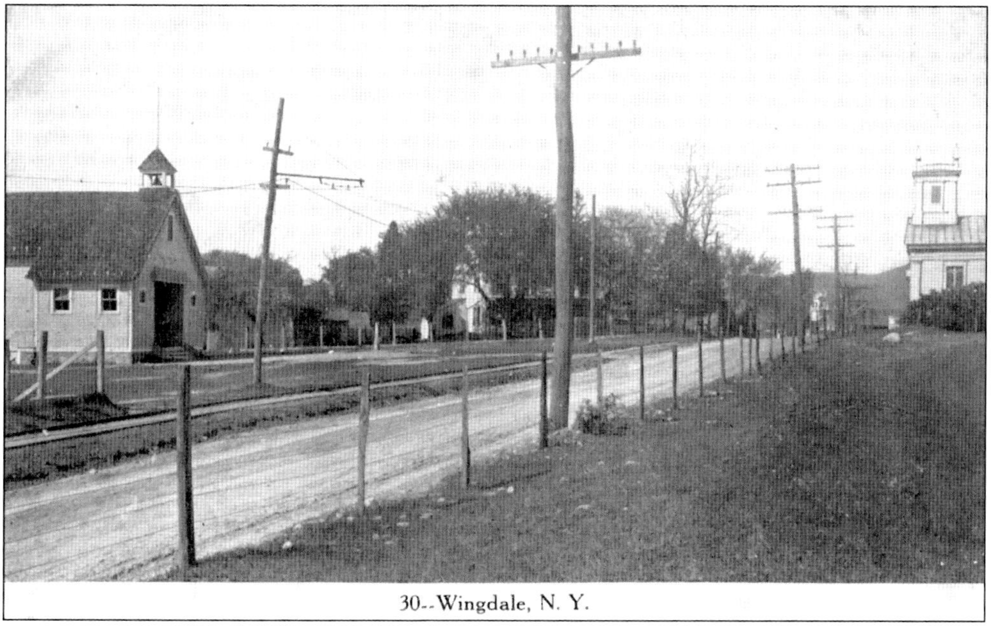

This photograph of Church Hill around 1915 shows the Wingdale School (left), Dover First Baptist Church (middle), and the Wingdale Methodist Church (right). Old Route 22 runs through the middle of the photograph. Parallel to the road are the two trolley tracks running from the marble plants to the railroad. Note two sets of electric poles. The pole in front of the school carried electricity to run the cart. (TDHS.)

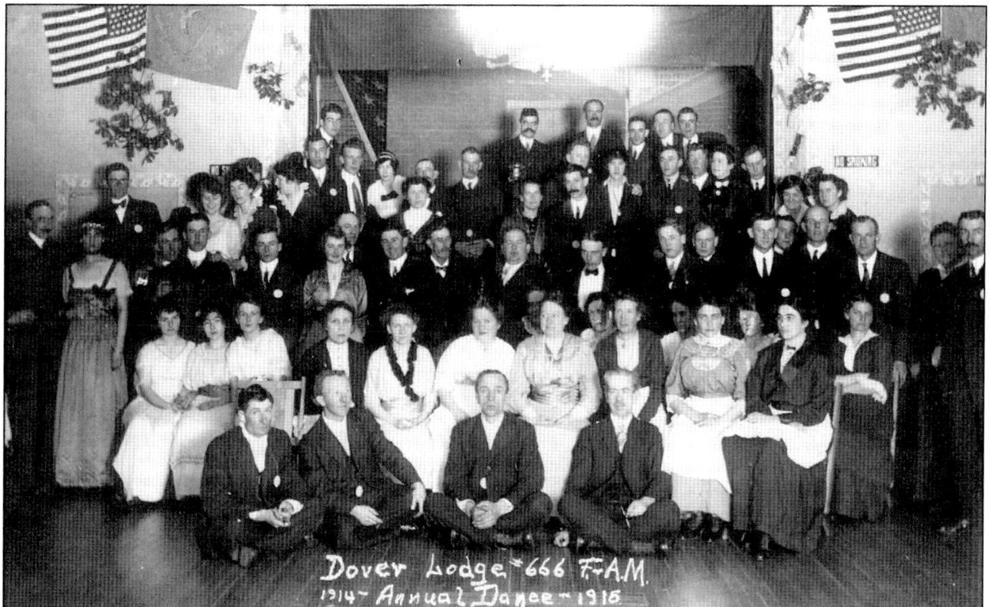

The Dover Lodge No. 666 Free and Associated Masons was organized in 1867. In 1914 and 1915, people attired for the evening dance posed for their picture. Swags of paper chains, flowers, and greenery decorate the doorways. Perhaps the dance celebrated St. Patrick's Day, as some of the flags say "Erin go braugh." The Masonic lodge also held meetings in the Reed Block building and the Chertock's building. (KD.)

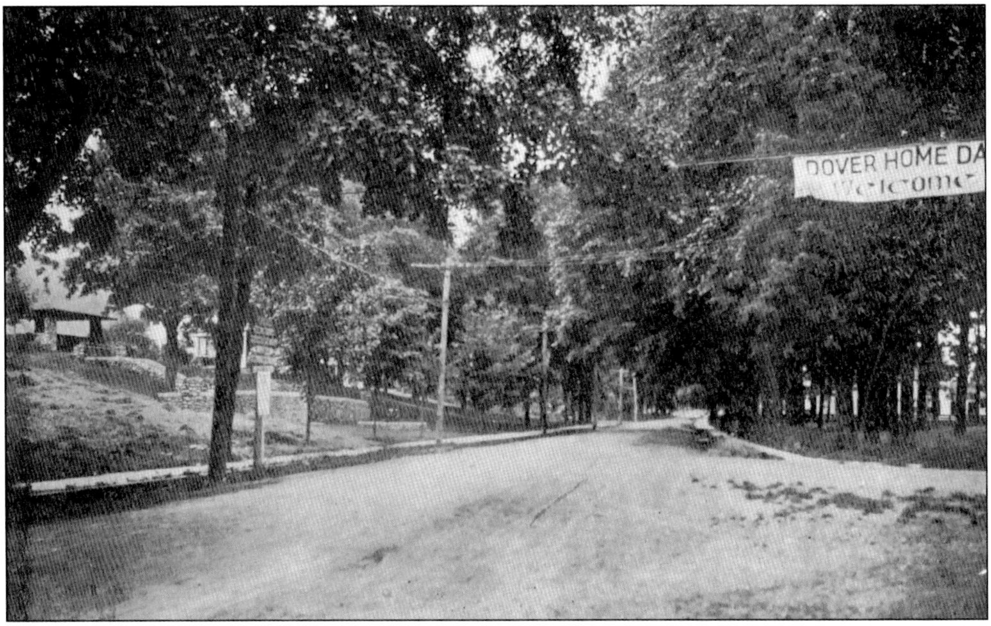

This image was taken about 1914 in Dover Plains looking north from the Route 22 and Mill Street intersection. A banner proclaims Home Day, celebrated around the Fourth of July. Eagerly anticipated each year, the social activities included numerous good-natured competitions between friends and families. The stone walls (left) seen at the home of Arthur and Pauline Palmer were restored by Larry and Katie House, owners of the Hufcut Funeral Home. (TDHS.)

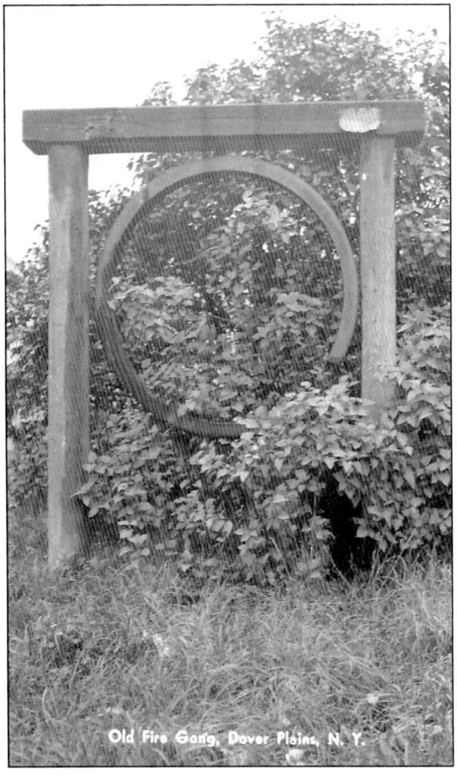

When the fire company first formed, volunteers raced to the firehouse and beat on the old fire gong. If the hand pumper was gone from the firehouse, a chalkboard message left details for those who arrived minutes later. As sirens and radios replaced the gong, the chalkboard remained the instant messenger for many fire and rescue volunteers. Today the gong is proudly displayed by J. H. Ketcham Hose Company, a tribute to past volunteer efforts. (KD.)

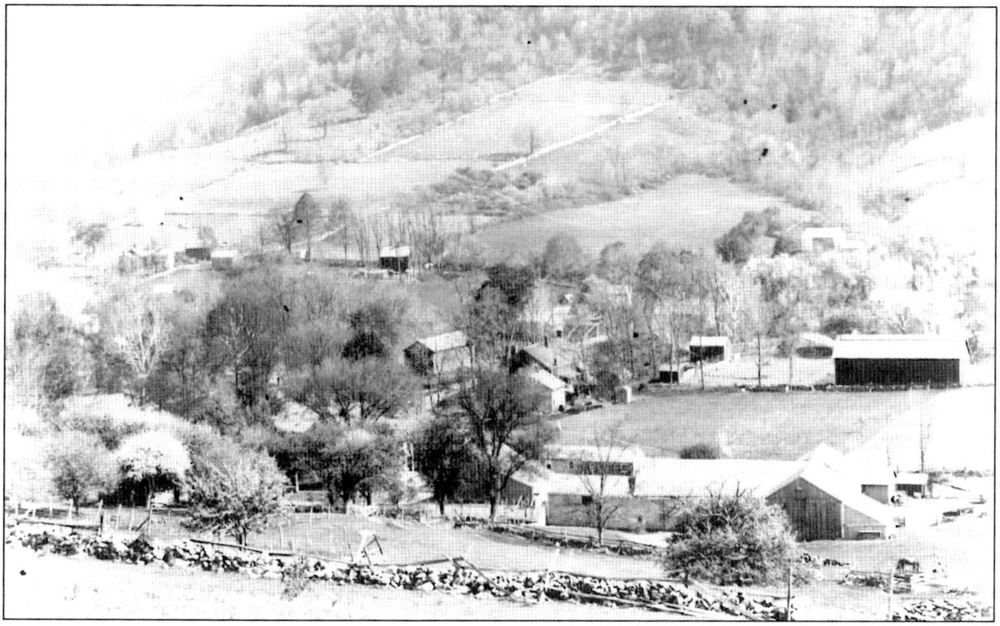

This bird's-eye view of Webatuck centers on the Ten Mile River bridge at Dog Tail Corners and the Hunt's complex (right). This 1920s photograph was taken from the top of the hill west of Berkshire Road, where, during World War II, volunteers at a spotting station kept watch on the darkened skies for enemy planes near the local landing strip and old farm fields. Today modular homes populate White Oak Circle. (CRR.)

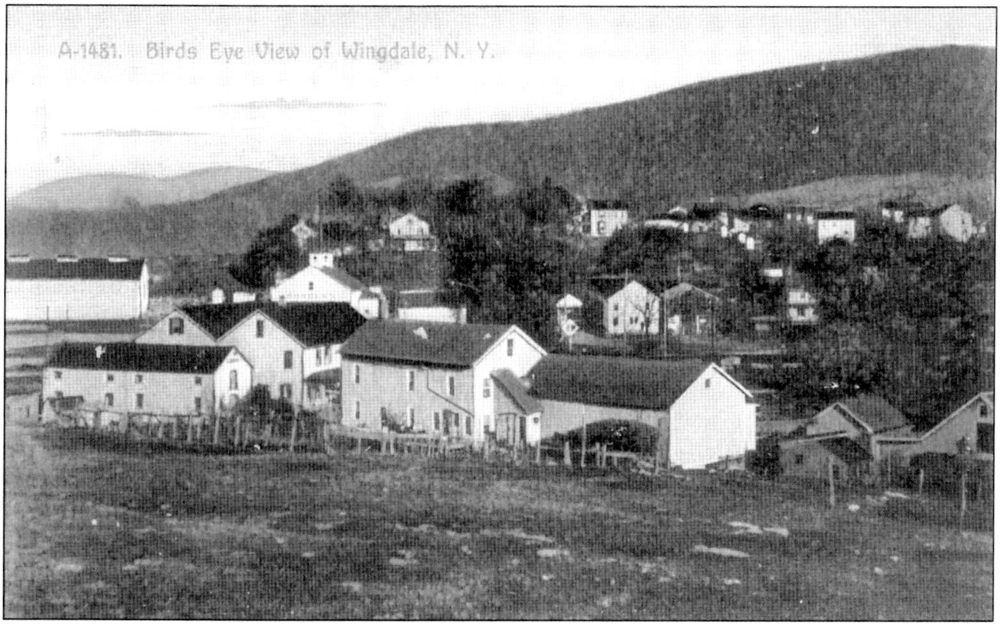

Wingdale is viewed from near Slocum's, the western hilltop in the hamlet. At center is the railroad crossing sign. Above is Depot Hill and Route 22. Marble worker housing and the Deuel Hotel are on the right. The Slocum home and farm are at bottom center, right. Just above Garrisons Store (left) is the "Borden's" plant name. The ice storage house is at the extreme left. (RA.)

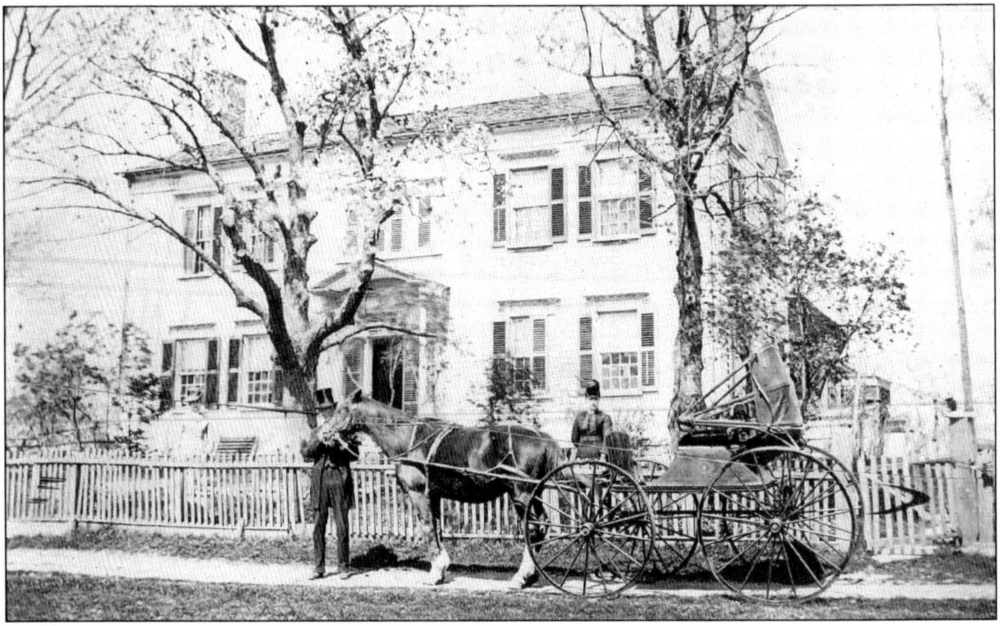

By the 1920s, the Tabor Wing House was a century old. This image shows the house in 1816. Notes on the reverse of the picture dated it and provided identification as "my mother and uncle Dan and old jed." A second woman is unidentified. In the 1930s, a historical survey highlighted the house. Architectural drawings were created of the structure and are on file at the Library of Congress. (TDHS.)

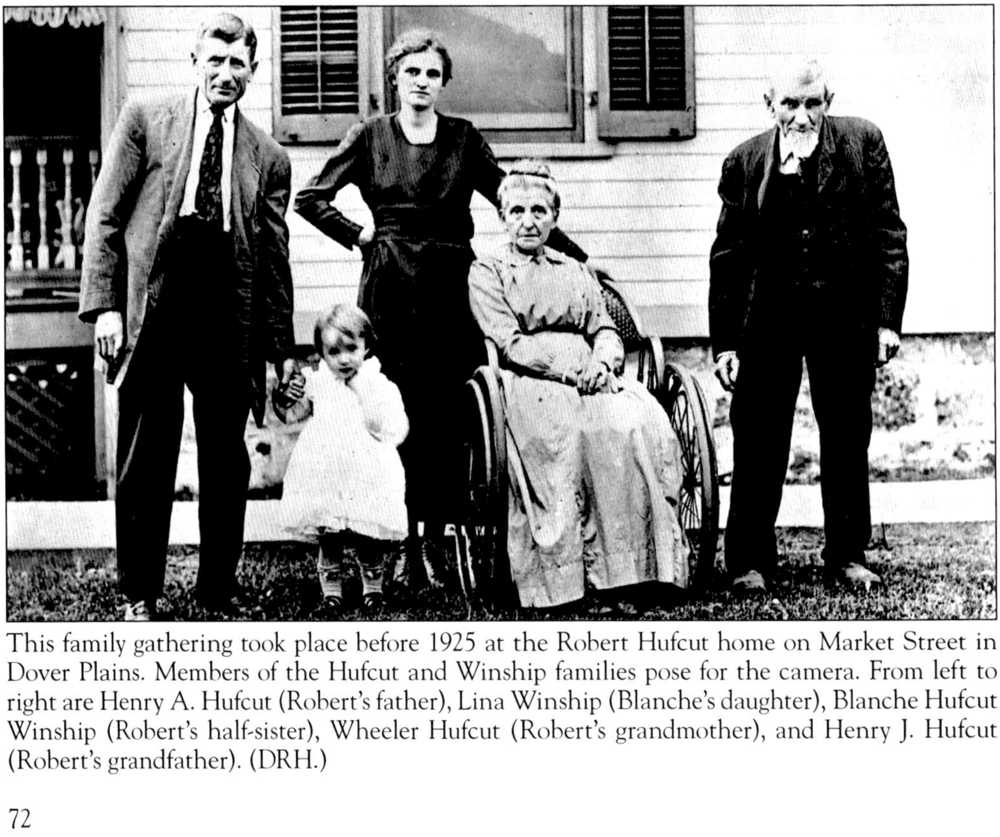

This family gathering took place before 1925 at the Robert Hufcut home on Market Street in Dover Plains. Members of the Hufcut and Winship families pose for the camera. From left to right are Henry A. Hufcut (Robert's father), Lina Winship (Blanche's daughter), Blanche Hufcut Winship (Robert's half-sister), Wheeler Hufcut (Robert's grandmother), and Henry J. Hufcut (Robert's grandfather). (DRH.)

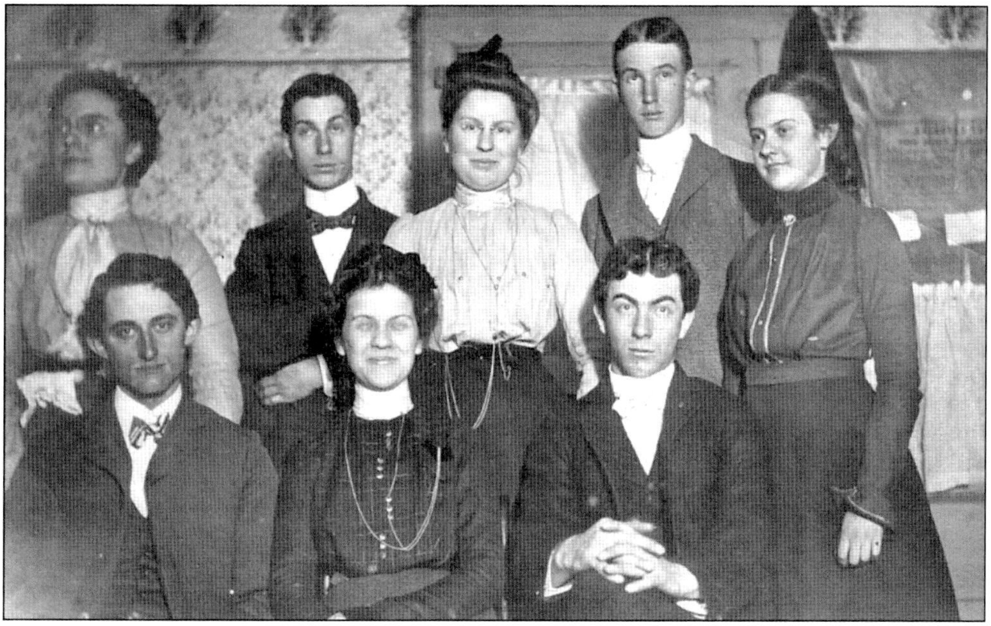

In 1901, these eight young people posed for the camera. From left to right are (first row) Edward L. Brush, Mary (Brush) Hodge, and Chester Gardner; (second row) Winifred Spooner, James Hodge, Ruth (Taylor) Spooner, Harry Tabor, and Belle (Baker) Hodge. The Brush family farm was on the east side of Crickett Hill at the top. Tabor became a town justice of the peace in Dover Plains. (TDHS.)

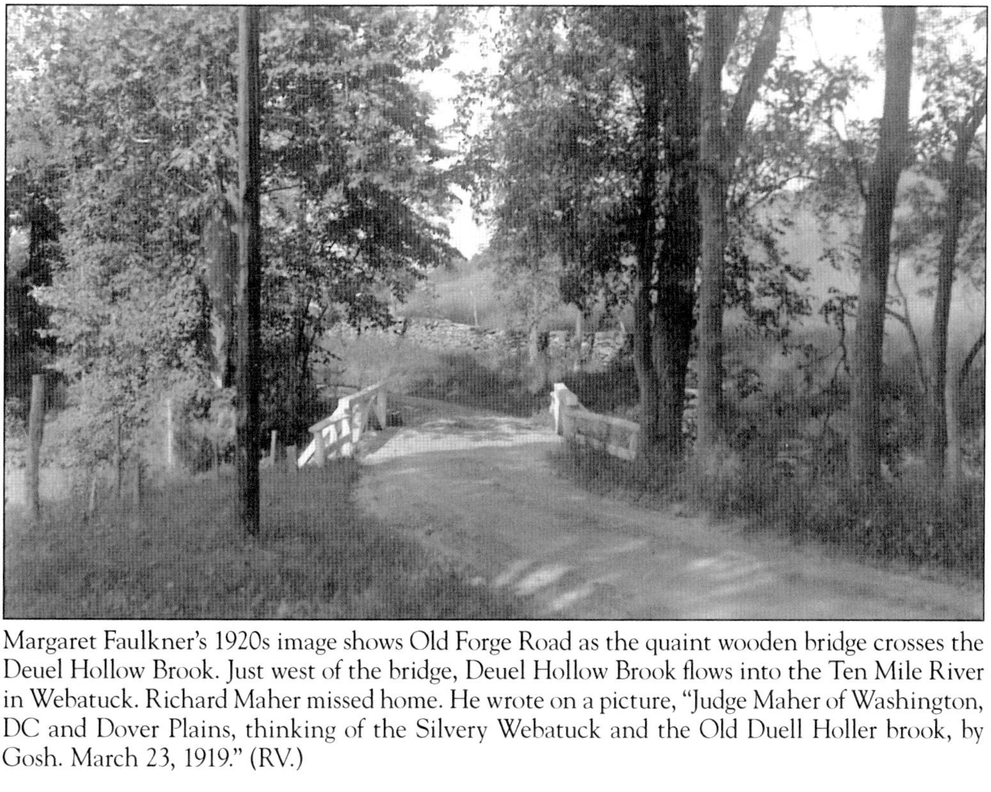

Margaret Faulkner's 1920s image shows Old Forge Road as the quaint wooden bridge crosses the Deuel Hollow Brook. Just west of the bridge, Deuel Hollow Brook flows into the Ten Mile River in Webatuck. Richard Maher missed home. He wrote on a picture, "Judge Maher of Washington, DC and Dover Plains, thinking of the Silvery Webatuck and the Old Duell Holler brook, by Gosh. March 23, 1919." (RV.)

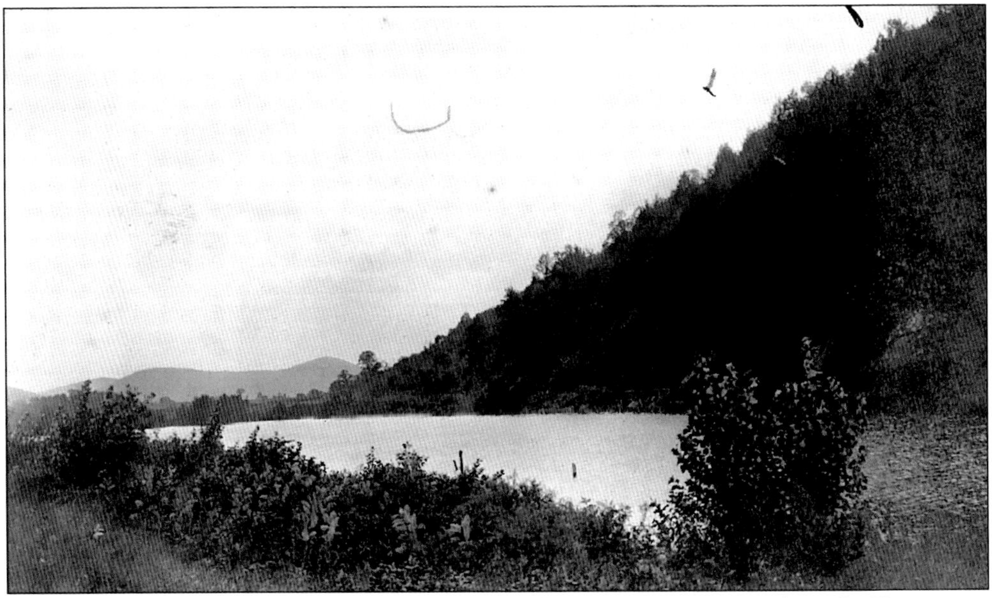

Richard Maher knew the Webatuck area and traveled Connecticut Route 7 along the Housatonic near Bulls Bridge. From the east side of the Housatonic River, he focused his camera westward for an unusual view of the Ten Mile Hill in Webatuck. Beyond Ten Mile Hill is Leather Hill. On the right is the eastern face of East Mountain. In Connecticut, it is known as the Schaghticoke Reservation lands. (TDHS.)

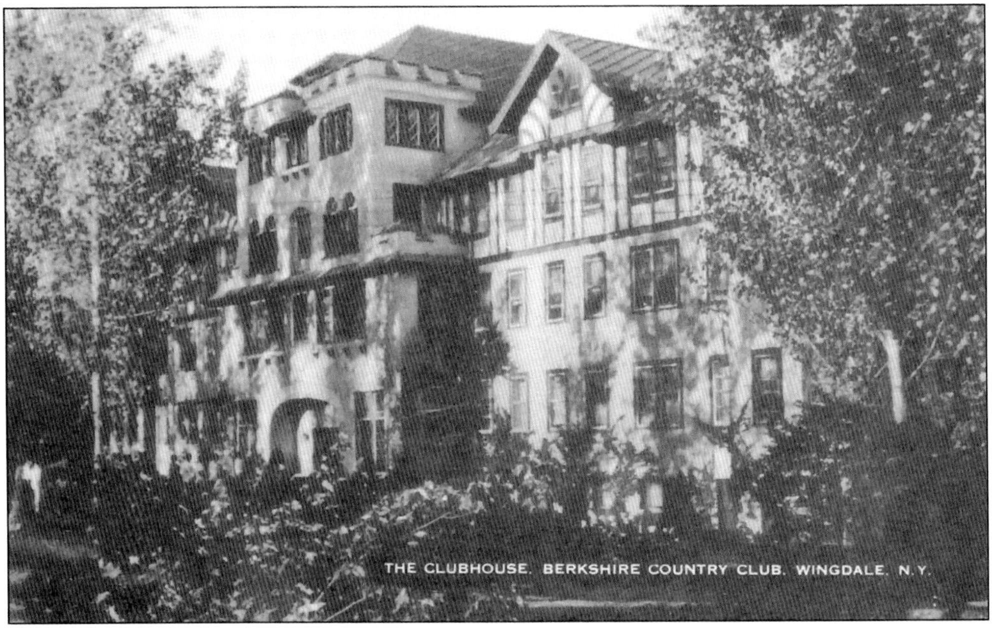

The clubhouse at the Berkshire Country Club on Berkshire Road in Wingdale overlooks Lake Ellis. A vacation destination in the early 1900s, the country club was recognized for its fine dining and magnificent golf course. When the club closed, the Greater New York Conference of the Seventh-Day Adventists Church purchased the facility. The clubhouse became a hotel, which burned about 30 years ago. Today the church still runs Camp Berkshire. (KD.)

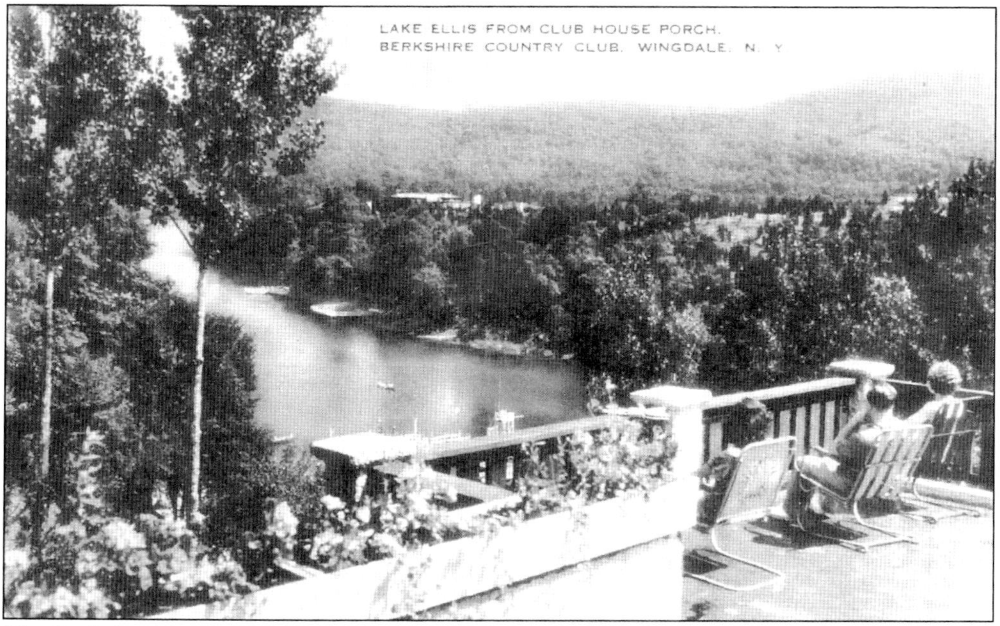

The Berkshire Country Club house porch provided a spectacular view of Lake Ellis against a backdrop of the East Mountains. According to Maher, Schaghticoke women wearing their blankets searched the lake edges for fish and turtles in the mid-1700s. In 1925, some 20,000 lake trout were stocked in the lake. Known by names such as Dutchess Point and Devil's Pit, the lake had a mystique of its own. (KD.)

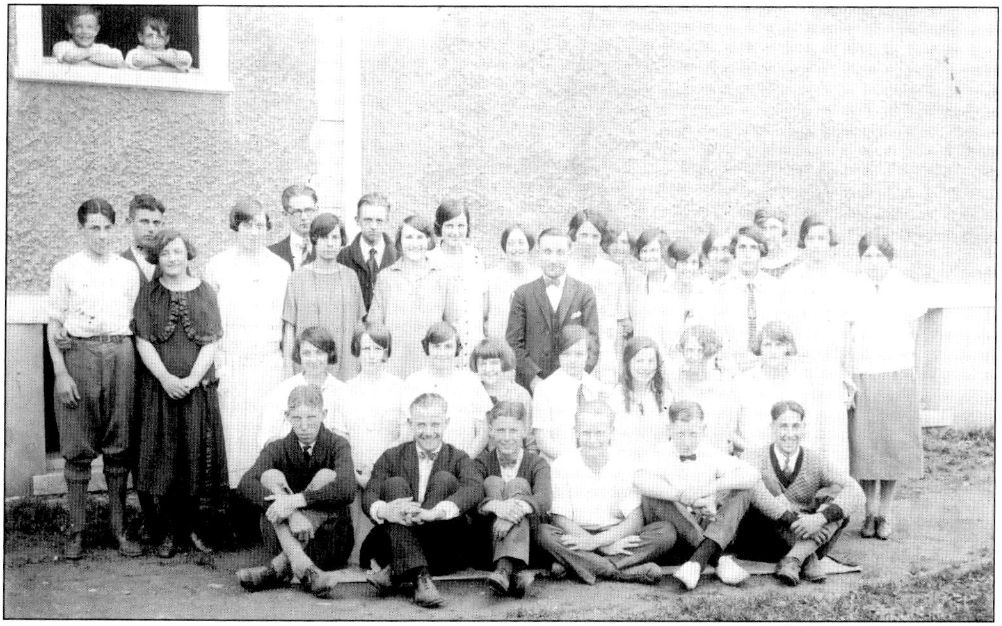

Students of Dover High School were photographed in 1925. The students include Hodge Brush, Muriel Boyce Murphy, Ken Lasher, Martha Hodge Southworth, Lyda (Scott) Dolan, Alice (Keegan) Brady, Margaret Carey, Hilda (Hunt) Lasher, Elizabeth Allen, Harry Tabor, Richard Humeston, Tom Dolan, and Lester Benson. From a first-floor window, John Polhemus (left) and a classmate grin for the camera. (DRH.)

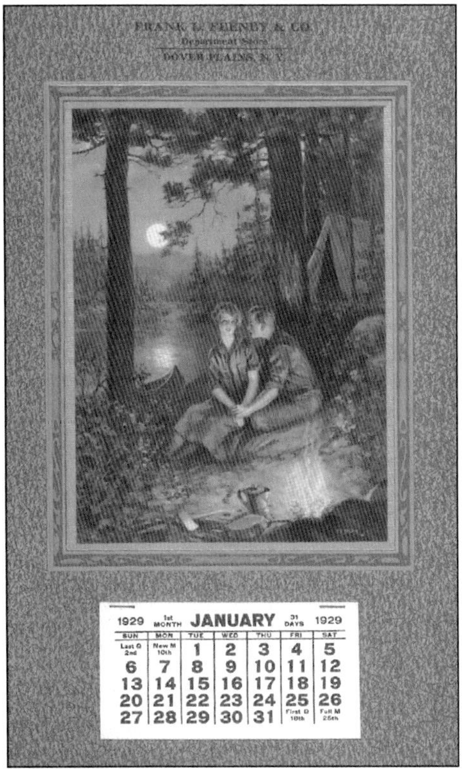

This 1929 promotional calendar came from the department store of Frank L. Feeney and Company in Dover Plains. Feeney's was located on the corner of Market Street and old Main Street. Stuart Chertock eventually purchased the building for a department store. Across the road was the crossing guard shack, where a paid crossing guard held up a stop sign to traffic for oncoming trains before the installation of mechanized crossing barriers. (LEB.)

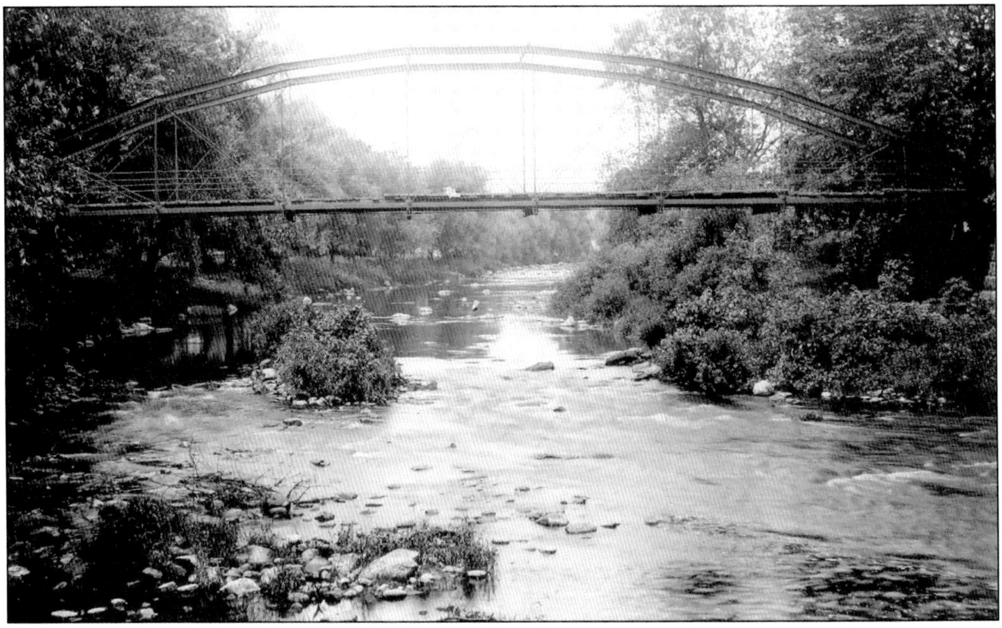

In the early 1930s, Bill Schreiber crossed the wooden-planked Ten Mile River bridge daily at the Hunt's property, getting fresh milk from the nearby Litwin farm. He remembers "that old temptation" calling to him. Soon carrying two full gallon milk pails, his return walk took him up and over the bridge arch. From the top, the teenager often stopped to watch Lillian Hunt washing clothes and furniture in the river. (CRR.)

Five

The Iron and Marble Industries

Dover's iron industry began with the transportation of ore from early mines on Quaker Hill and Deuel Hollow to a forge in Kent, Connecticut. From there, the pig iron went from Dover to Poughkeepsie, an easier market than Hartford. Later the secondary industry of coaling wood for charcoal expanded to the hills of Dover. Although evidence is scarce, by the Civil War, the ore was utilized from the mine in Deuel Hollow and those in Dover Furnace. The South Boston Iron Company built a new furnace at Sharparoon in 1881. Soon the industry slowed and faltered but continued until the early 1900s when the effect of the Bessemer process on higher-grade ore of the Mesabi Range in the west silenced the iron industry in the east.

The Dover marble companies breathed new life into the small hamlet of Wing's Station in 1899. As business grew, it was no longer practical for the companies to haul the marble by steam car over the actual roads. By 1910, the marble companies purchased a right-of-way and built their own railroad system to haul the massive blocks from the quarries to the railroad. South Dover Marble Company opened an office on Fifth Avenue in New York and catered to premiere architectural firms. In October 1913, the South Dover Marble Company shipped the last of the 60 columns weighing between 20 and 24 tons for the showcase Tiffany and Company building in New York City. Limestone or marble was necessary for the iron industry as an ingredient to remove impurities from the molten iron. The marble industry also had leftover marble from its quarries. The marble was crushed and cooked to make lime for fertilizer. When concrete was rediscovered as a building tool and stronger steel made it possible to build skyscrapers, marble was no longer in demand for building. Dover then tapped the quarries for limestone. During World War II, the magnesium component of the stone was sought for metal alloys. Today the extractive industry utilizes sand and gravel reserves and quarries stone in Wingdale.

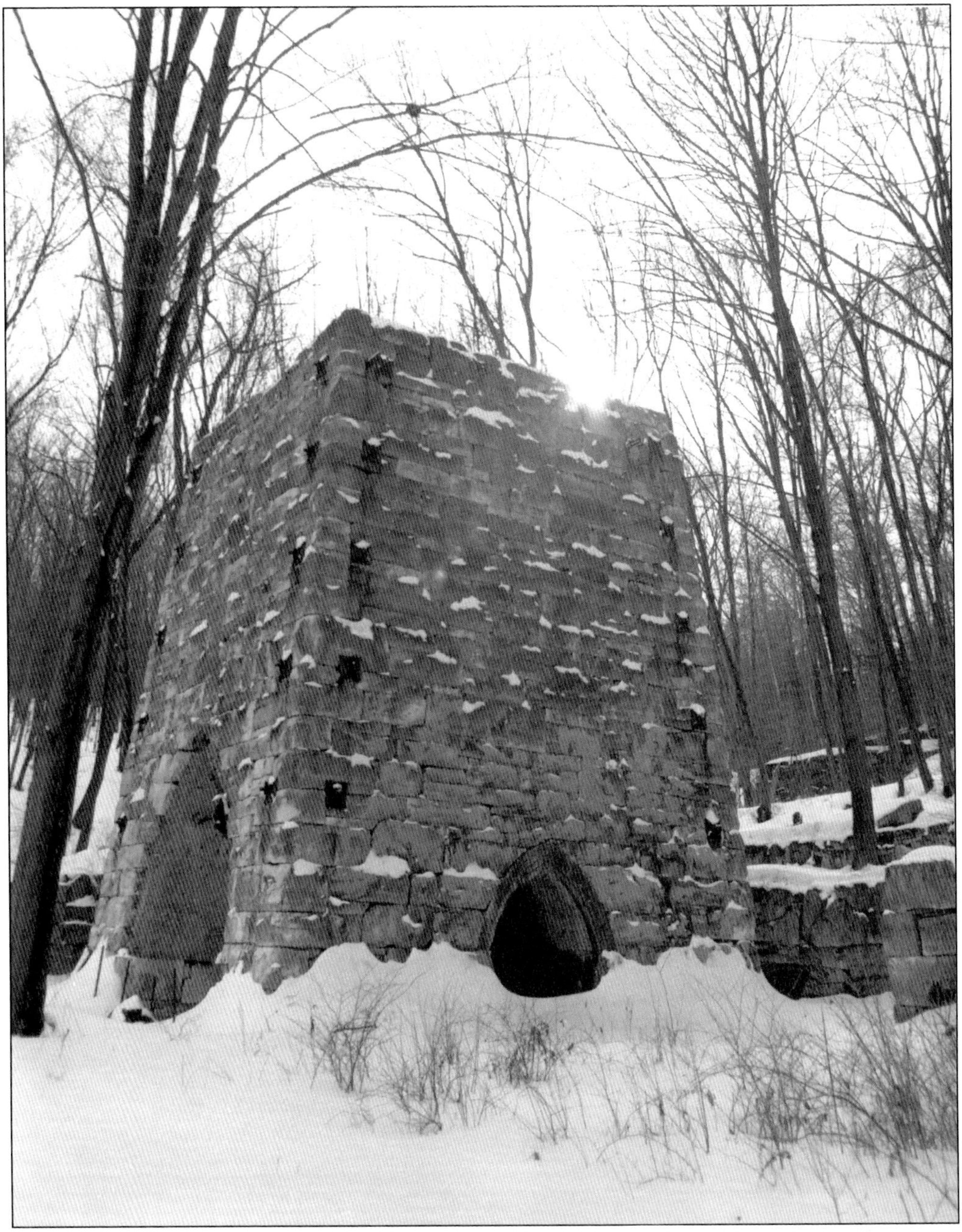

In 1881, the South Boston Iron Company built a blast furnace in Dover Furnace adjacent to the railroad track spur. Records indicate at least two previous furnaces in the immediate area that used Foss ore and other local ores. Charcoal was shipped in from Vermont due to limited supplies in the area. The South Boston furnace used bellows to add an extra blast of steam to elevate the furnace smelting point. The Sharparoon furnace worked slightly over two decades before the eastern iron industry declined. Part of the Salisbury iron district, Dover Furnace ore was rich in magnesium. The slag by-product was greenish-black and translucent. Pig iron from mines in the area was used primarily for cannons during the Civil War. The furnace site is located on privately owned property. (EH.)

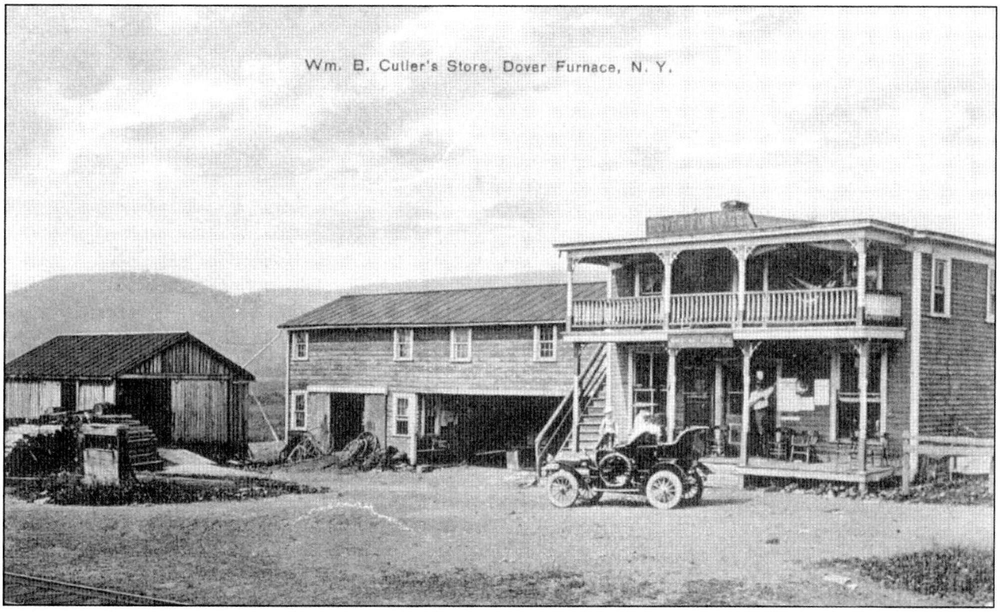

William B. Cutler was a prosperous merchant whose store and outbuildings were south of Dover Furnace Road adjacent to the railroad tracks. Food, transportation, equipment, and news were available to area farmers and laborers from adjacent mines and furnaces. When richer ore was discovered in the 1890s in the western Mesabi Range, the eastern iron industry collapsed. The New York City Mission Society purchased the premises for a summer camp. (KD.)

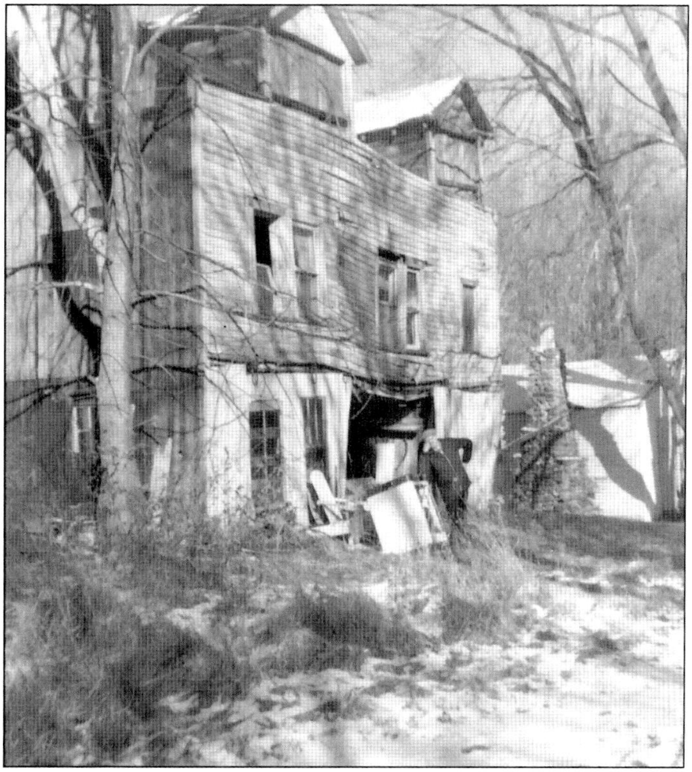

During the Civil War, the Bridgeport Ironworks owned the Deuel Hollow mine. The parent company of the Bridgeport Ironworks was the Monitor Iron Company of Bridgeport. When Frederick VanPelt Bryan purchased the land in the 1960s, this sagging, century-old barn remained from the ironworks era. It was later dismantled. Today documentation on the Deuel Hollow neighborhood indicates the area is a historic industrial complex. (DB, DPH.)

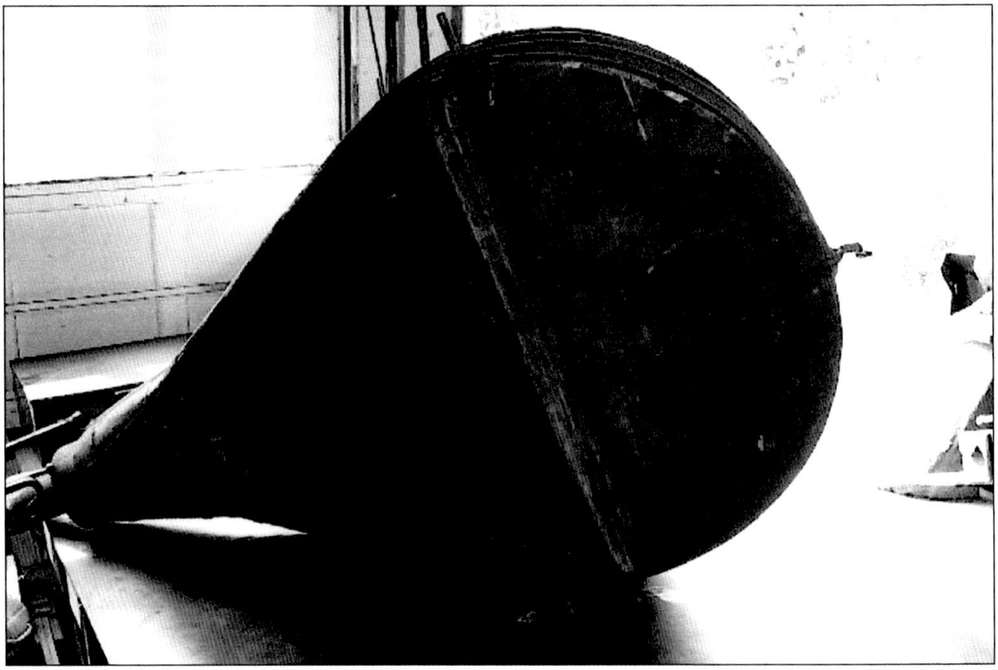

Blacksmith experts Skip Kern and Skip DiPierne believe these bellows date from around 1910, despite the 1843 Cutler store date. In 1915, similar Sears, Roebuck, and Company bellows retailed for about $5. Leather was dyed, and stencils were used for the names. The large, power-driven bellows clearly read, "William Cutler, Dover Furnace NY 1843." Now restored, the bellows are in the Boothe Museum in Stratford, Connecticut. (SK.)

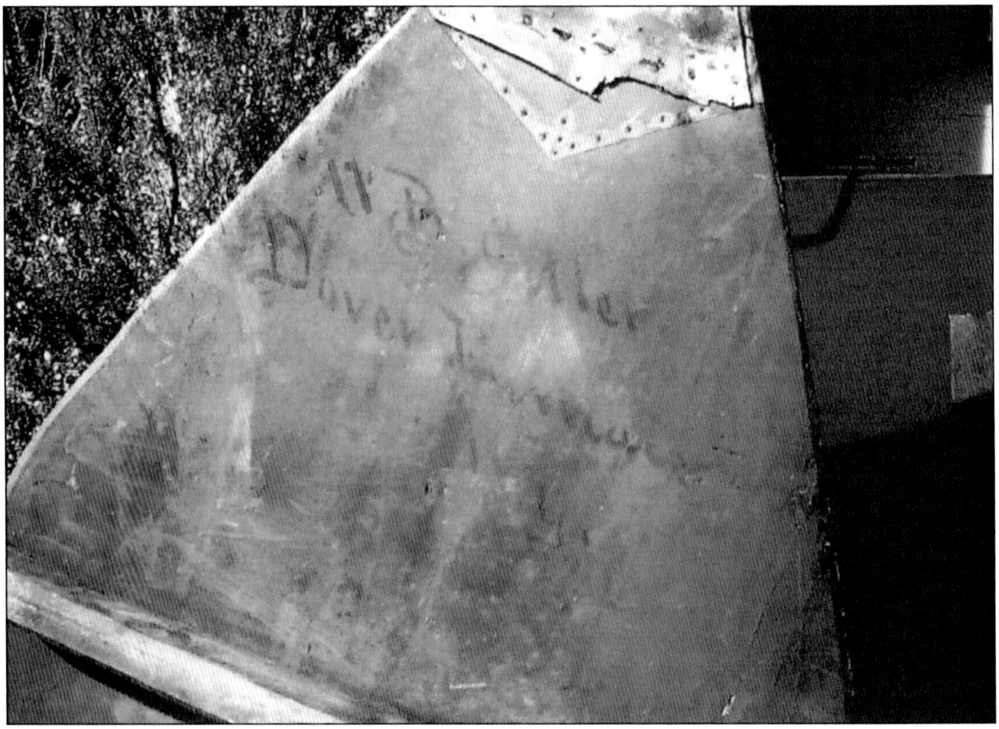

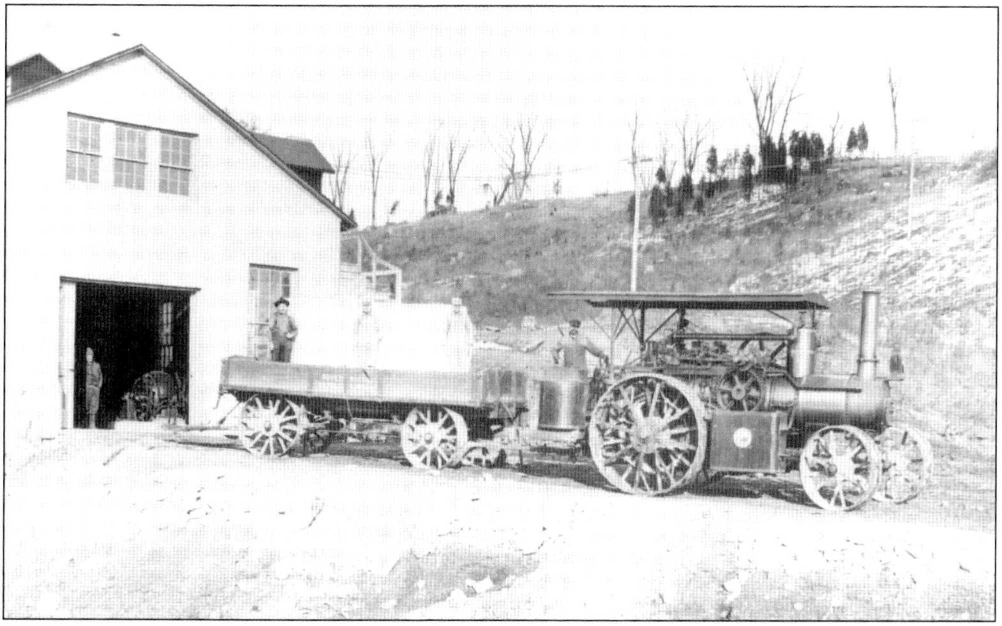

Dover marble was in high demand in the early 1900s. This image shows a marble plant worker on his modern steam tractor ready to haul a massive marble block uptown to the railroad tracks or the marble finishing mill. Note the heavy treads on the engine wheels. Three men in the wagon give perspective to the mass of the marble block. The wagon bears the name Dover White Marble Company. (IH.)

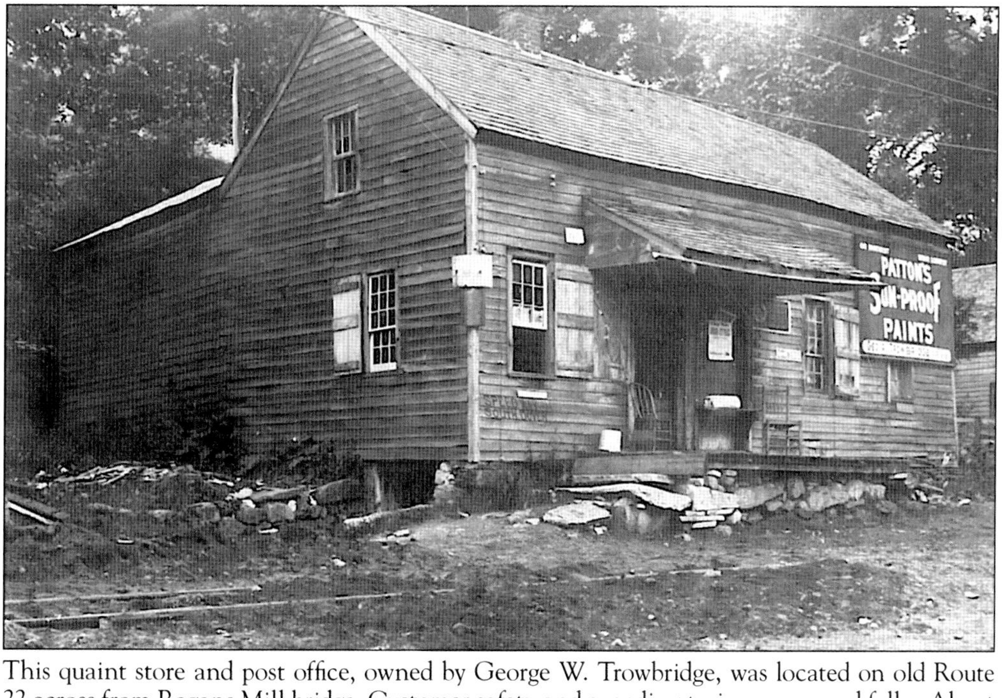

This quaint store and post office, owned by George W. Trowbridge, was located on old Route 22 across from Ragans Mill bridge. Customer safety and speeding trains concerned folks. About 1919, a sign on the side of the shop read, "South Dover Speed Way." Perhaps the message refers to the trolley route for the marble company built in 1910 right in front of the store. (LM.)

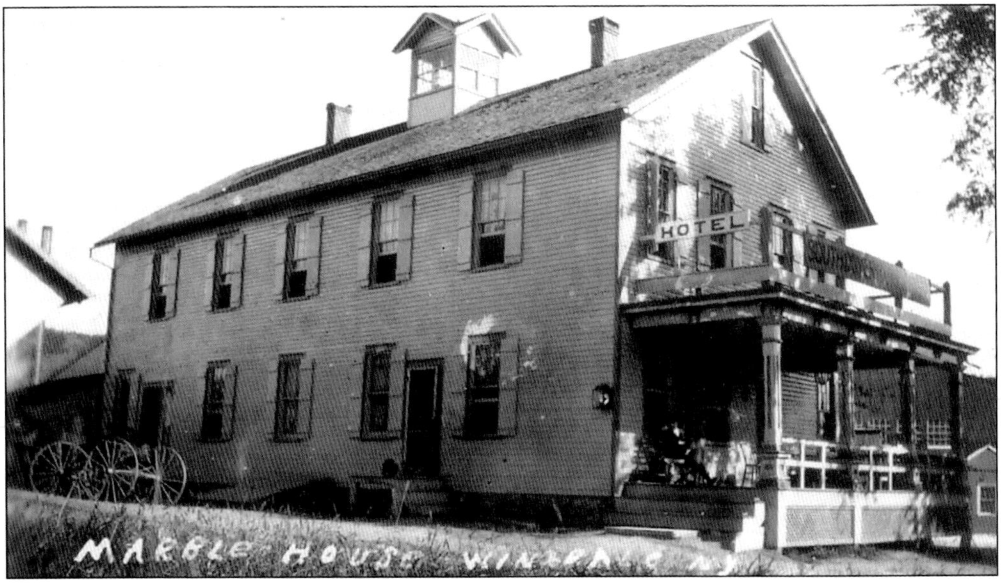

The South Dover Marble Hotel was located south of Cottage Avenue adjacent to the finishing mill and railroad tracks. The hotel provided rooms for visitors and guests of the marble companies. According to Richard Maher, in 1908, Louis F. Ahner was proprietor of the marble house. Behind the hotel and beyond the porch, the distinctive windows of the marble finishing mill are visible. (TDHS.)

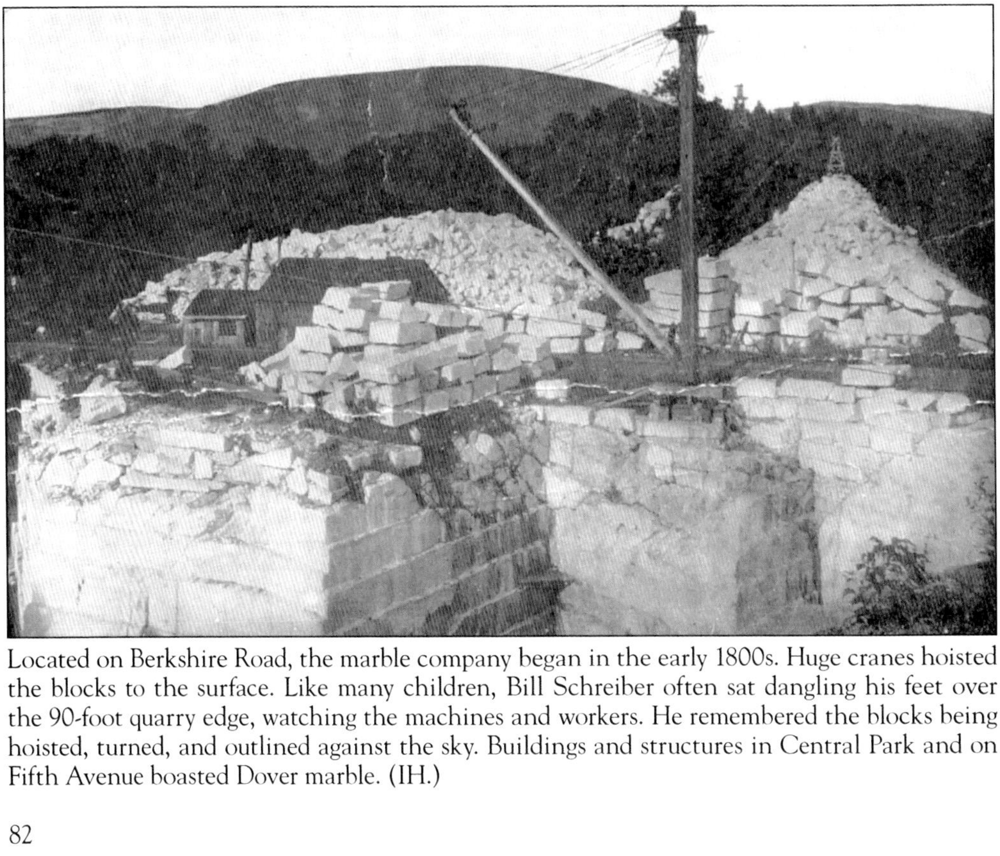

Located on Berkshire Road, the marble company began in the early 1800s. Huge cranes hoisted the blocks to the surface. Like many children, Bill Schreiber often sat dangling his feet over the 90-foot quarry edge, watching the machines and workers. He remembered the blocks being hoisted, turned, and outlined against the sky. Buildings and structures in Central Park and on Fifth Avenue boasted Dover marble. (IH.)

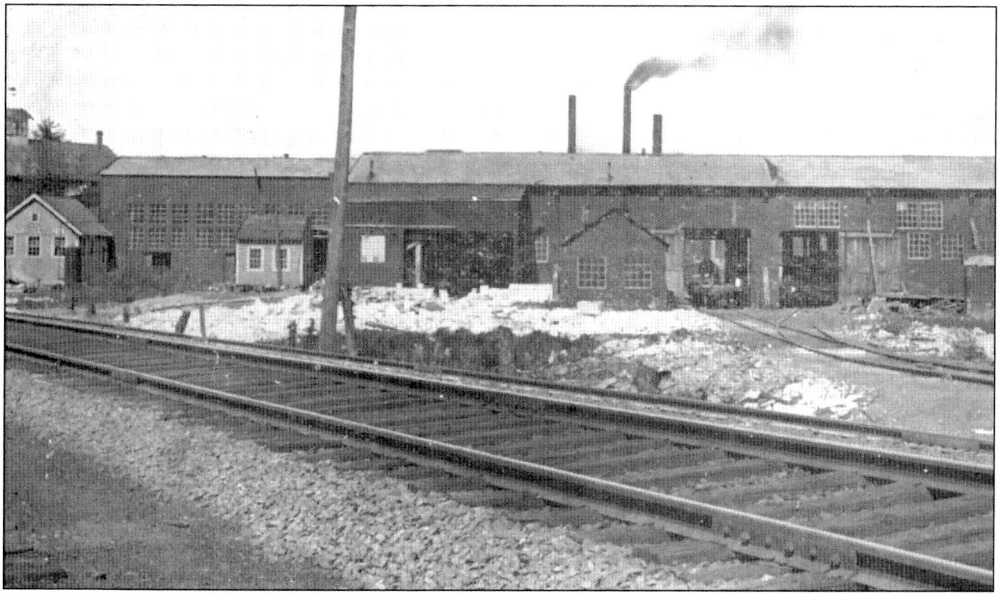

At the South Dover Marble Company mill in Wingdale, block marble was carried inside by crane to a gang saw where it was cut. Diamond saws were only for fine-quality marble. Then pieces were smoothed by rubbing with a specially molded form before pickup and transport by the railroad. This picture was used in a school project on the workings of the South Dover Marble Company mill, prepared by Martha Southworth's sister. (TDHS.)

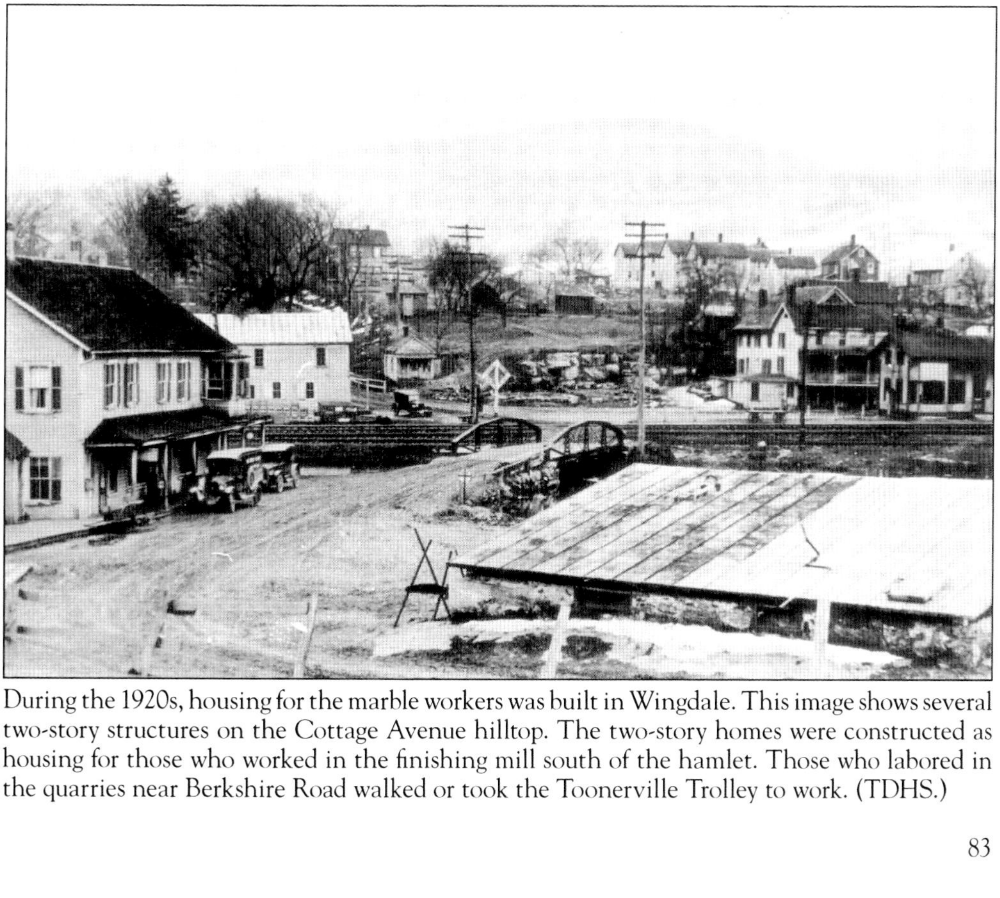

During the 1920s, housing for the marble workers was built in Wingdale. This image shows several two-story structures on the Cottage Avenue hilltop. The two-story homes were constructed as housing for those who worked in the finishing mill south of the hamlet. Those who labored in the quarries near Berkshire Road walked or took the Toonerville Trolley to work. (TDHS.)

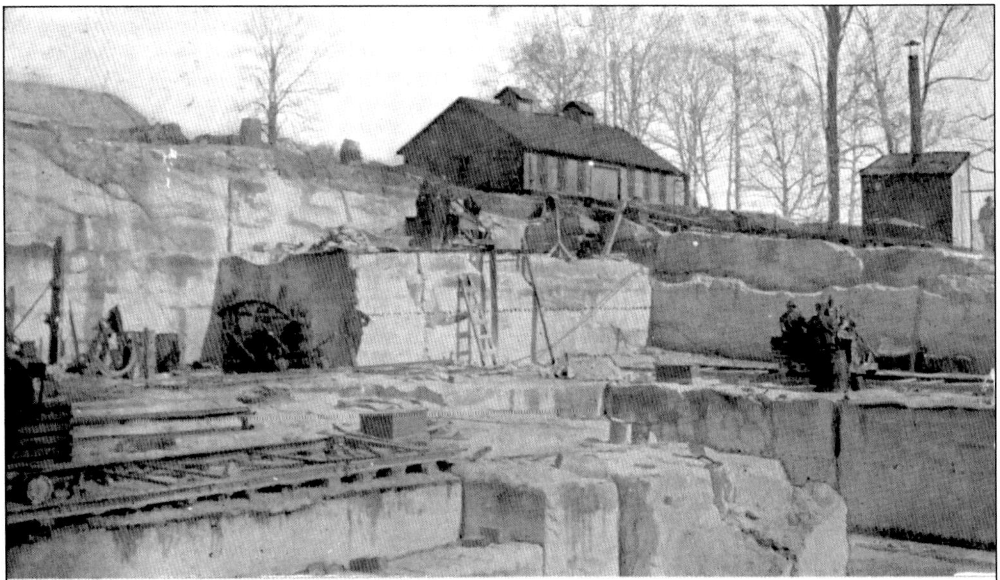

32--Dover White Marble Quarry, Wingdale, N. Y.

Dover White Marble Company quarry was located between Berkshire Road and today's old Route 22. Known for its fine, white color and purity, the marble was much in demand and used primarily on statuary and decorative portions of buildings. In this image of the upper quarry levels, three men stand atop a partially quarried block. The separation line was to run through the drill holes crossing the block midway down. (IH.)

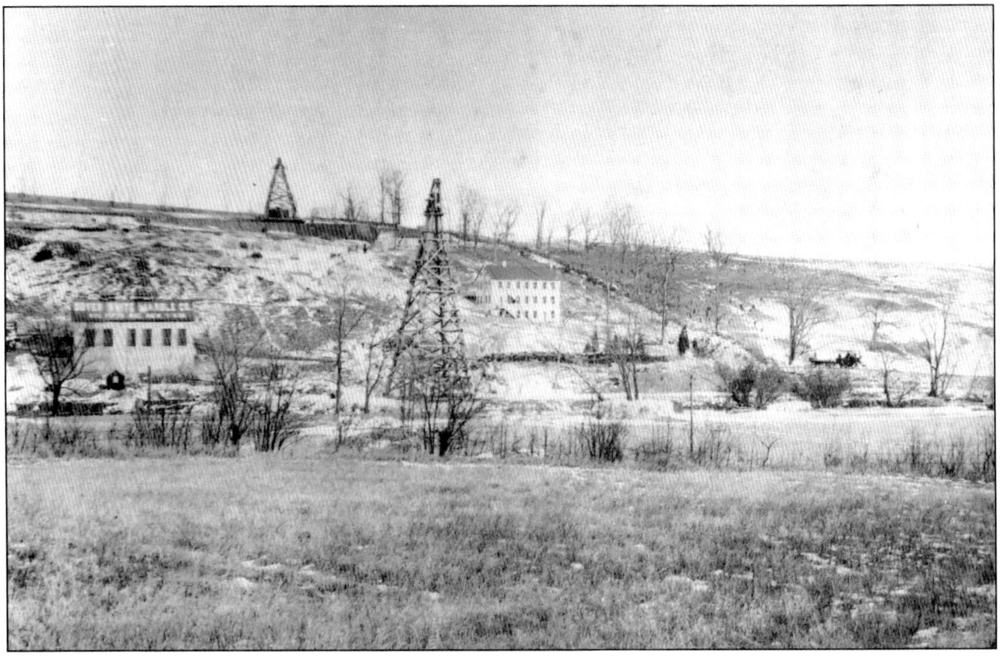

This fabulous picture of the Dover White Marble Company plant shows two buildings and two tall, wooden towers used to hoist and move the marble. The upper tower is on a ledge near the top of the quarry, while the lower tower is at road level. On the extreme right, a steam engine hauls a large block of marble off-site to the railroad or finishing mill. (IH.)

The 2006 draft Washington Park Cultural Landscape Report indicated the architectural firm of McKim, Mead, and White contacted Herman Atkins McNeil in 1913. It wanted a high-relief group of figures carved behind the 12-foot statue of *Washington as Commander-in-Chief*. South Dover Marble Company was to be used for the George Washington statue and displayed on the eastern pier of the Washington Square Arch. The secondary figures used Dover marble and Georgian marble. (New York City Department of Parks and Recreation.)

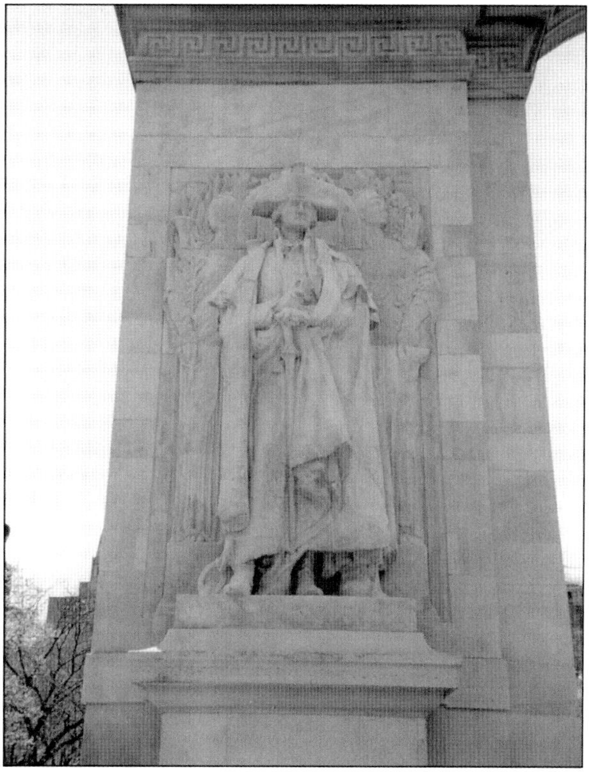

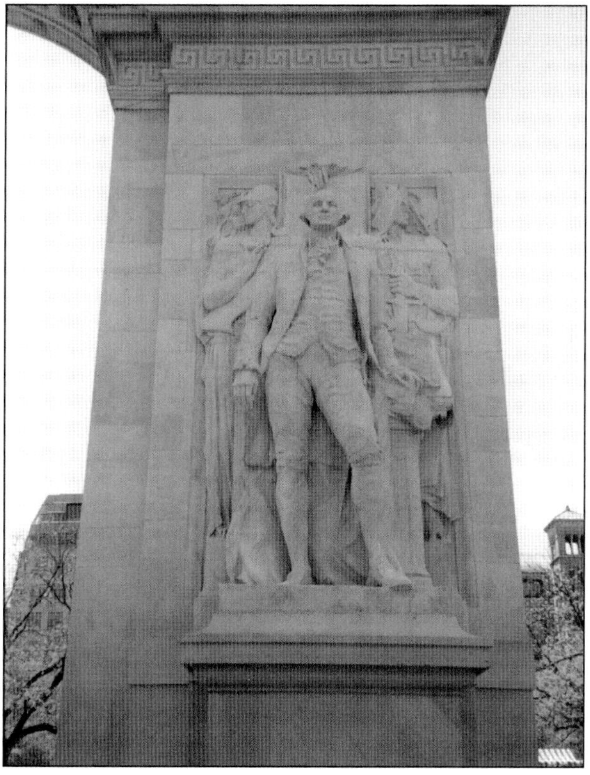

In 1916, the firm contacted sculptor Alexander Stirling Calder to design and sculpt the western pier figures. Allegorical figures of *Wisdom* and *Justice* would accompany the central statue of *Washington-as-President*. The western sculptures were dedicated in 1918. According to parks director Jonathan Kuhn, Dover White Marble Company and South Dover Marble Company marbles were utilized with Georgian marble for the bas-relief figures behind the central figures of Washington. (New York City Department of Parks and Recreation.)

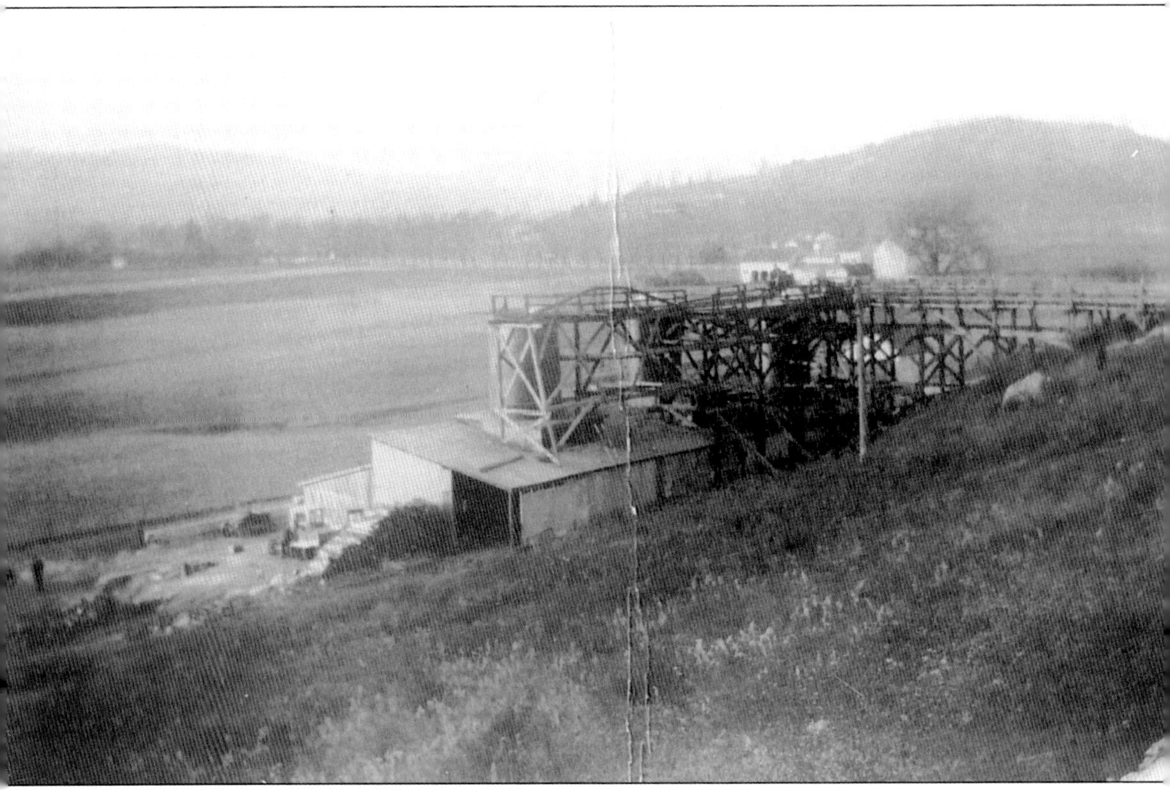

This three-stack kiln on the east side of Limekiln Road was located south of the Maple Lane intersection and below Sand Hill Road. A loading bridge from Sand Hill enabled workers to load crushed marble into the stack. Looking across the empty field toward Fox Hill, rows of young maple trees border Maple Lane leading past the farm once belonging to John H. Ketcham. (RDR.)

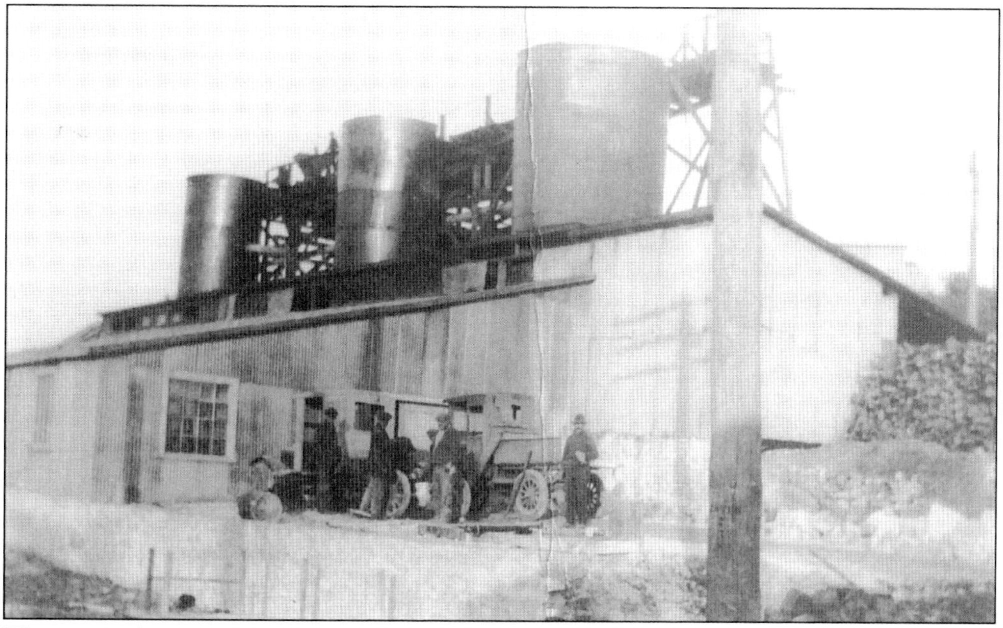

This image shows two workers on the bridge loading crushed marble in the stack and five men below with the truck and cart. Alongside the kiln is a stack of wood for the fires at the lower sides of the kiln. After the Civil War, marble orders for monuments declined. However, the Ketcham quarries still provided work and revenue as crushed marble was converted to lime. (RDR.)

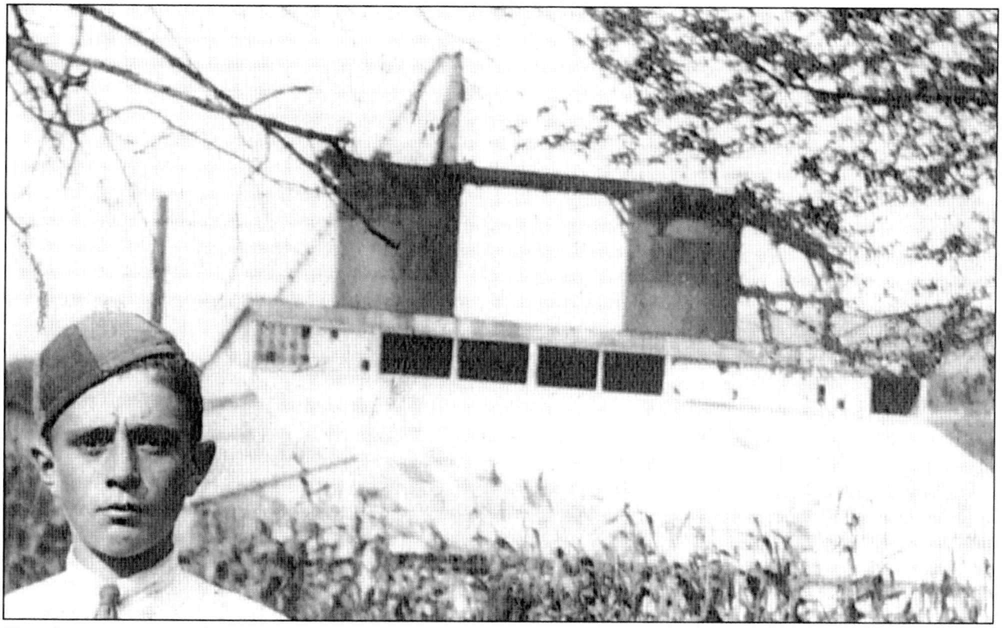

On the east side of Limekiln Road south of McCarthy Road were areas of level stone blocks, which formed the base of this limekiln. Charged with lime via a wooden bridge, it was calcined by wood fires in the kiln sides. Hand-powered dinky cars rolled lime across the road westward to the railroad tracks. Lime was also in demand for tanning and by farmers to sweeten the soil. (RMC.)

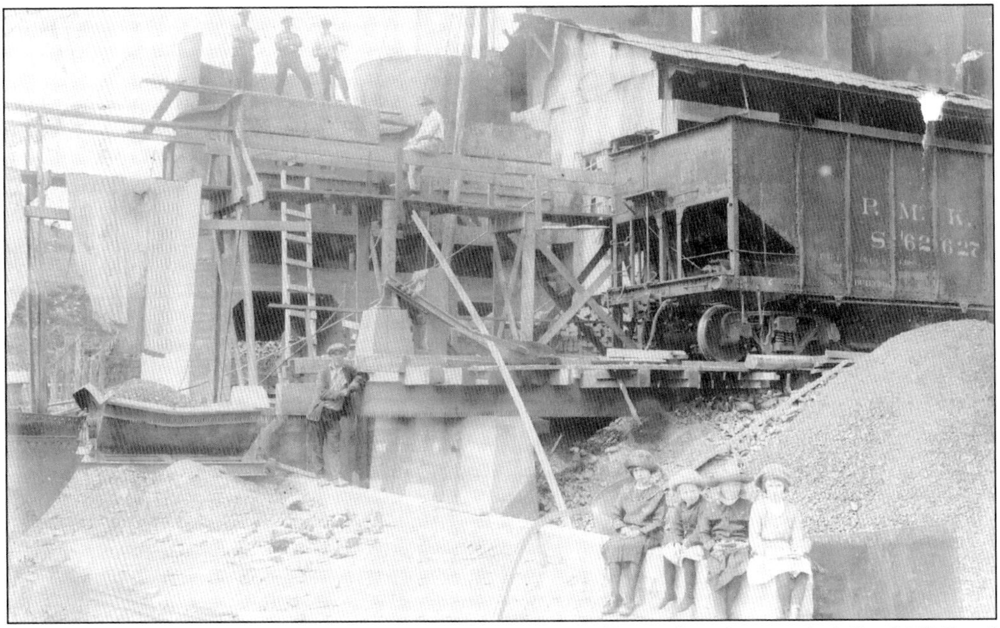

This dilapidated-looking plant was located west of Powell Road and east of Nellie Hill Road below the railroad underpass. Jagged tin sheeting on the walls may indicate demolition. On this day, four children stopped by for a visit. The young girl sitting on the right is Madeline Callahan's aunt Madeline around age 10. According to Callahan, this was not the Dover Plains Lime Company plant. (RMC.)

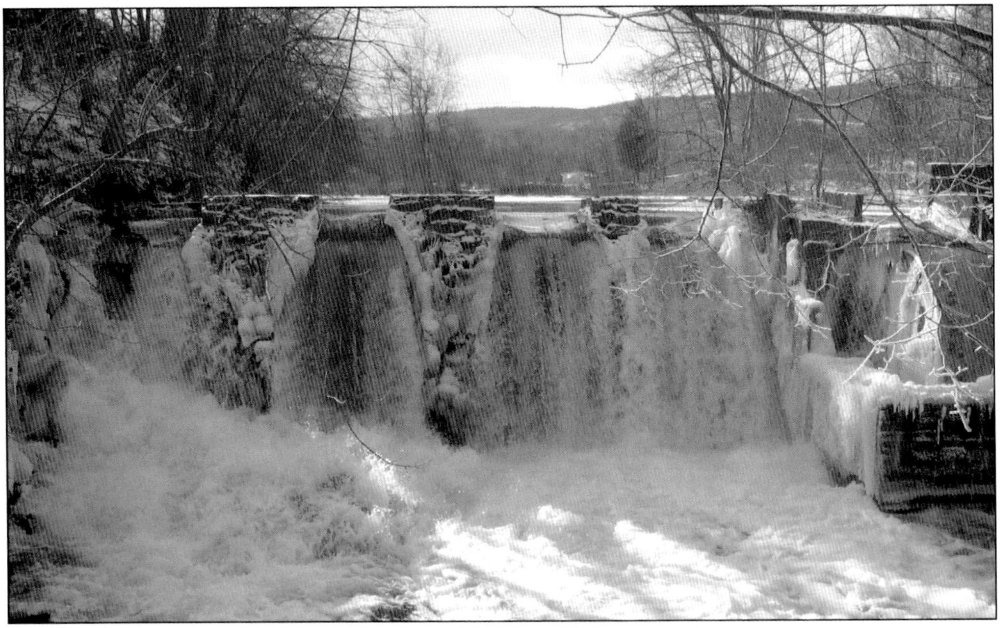

Today Dover Furnace Dam on the Swamp River with its cascading waters is impressive any season of the year. Constructed by W. S. Stirling before 1921 of block from a previous furnace, the dam creates the headwaters for the north section of the Great Swamp. On the west side of the dam (right) are the remains of a platform, spillway, waterwheel, and the drive mechanism of an earlier furnace. (TDHC.)

Six

The Coming of the Hospital

In 1910, New York State began looking for a site to house the new Sing Sing Prison and relieve overcrowding of the present prison. The Wingdale site was chosen, but it was not the first choice for the state. That first site was at the foot of a place called Bear Mountain in the Palisades where prison work was underway. During that time, land along the Hudson River Palisades was wanted for the Palisades Interstate Park Commission. Mary Williamson (Averell) Harriman, wife of the late railroad tycoon Edward H. Harriman, wished to preserve Bear Mountain and nearby Fort Clinton. She wrote to New York governor Charles Evans Hughes, offering to donate 10,000 acres and $1 million to the Palisades Interstate Park Commission, but she wanted work on the prison stopped. Officially, the Bear Mountain site was classified unfit for the farming that prisoners were required to do. The generous offer was accepted, and the prison wall was demolished. Soon after, construction on the Bear Mountain Inn began at the former prison site.

In Wingdale, the state purchased over 600 acres from four farms. The Wheelers' 366-acre farm was the largest and sold for $100 an acre. The farm contained the Wheeler house, with barns, stables, and storage for a large herd of cows. The remaining acreage came from the Titus, Wilcox, and Brown farms. William J. Beardsley, an architect from Poughkeepsie, won an $800 design award for the prior site. He adapted the prison plans for the Wingdale site easily. Contractor P. J. Carlin from New York City began work in April 1911 but soon discovered the original concerns about the nearby river left the site one step above a swamp. By 1912, although four buildings were completed, the project halted. The official cause listed high water tables and a questionable water supply as construction constraints. The site alternative chosen by the state was for the housing and care of the insane who were hardy enough to work the farm. On August 23, 1924, the Harlem Valley State Hospital opened its doors to 32 patients.

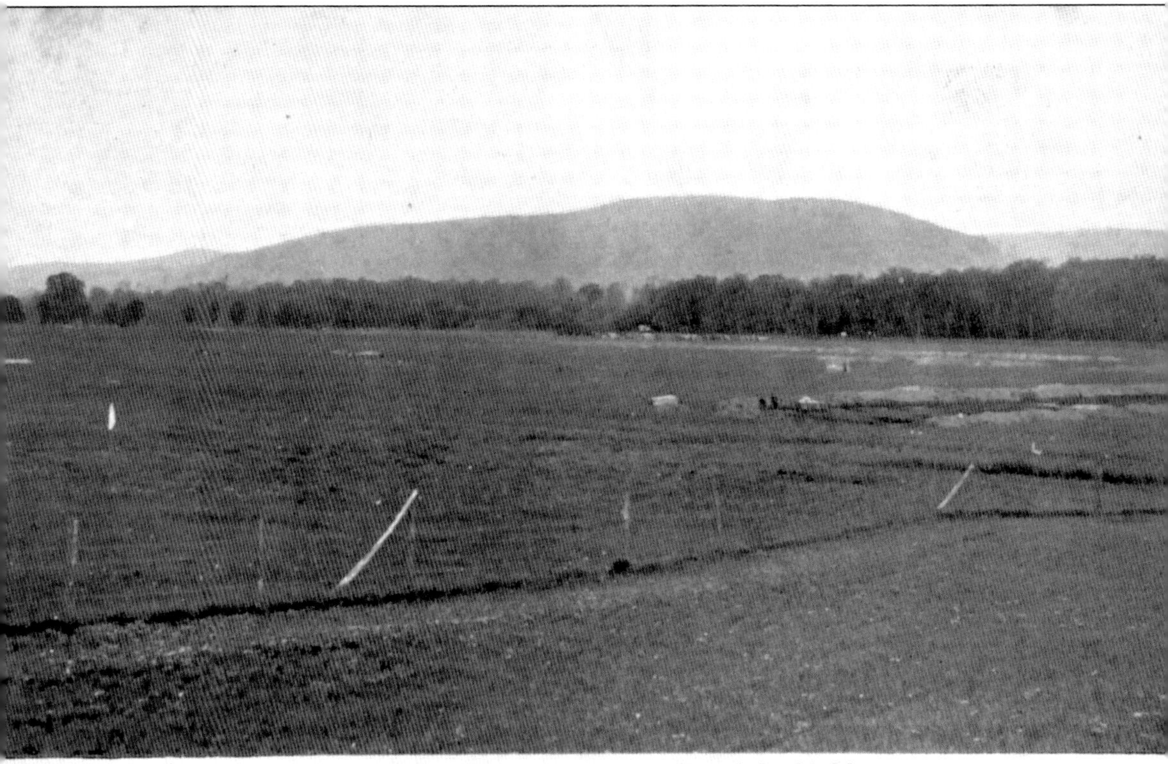

Site of New Harlem Prison, Wingdale, N. Y.

After prison construction stopped on Bear Mountain in Harriman, Wingdale was chosen for the new Sing Sing Prison. Work began in 1910, but by 1912, rumors of failed business contracts surfaced. High groundwater and related construction costs were the official reasons for the change from a prison to a mental health hospital. This image looks southwest toward Waldo Hill from the Hutchings Avenue and Reservoir Road intersection. (TDHS.)

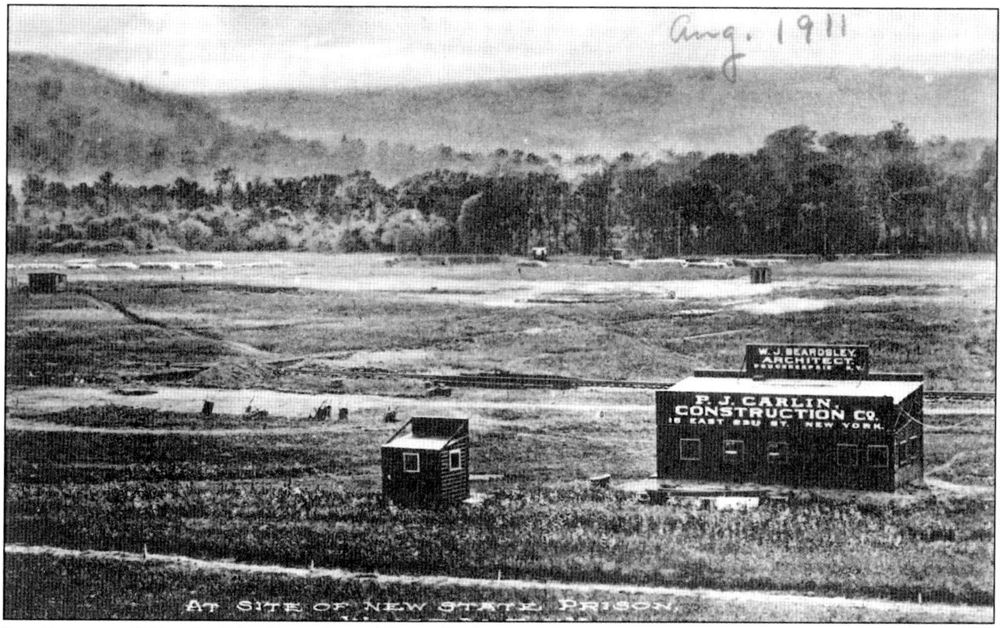

In August 1911, G. Hasbrouck published this postcard showing the trackside construction building of the New York City firm P. J. Carlin Construction Company. Poughkeepsie architect W. J. Beardsley won an $8,000 award for the Bear Mountain prison design. Wingdale prison plans evolved from Beardsley's original plans. This image looks west toward the Swamp River and Wheeler farm beyond the trees. (TDHS.)

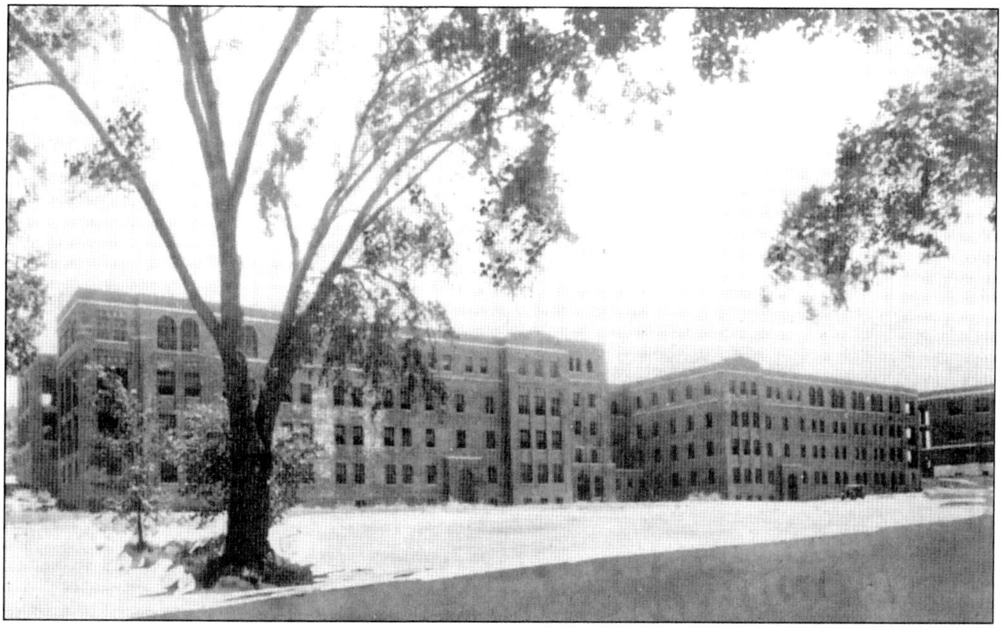

Construction continued over the course of a decade. Looking through the arching branches of an American elm, building F nears completion as construction continues on nearby buildings. A parked car and a newly planted tree appear farther back from the road. While the near end of building F appears finished, the far end and both adjacent structures are lacking screening and windows at their ends. (RA.)

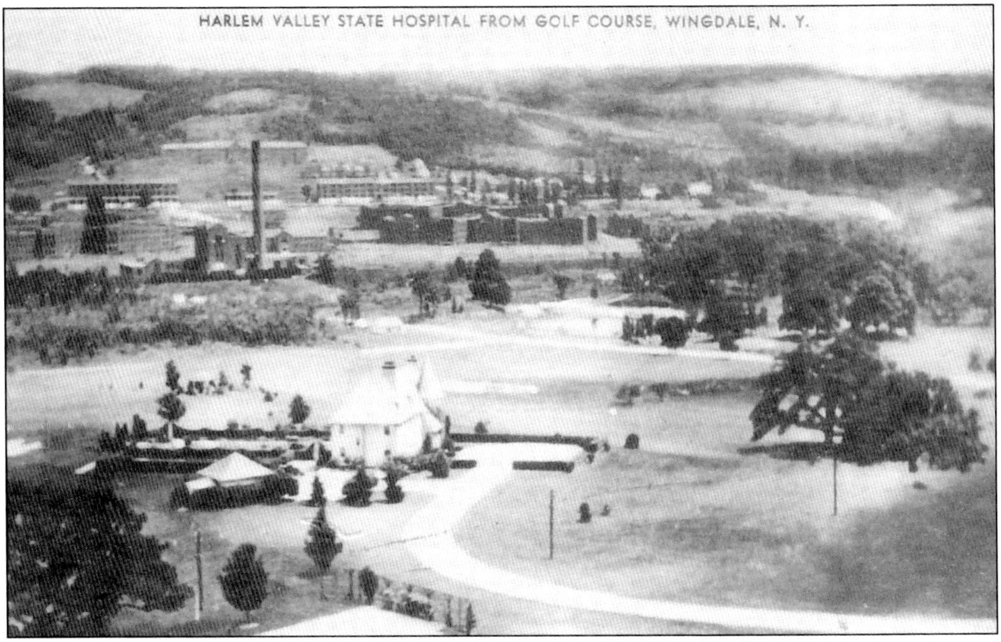

Quality leisure time was important to the staff. A golf course fulfilled a recreational need for on-call doctors who could not leave the campus. Employees enjoyed the course as well. Taken from the golf course, this image focuses on the director's house and gardens, with the remaining campus as backdrop. The house architecture was a mix of styles and served as the director's house. (KD.)

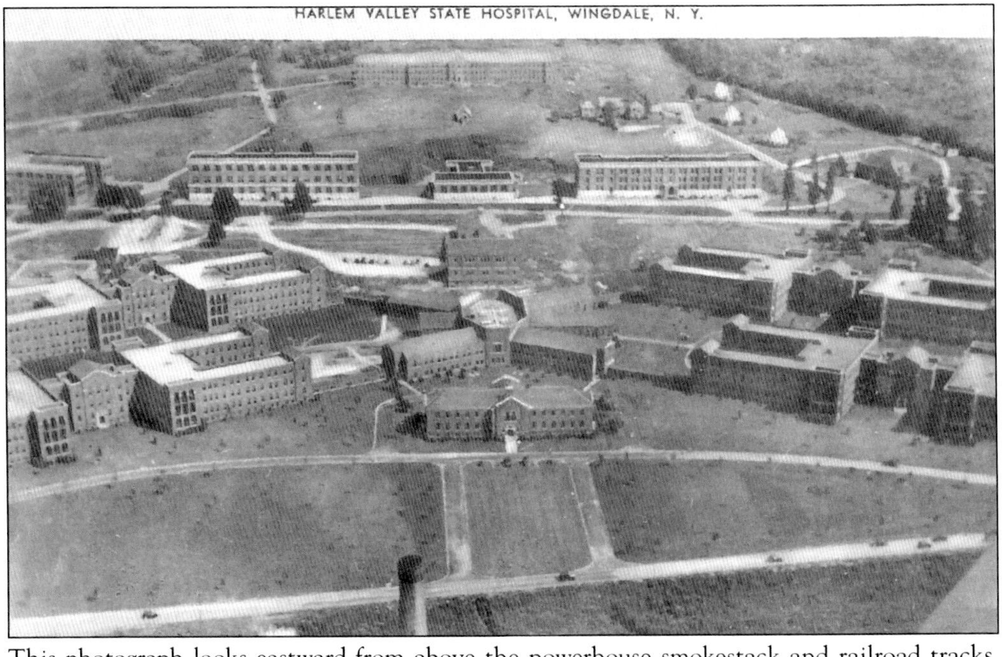

This photograph looks eastward from above the powerhouse smokestack and railroad tracks. Newly completed Route 22 takes traffic west of the main facility. Landscaping and elm trees line the east side of the main road. The administration building sits among four H buildings. To the rear were I-shaped buildings planned for the original prison. (KD.)

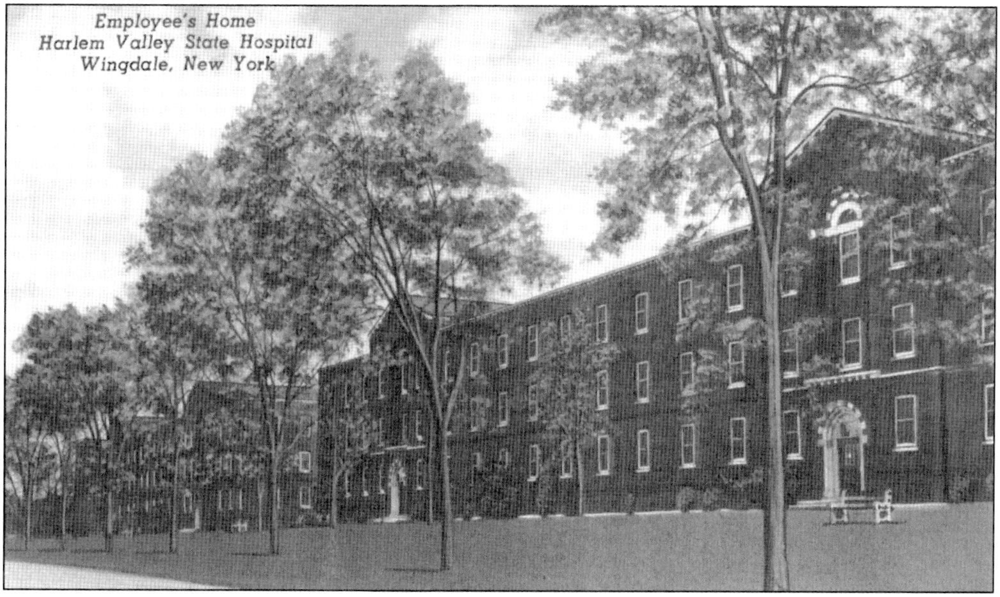

The hospital needed more workers than the local area could supply. Employee recruitment took place in areas beyond Dutchess County, such as in Upstate New York and the southern states. Minimal housing costs added incentive to the job offer. The employees' home housed workers from the psychiatric facility and the Division for Youth prison. Today corrections officers from area correctional facilities live there. (RA.)

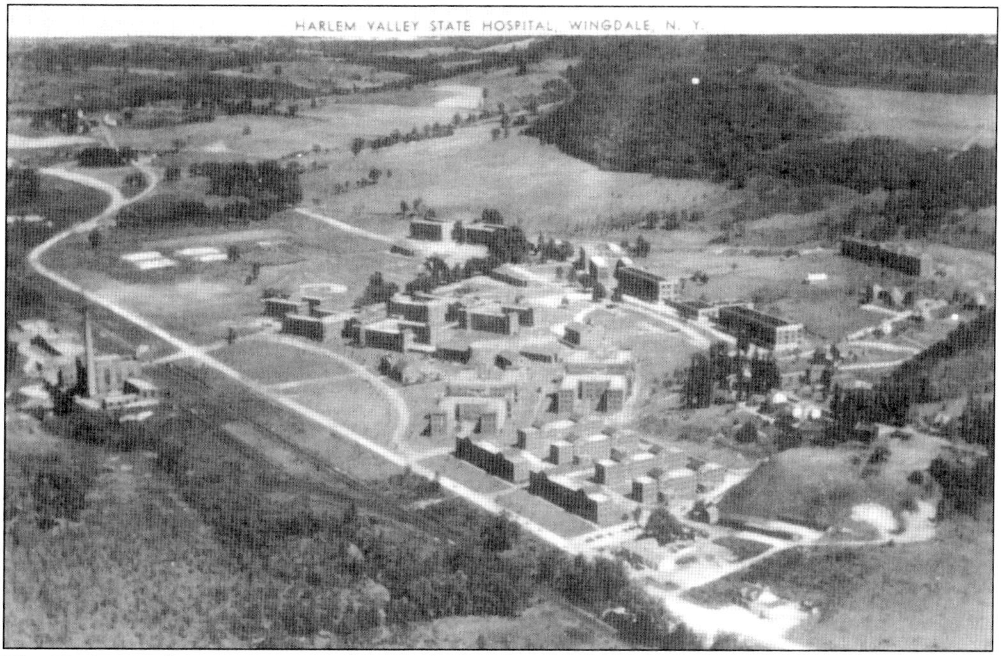

The Harlem Valley State Hospital opened on April 24, 1924. This later view shows the completed facility against the rural landscape of the area in the 1930s. New Route 22 was completed by 1929 to avoid excess traffic within the facility. Church Hill can be seen at the upper left. The road led south past Jackson Wing's inn. Adjacent to the hospital on the south side was Guy C. Ligon's Diner. (RA.)

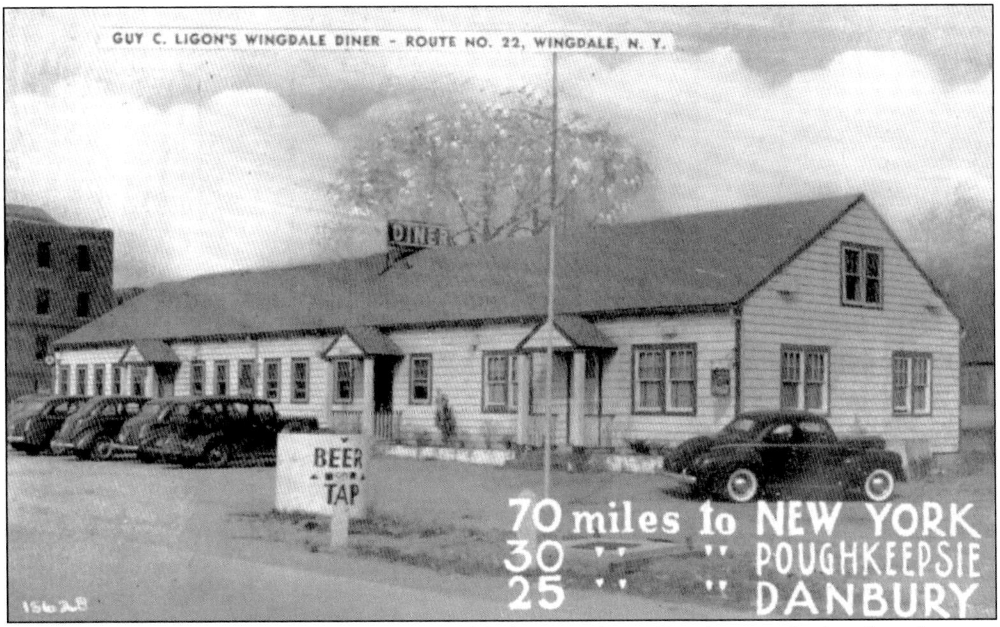

Guy C. Ligon advertised his place as the world's longest diner. Employees who lived in the state housing ate at the employee dining hall or walked next door for dinner. The diner was also a bar and gathering place. By the 1950s, numerous bars had opened near the hospital. Today this building does business as the Wingdale Beer and Soda. (KD.)

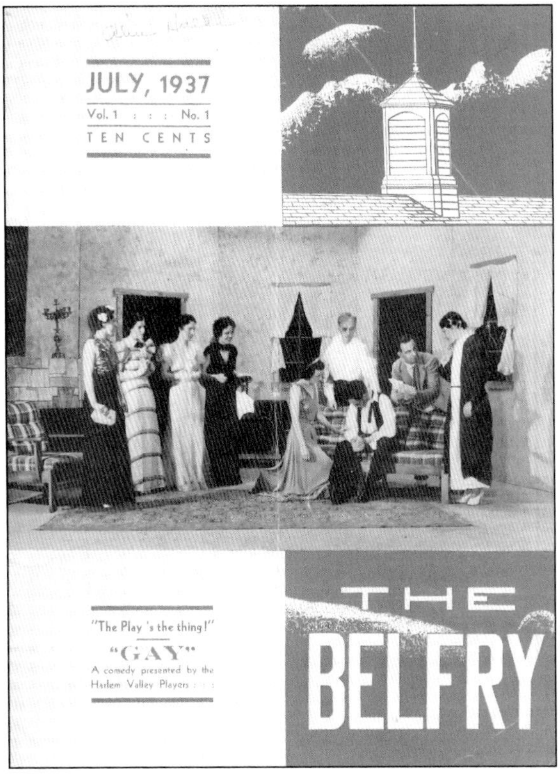

Mental health care and terminology have changed since July 1937, when an employee newspaper, titled *The Belfry*, published its first magazine. As the voice of over 1,000 workers with an annual payroll of over $800,000, it intended to harness their strength for their common good. The cover showed their play, performed at the playhouse at Pine Forest Colony, in Wingdale. Thanks were extended to the Weils for heir help in making the production possible. (TDHC.)

Seven

Dover a Short While Ago

From 1930 to 1960, many changes occurred in the town of Dover. Impacts from the state hospital were enormous, as the institution grew to into a self-sufficient complex and the town's largest employer. During World War II, listening posts on the hilltops east of Ragans Mill and Vincent's farm were manned 24 hours a day as the magnesium plant went into operation. Dover's men and women served around the world. Most returned home, while some made the ultimate sacrifice. Dover's legion post honors them.

By 1940, Hunt Country Furniture was a thriving business in Webatuck. In the 1950s, farming continued to decline, and many farmers leased to sand and gravel companies to supplement their income. Other fields became new subdivisions as the population increased and diversified. In 1960, zoning was adopted to regulate growth and impacts as the town aimed to improve through space planning, preservation of important architecture, improvement of services, and enhancement of economic and cultural needs of the community. The Dover Lions had land donated and built a pool for the town's youth. It was not long before transportation improvements created the bedroom-community effect in Dover. The locals welcomed the energy and spirit of the newcomers, as the suburbs galloped northward up the great road from New York.

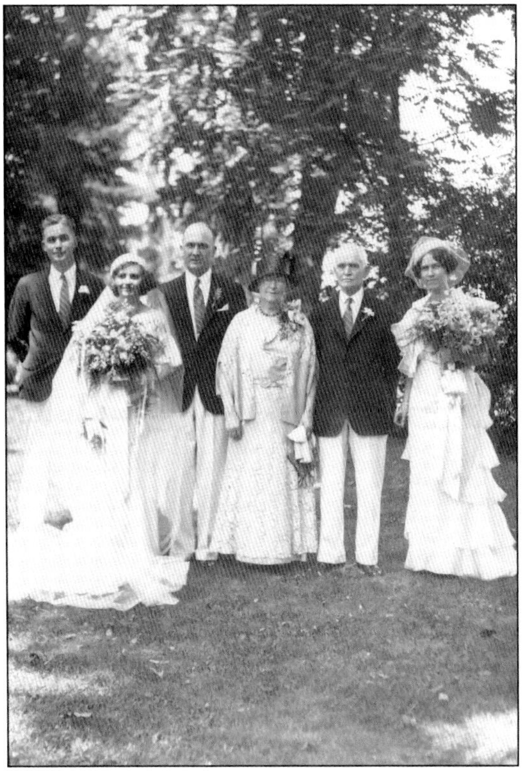

For almost a half century, Dover's favorite couple was inseparable. Mildred Boyce taught Latin at Dover High School, and Tom Boyce ran the Dover Plains National Bank. Married on August 5, 1933, this wedding photograph shows the family of Mildred Carey Boyce. From left to right are Mildred's brother, Richard Carey; Mildred; Tom Boyce; Mildred's parents, William and Catherine (Lehan) Carey; and Mildred's sister Margaret Carey. Marie Feathers Darling celebrated her birthday as their flower girl. (RMC.)

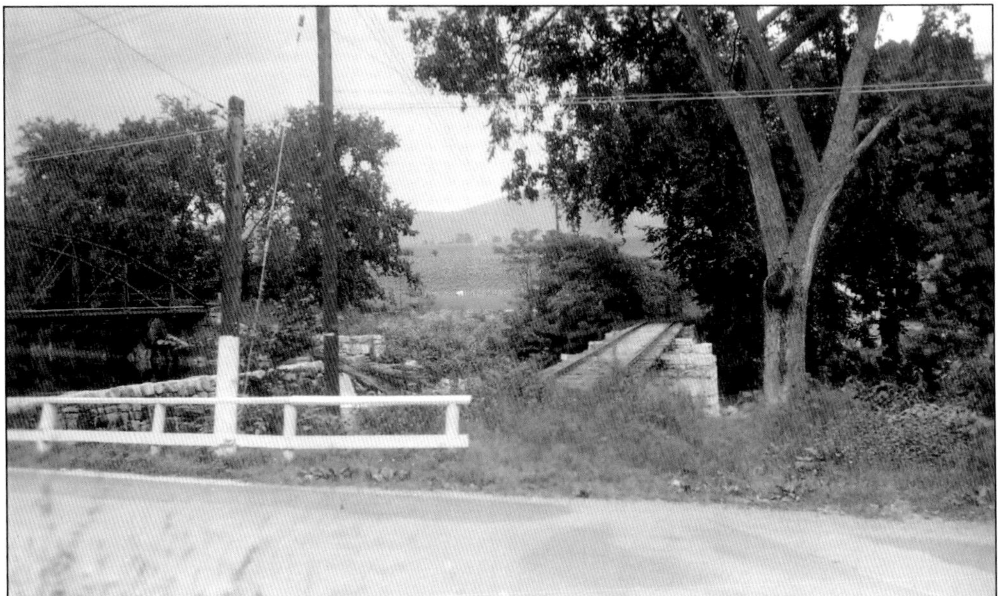

In this picture from about 1935 are the Ragans Mill bridge (upper left), Ragans Mill dam, and the Toonerville Trolley bridge (center), which dead-ends in a tangle of weeds at old Route 22. A long ridge in the resurfaced road indicates the old track beds. Between the dam and the trolley bridge is a long-range view of the north side of Ragans Mill Road. Today houses cover the fields. (IH.)

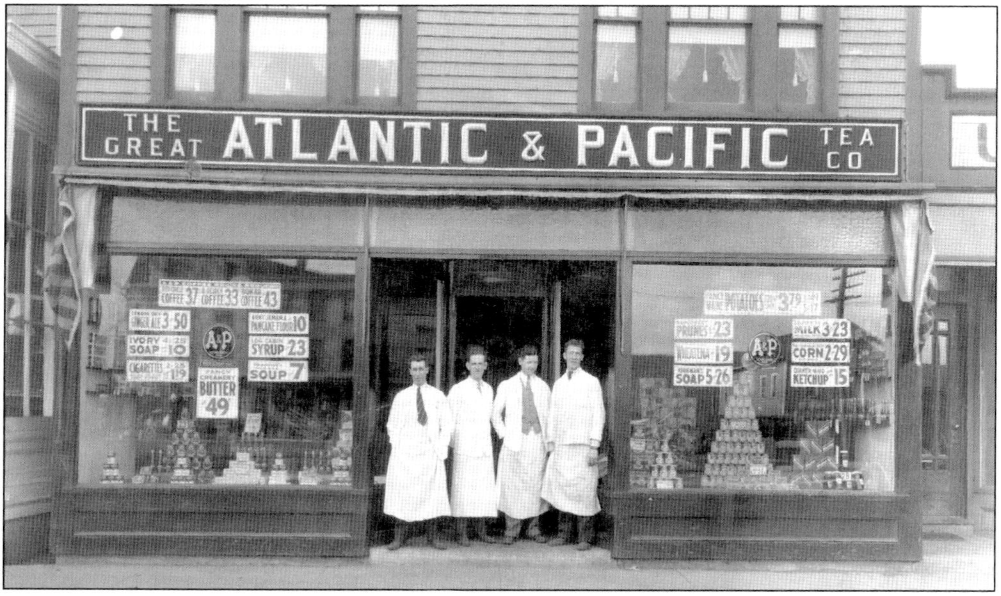

The Great Atlantic and Pacific Tea Company store was located on Market Street near the railroad tracks in Dover Plains. Taken in 1930, the picture shows, from left to right, Patrick Gorman, manager Mike O'Brien, Harry McIntyre, and Gerry Nelligan. The building later became an IGA store owned by Francis Scott and Darwin Benson. Today the owners have their home over a delicatessen catering to the local community and commuters on the Metropolitan Authority Railroad, Harlem line. (ELB.)

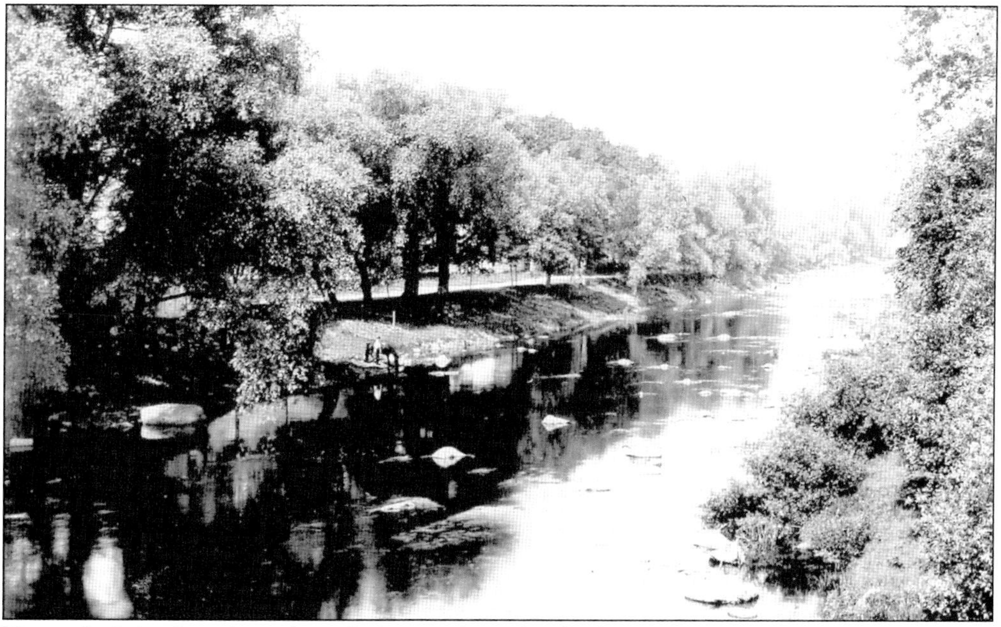

The early Schaghticoke Tribe called it Weebutook, which meant "Beautiful Hunting Ground." In old Dover, the river was called the Oblong River and Ten-Mile River. In 1900, it was to be dammed and its valley flooded past Dover Plains. By 1938, the New York City Camera Club judged South Dover's Ten Mile River area the most photographic area in six counties. Today anglers, boaters, photographers, and artists appreciate the scenic resource. (TDHS.)

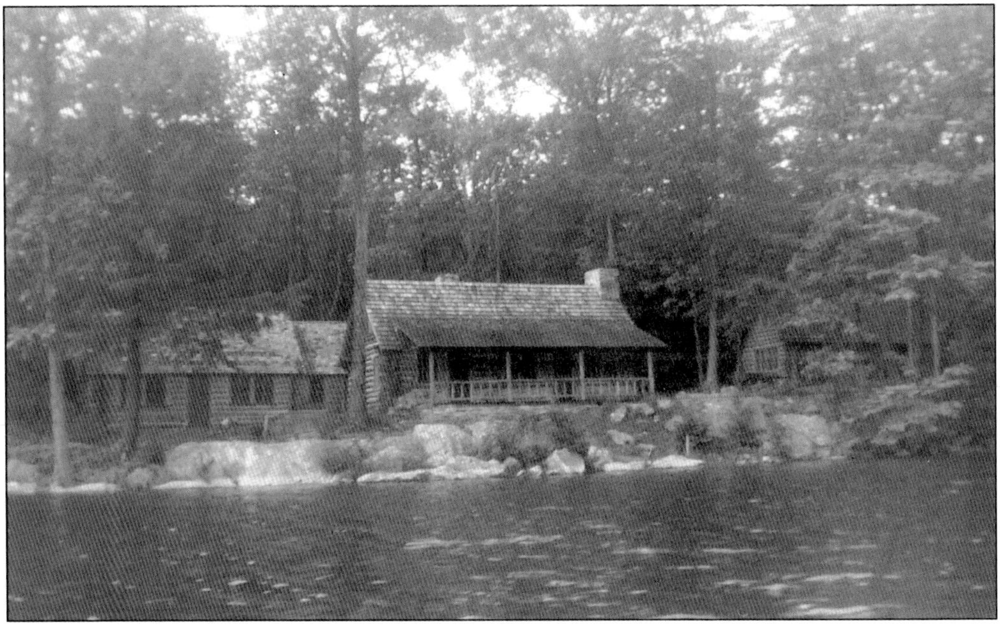

By 1846, Theodore Crane's family owned lands on East Mountain's northern end. After 1920, they dammed a small brook, creating a narrow, mile-long pond called Crane's Pond. A causeway called Kenaday Bridge crossed the pond. By the 1930s, leafless, standing chestnut trees remaining after the blight were used to build log cabins. Crane's cabin was on the pond's east side. Today the lands and cabins remain in private hands. (ECL.)

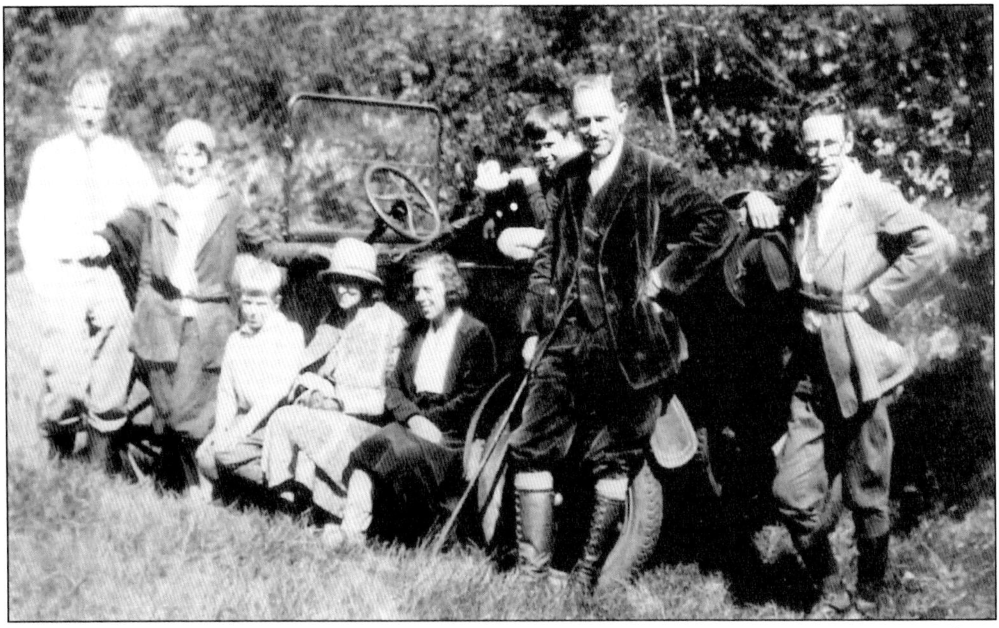

According to Robert Crane, Munroe Crane's family visited and camped at Cranes Pond on a regular basis during the summer months. This outing shows family members. From left to right are Robert, Helen Crane, an unidentified boy, Iola (Wing) Crane, Nancy Crane, Philippe (partly behind Theodore), Theodore Crane, and Donald Crane. The family posed in front of their Model T about 1931. (RC.)

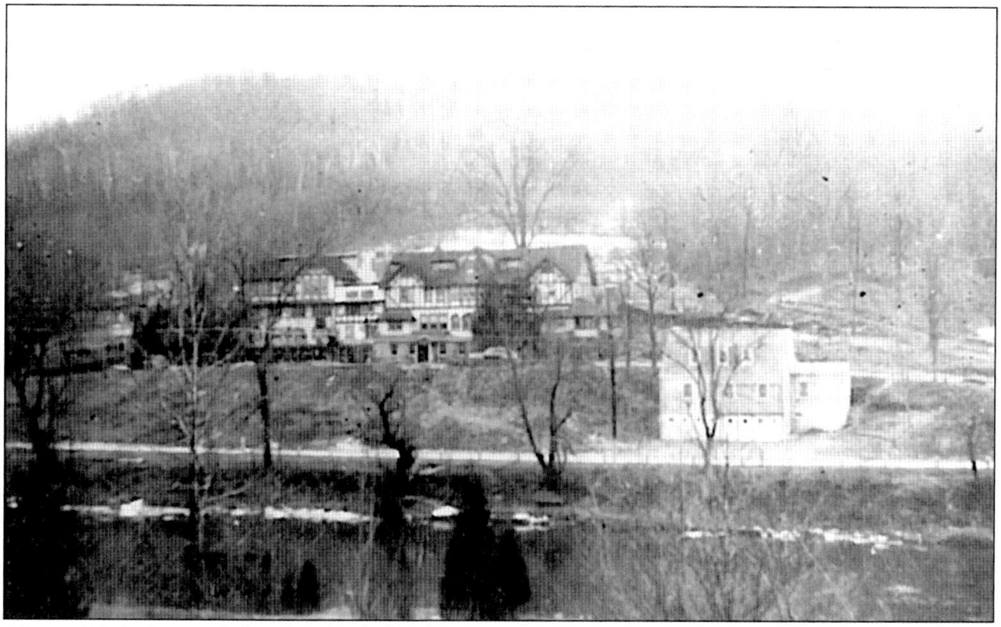

About 1920, Oscar Schreiber built his home in Wingdale. The house was expanded to the Webatuck Inn, with bright, airy rooms for summer tourists. Guests staying one week or more received free transportation from the railroad station. When Harlem Valley State Hospital opened, the inn boarded workers. Later reconfigured rooms became apartments for folks who moved into the area. The inn was destroyed by fire in the late 1950s. (WS.)

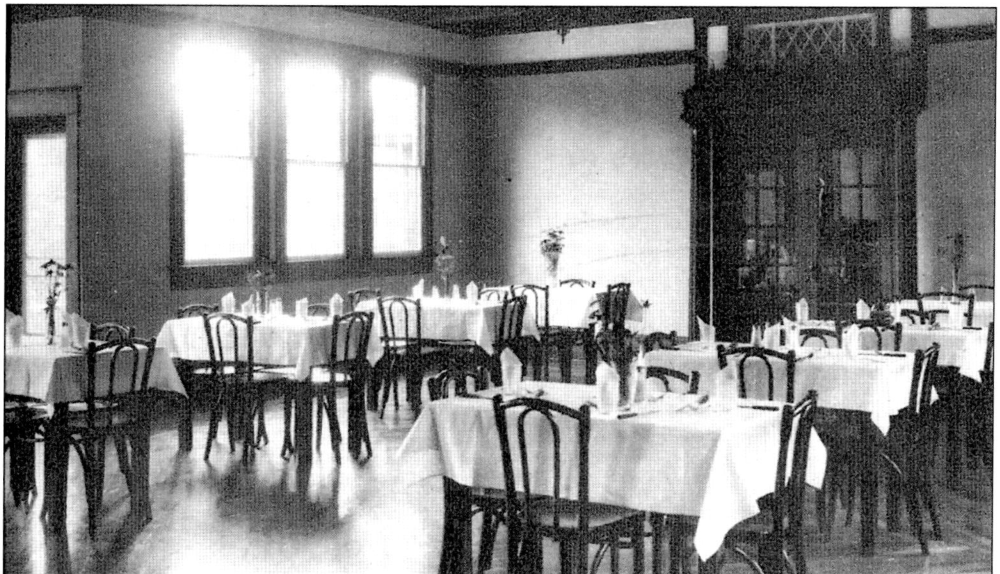

Nestled at the foot of the Berkshire Hills, the Webatuck Inn offered the best food of country life. A spacious dining room overlooked the Ten Mile River, and the cooks offered three meals a day. All baking and food preparation was done on premises using fresh fruit, vegetables, dairy, and meat supplied daily by local gardens and farms. Water was fresh, pure, and sweet from a spring-fed well. (KD.)

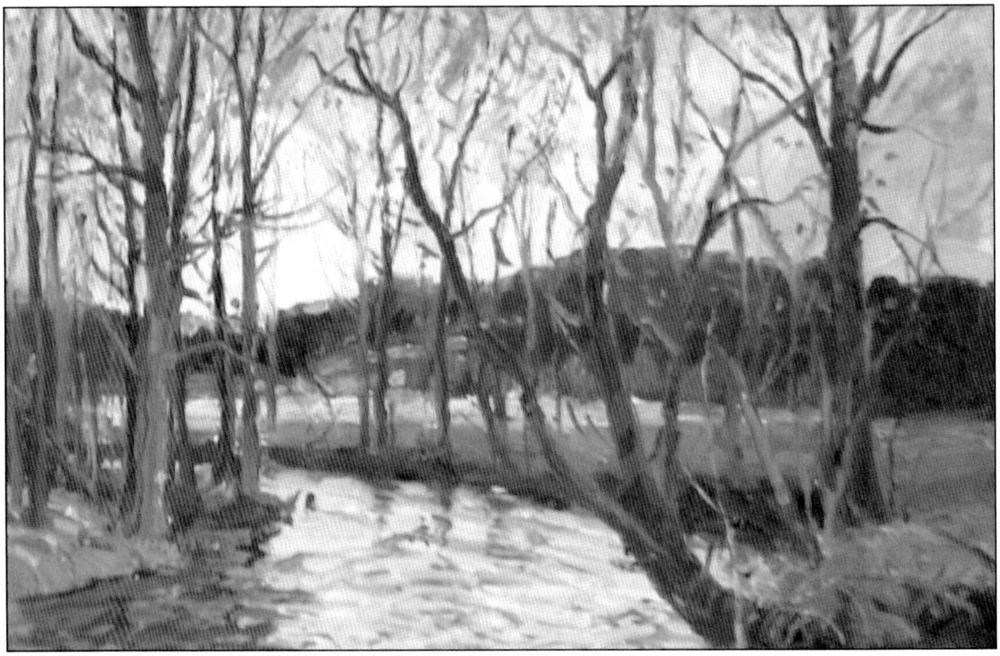

Impressionist Arthur J. E. Powell came to Dover in the 1930s as part of Franklin Delano Roosevelt's cultural program. The Ten Mile River was his favorite subject. This autumn scene shows the moving river with Nellie Hill in the background. Other painters who came to Dover were George Glenn Newell and Harry F. Waltman. (DPH.)

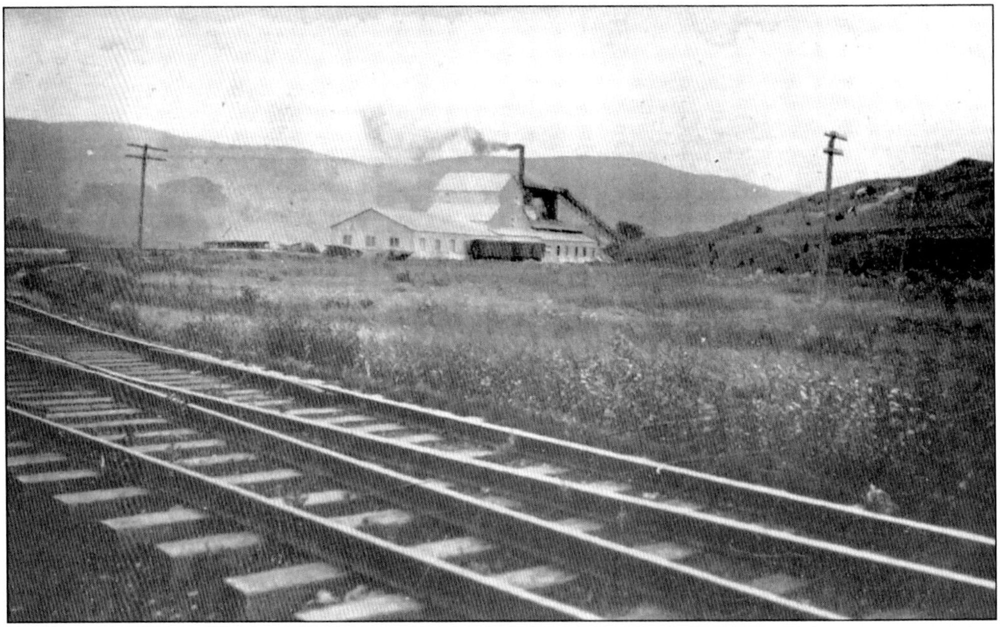

The Dover Plains Lime Company was located at the south end of Powell Road near Nellie Hill. When marble was no longer popular for buildings, operators hauled the lime-rich marble from the quarries on Limekiln Road and Sand Hill Road to the three-story factory where it was crushed, cooked, pulverized, and bagged. Carts hauled fertilizer to local stores, or railroad transport cars were loaded on-site. (KD.)

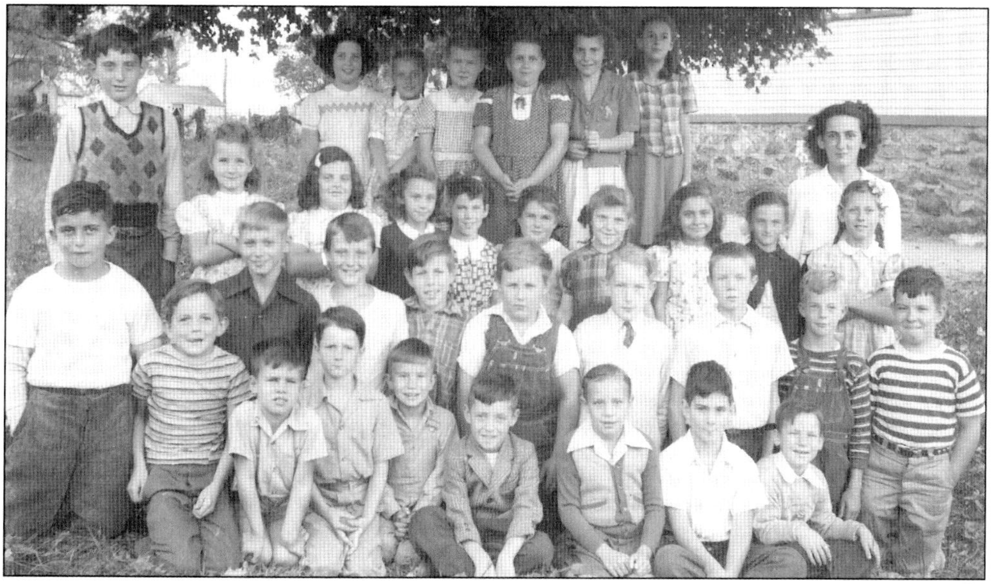

Webatuck School was located east of the Dog Tail Corners intersection on today's old Webatuck Road. The students from the one-room schoolhouse were photographed on the east side of the school in 1943. Among the students are George Ketchin, Rusty Franklin, Richard Darling, Martha Hodge, Hattie Rundell, Jane Baruffo, Dawn Caple, Louise Mostachetti, Doris Carlson, Fred Janus, Jim O'Dell, Betsy Conditto, Robert Jordan, and Linda Schatz. Teachers were Miss Southworth, Miss Rundell, and Mr. Key. (AF.)

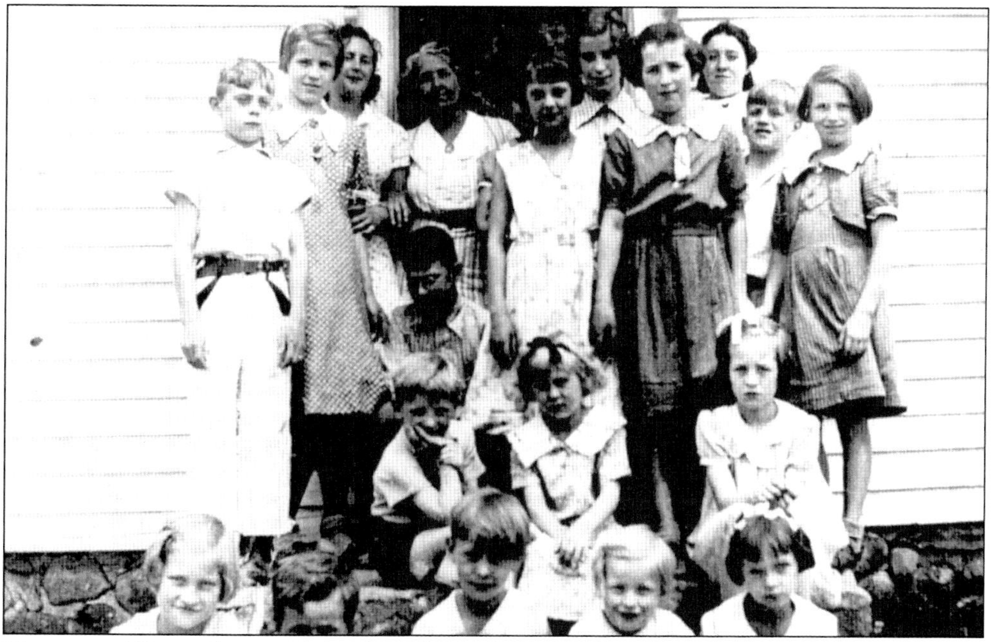

This second Dover Furnace School was located just south of the Mountain Brook bridge near Ridge Road. In 1938, Kate Pachin taught multiple classes. Her students had familiar names such as Tabor, Dennis, Gray, Metcalf, and Beebe. Later the school was converted into a house. According to Walter Vincent, the first schoolhouse stood between the Swamp River and the railroad tracks on the road's north side. (RMC.)

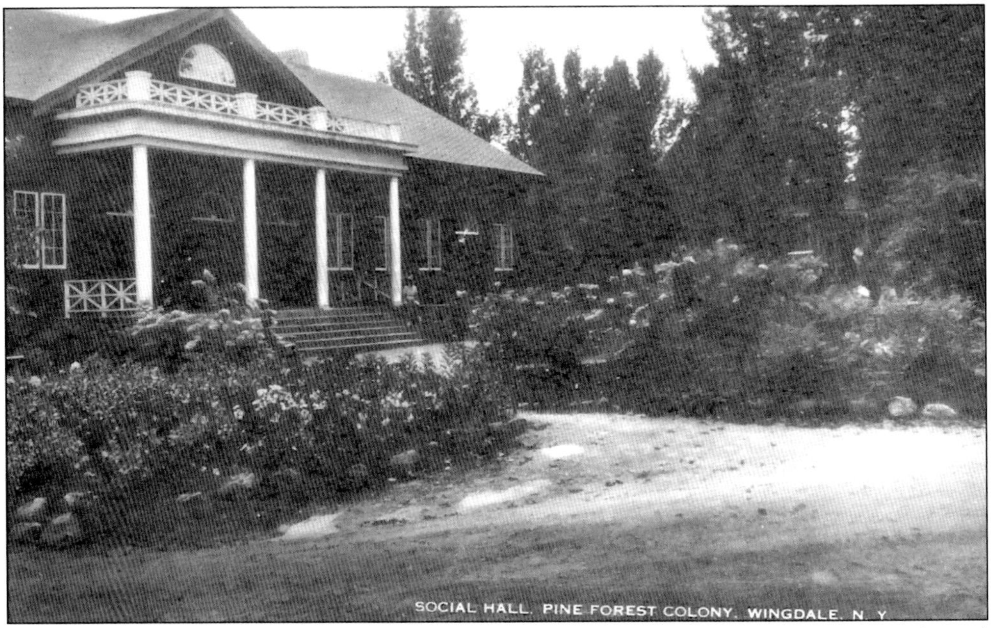

The Pine Forest Colony camp was located on the shores of Weil Pond. Shady pine groves formed a large part of the campground. Campers enjoyed social activities and dances in the social hall on the campgrounds. In 1937, Mr. and Mrs. Joseph D. Weil and Linton D. Weil opened the doors to the Harlem Valley Players, who presented the play for other employees and the public. (KD.)

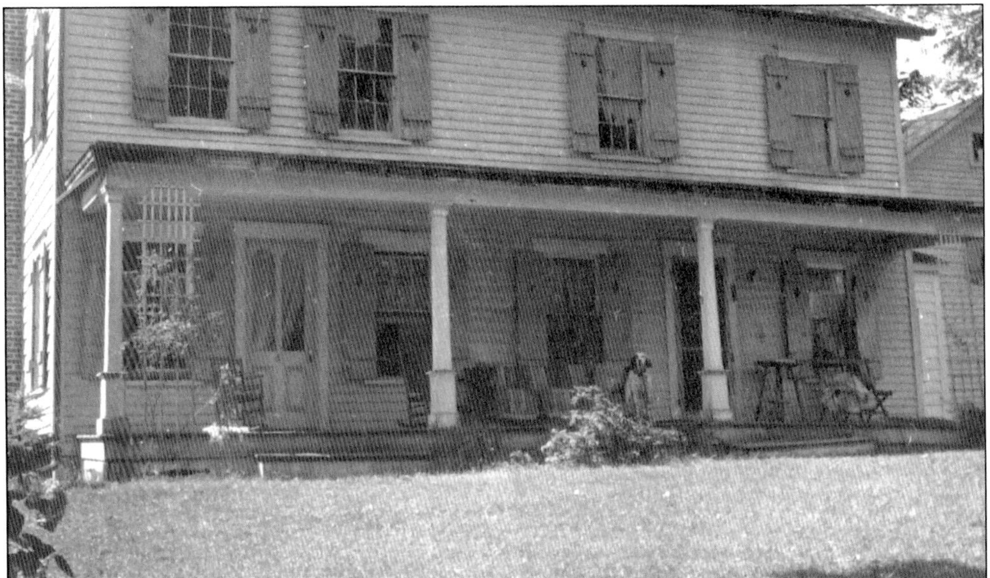

Falconwood Farm, owned by Margaret Faulkner, was purchased by David and Charlotte Shelby in the 1960s. Faulkner had documentation on former landowners and told them the song "Put on Your Old Grey Bonnet" was written about an older couple who sat on the front porch of the farmhouse on their 50th anniversary celebration. Still a working farm, the house and farm look much as they did when this photograph was taken in 1937. (CDS.)

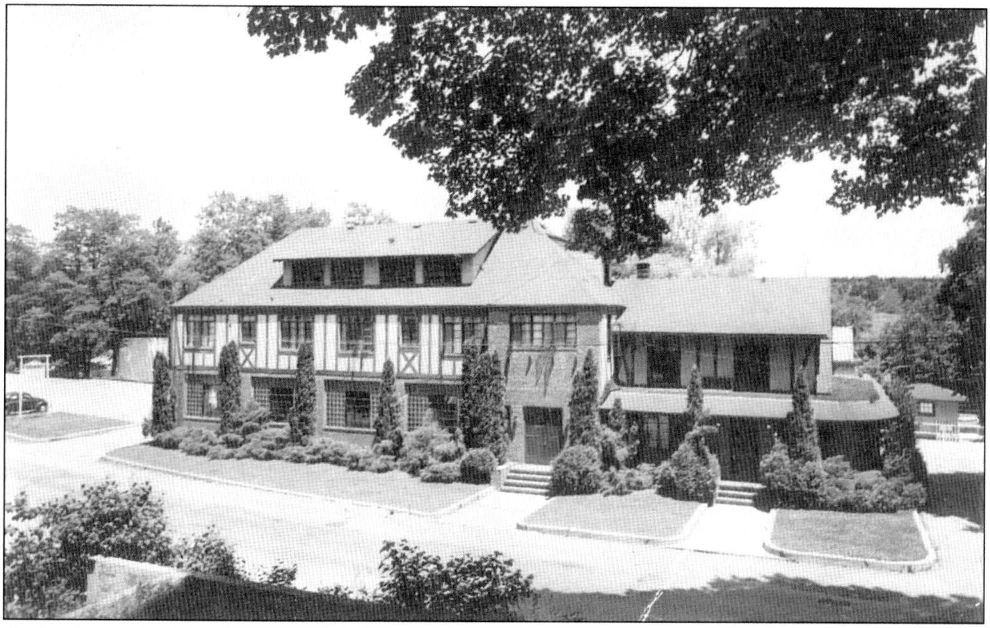

Built along the Ten Mile River in the late 1940s by Oscar Schreiber and Sons, Brookhaven Lodge was a retreat for guests who enjoyed river walks, the swimming pool, tennis, or handball. Later renamed the Berkshire Lodge, it became a popular dance club and bar for the younger crowd. A fire burned portions of the building in the 1960s. Today it is the JTR Bus Garage on old Route 22. (CMS.)

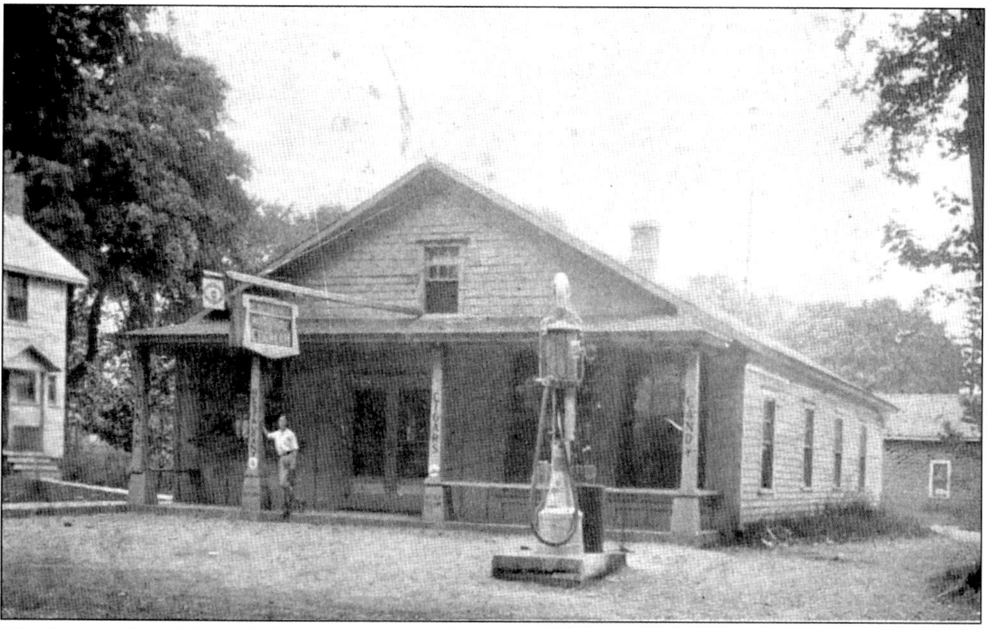

The Stone Church Lunch Room was situated on the Old Post Road, today's Route 22, across from the Dover Stone Church laneway. Nearby was the Stone Church Hotel. The quaint lunchroom and restaurant fed hungry tourists and fueled their thirsty automobiles through 1939, when Edwin and Marion Moran purchased and ran the restaurant until the 1960s. It then became Earl "Chubby" Feather's Red Beard Pub. Today it is Whalen's legal offices. (KD.)

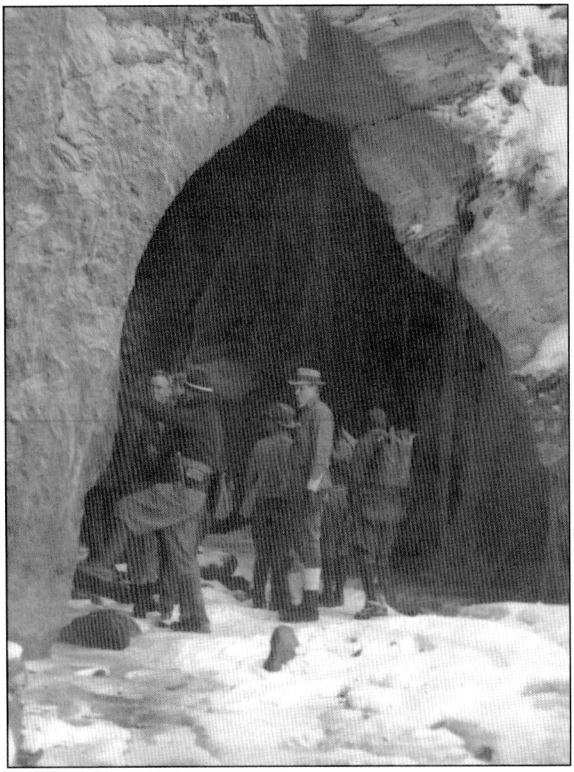

Visiting the cave has been enjoyed since the time of the Pequot chief Sassacus. Exploring the smooth cave recesses was dangerous because of dampness and water flow. Temperature controlled the water, so these nine explorers chose winter for their inspection. Huge icicles hang from the ceiling, drape the cave sides, and cover the floor. According to one local historian, the earliest cave explorer was recorded around the mid-1700s. (KC.)

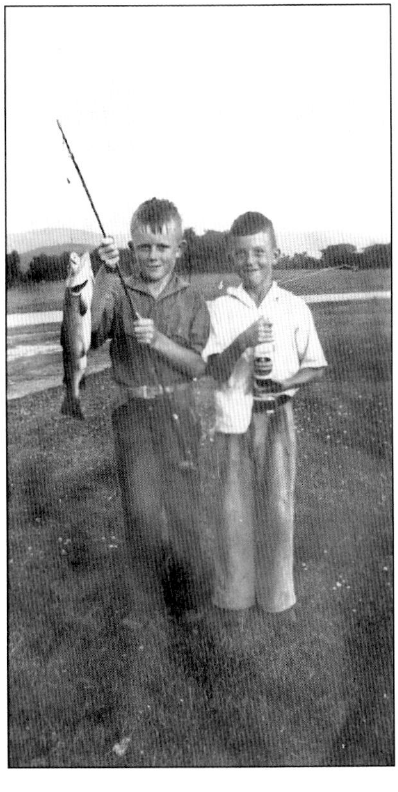

In the spring of 1942, Donald (left) and Roger Callahan went fishing in the Ten Mile River above the Dover Plains railroad station. At age 10, Roger remembered walking to the trestle with his brother, where they caught this whopper. The brothers walked out and crossed Route 22 to Mr. Sherin's store. The owner gave Roger an ice-cold bottle of his favorite pop, Mission Orange Soda. Today Mr. Sherin's store is known as Renny's. (RMC.)

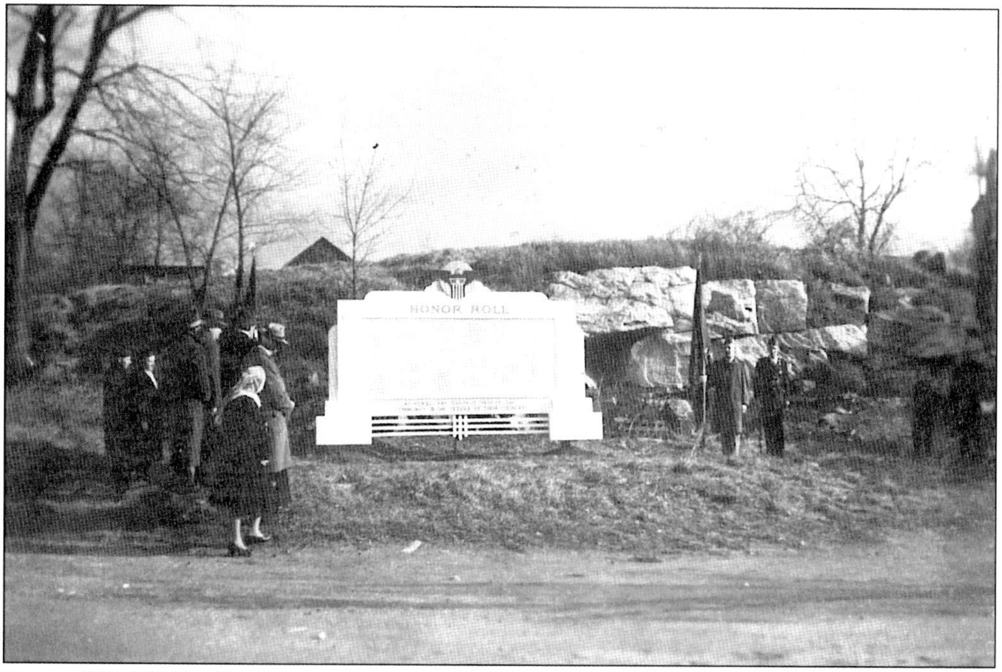

During World War II, many patriotic civic associations made efforts to honor the hometown youth in the armed services. In Wingdale, the Wingdale Civic Association built this honor roll opposite the Wingdale railroad station. According to former post commander William Schreiber, after the war, the Wingdale Civic Association purchased land and helped homecoming veterans draw up plans, purchase supplies, and build the Masiero-Winship American Legion Post 1811. (LM.)

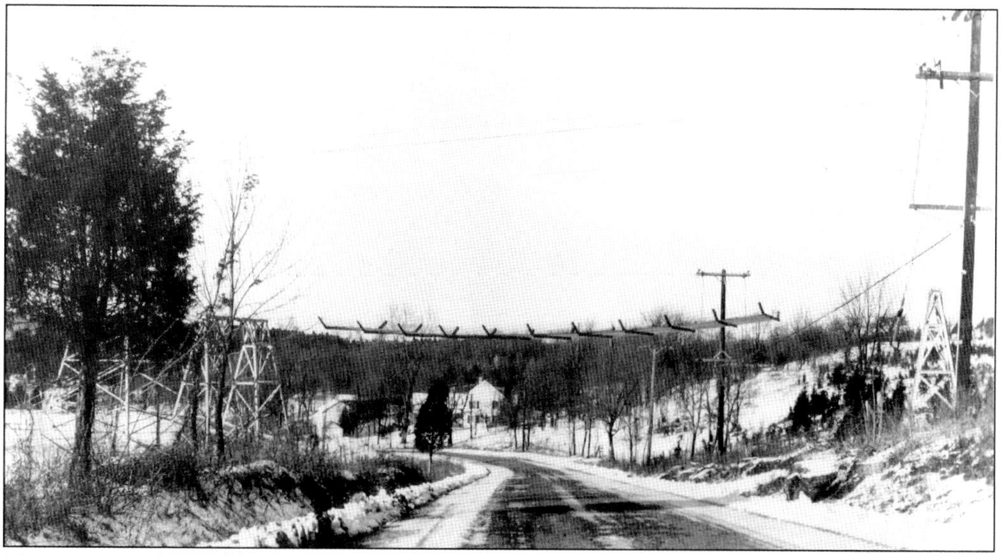

Magnesium-rich marble was hauled two and a half miles via the tramway from the former Dover White Marble Company. Using steel towers and cable, the tramway was constructed to haul 40 tons of ore per hour to the plant. Screening under the tramway protected vehicles and pedestrians where it crossed old Route 22, Route 22, and near the north end of Crickett Hill Road, where this picture was taken. (CRR.)

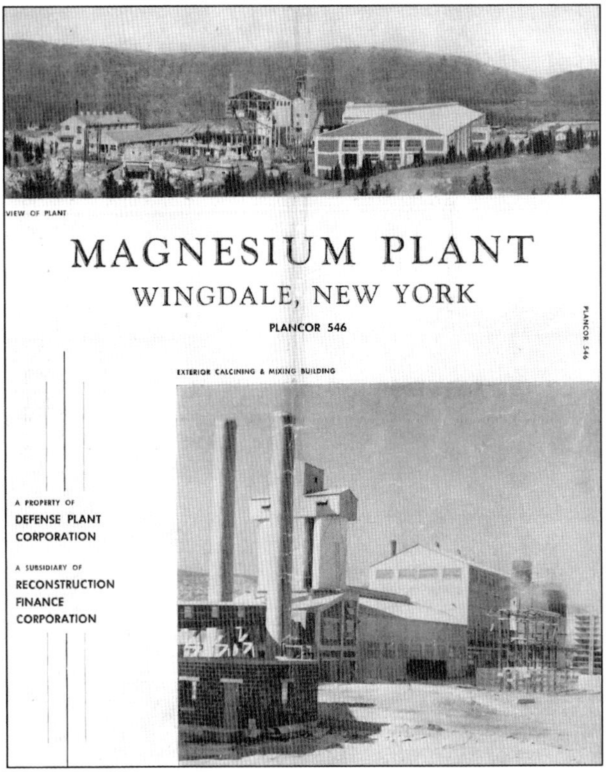

The federal government built the magnesium plant in Wingdale on Route 22. Designed to extract magnesium from the marble, the facilities had numerous buildings, including the 100-by-700-foot main building, kilns, furnaces, and equipment. A railroad spur attended the site. The plant employed over 200 workers, including Oscar Schreiber, who was determined to help with the war effort. (BCK.)

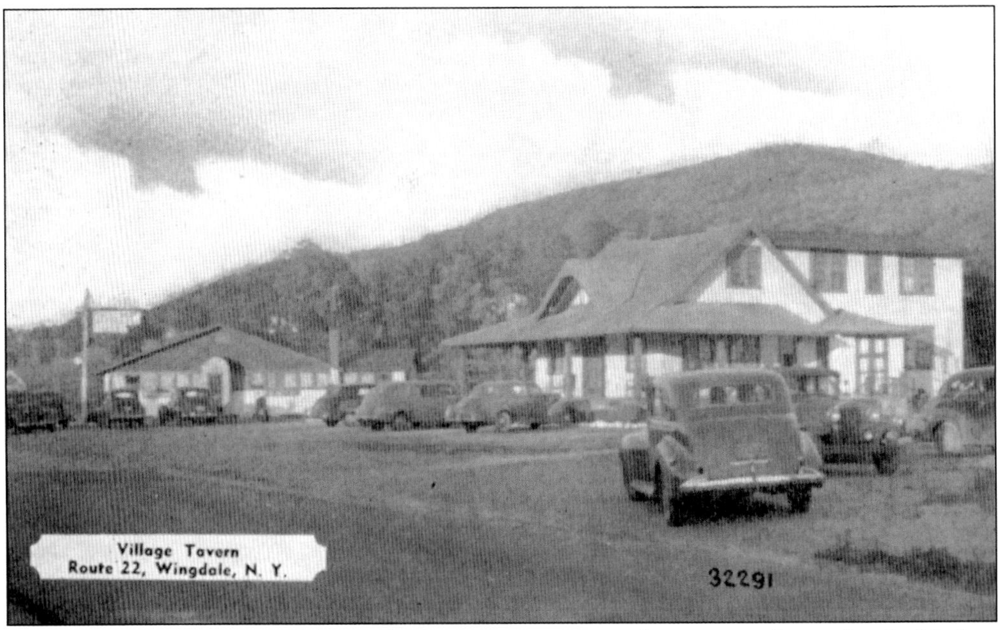

By the mid-1940s, the Wingdale area had grown to accommodate new employees for the Harlem Valley State Hospital. An apartment house was built (right) between Church Hill and the hospital. The Village Tavern (left) became a popular place among the younger crowd. Eventually the tavern closed, and the building became an antiques store. Today this popular spot is known as Cousin's Deli. (TDHS.)

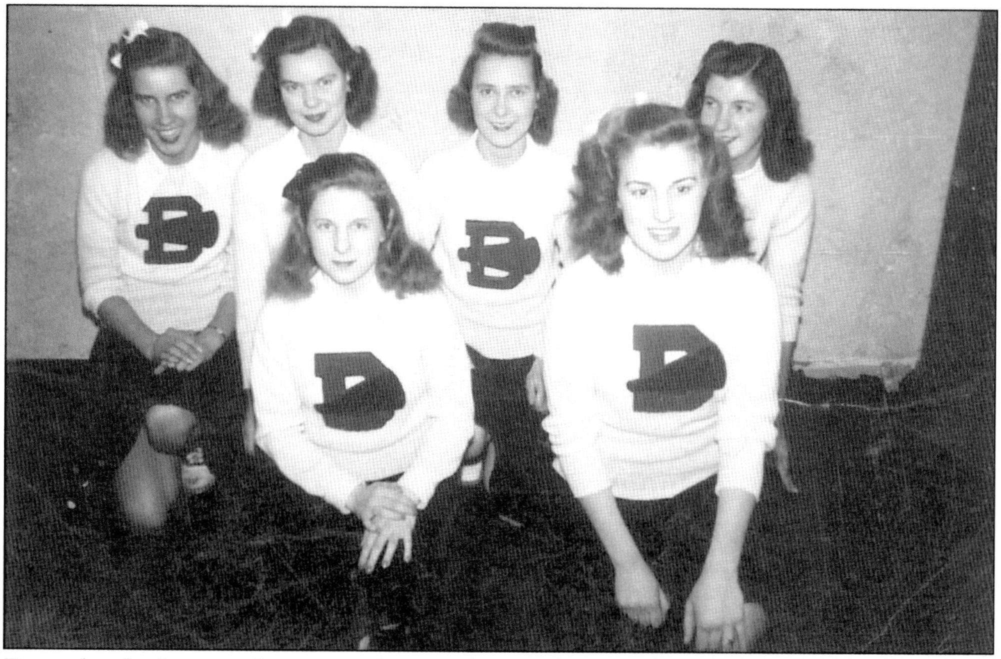

Dover cheerleaders pose for a group photograph around 1940. White sweaters, white blouses, black pleated skirts, and black-and-white saddle shoes were the uniform. A black megaphone on an orange *D* was the only decoration. From left to right, members of the squad are (first row) Shirley Ensign and ? Taddeo; (second row) Ann Faix, ? Landry, Evelyn Novak, and Jean Hoag. (DPH.)

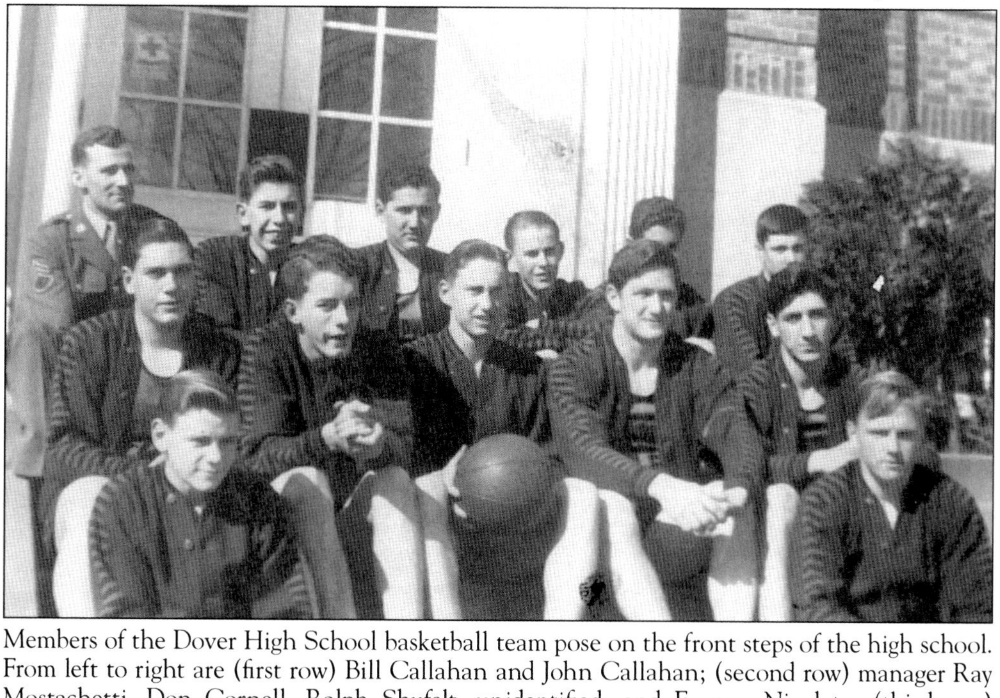

Members of the Dover High School basketball team pose on the front steps of the high school. From left to right are (first row) Bill Callahan and John Callahan; (second row) manager Ray Mostachetti, Don Cornell, Ralph Shufelt, unidentified, and Eugene Nicolato; (third row) unidentified, Robert Hufcut, Joseph "Babe" Cutolo, Francis Callahan, Raymond Hufcut, and unidentified. (DRH.)

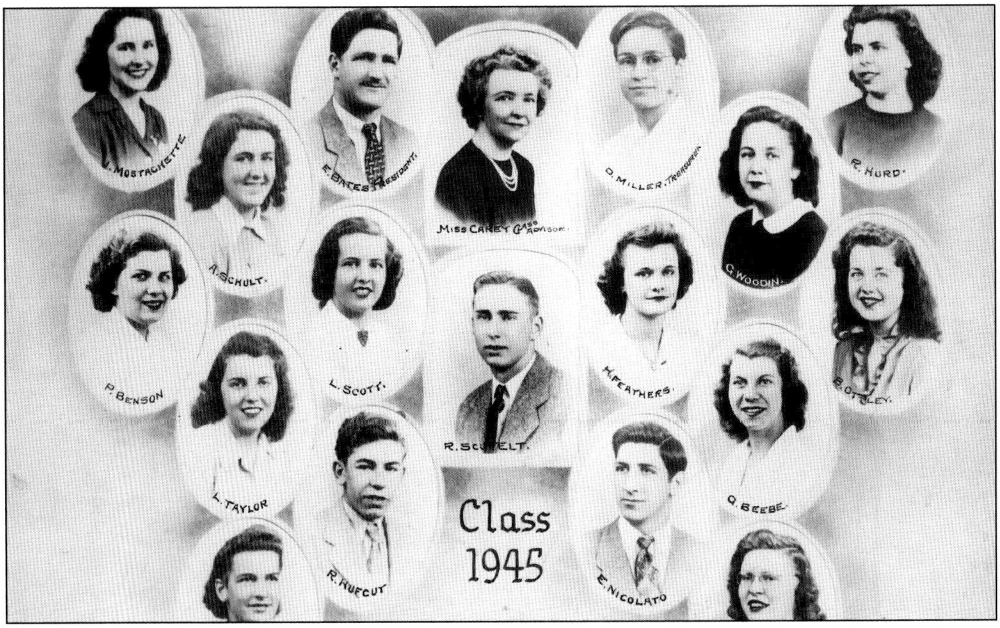

The Dover High School class of 1945 is shown with class advisor Margaret Carey. Many graduates remained in Dover. Recognizable names include Benson, Woodin, Feathers, Beebe, and Ottley. Class member Eugene Nicolato became a lawyer and practiced in town. Ralph Shufelt went on to become a long-standing member of the Dover Planning Board. Robert Hufcut became a local businessman with his own "garbologist" disposal service. (DRH.)

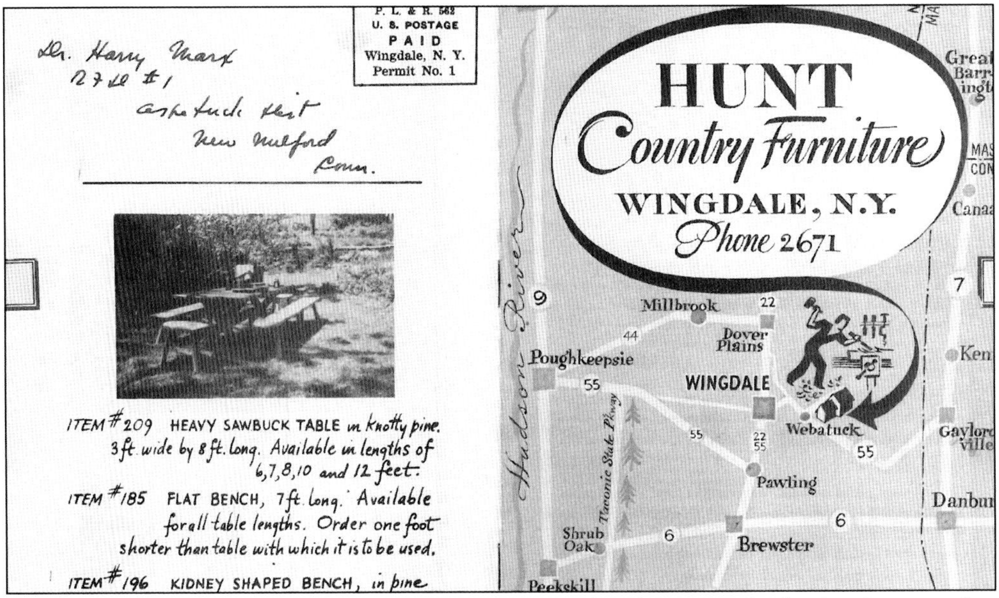

By 1949, Hunt Country Furniture had a following that began with the heirloom-quality workmanship of Lockwood Hunt. People appreciated the comfort and warmth of solid-wood chairs and other furniture made by skilled artisans. They sought out the furniture for their homes and businesses. The business made furniture to order, and customers could choose styles, sizes, and woods. The Hunt farm evolved from workshops for the business and eventually grew into a craft village at Webatuck. (BCK.)

Evelyn Eaton waves from the 1740s Deuel house noted on Robert Erskine's 1778 map of Fishkill and vicinity. She lived on Quaker Lake Road while writing *Give Me Your Golden Hand,* about an orphan who is the son of King George III. Axford Daigle fled to America, eventually settling in the Oblong among the Quakers. With the Deuel and the Hoag families, he finds new hope in life. Many passages in the book refer to the local area. (EF.)

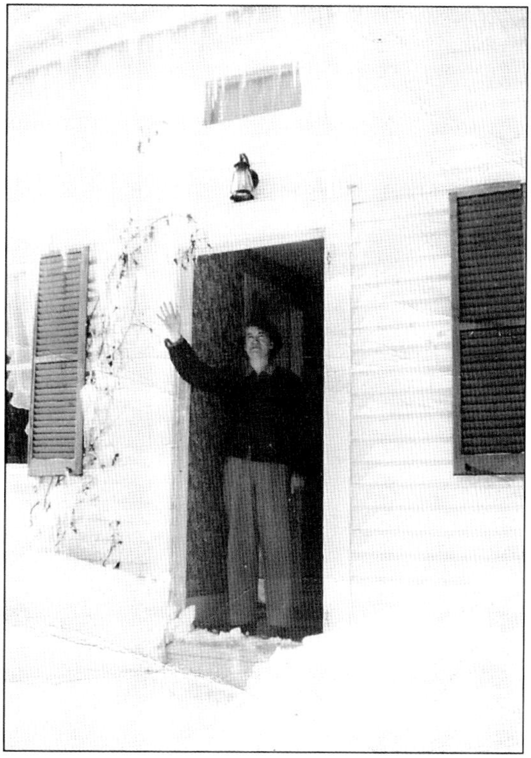

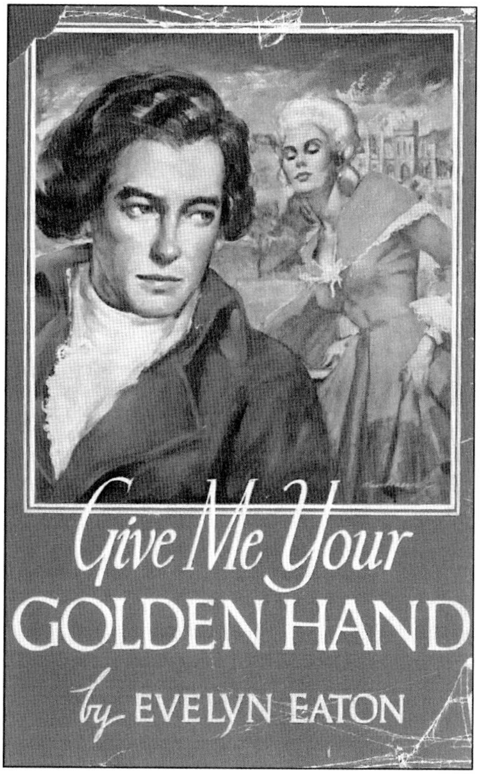

When Eaton came to the Dover area, she purchased part of the old Deuel farm in Deuel Hollow from Lowell Thomas Jr. in 1948. She and her daughter lived there for several years. Eaton's novel focused on the Quakers, the Deuels, the Hoags, and Deuel Hollow. Her sources were descendants of the Deuel and Hoag families. The book was published in 1951. (Terry Eaton.)

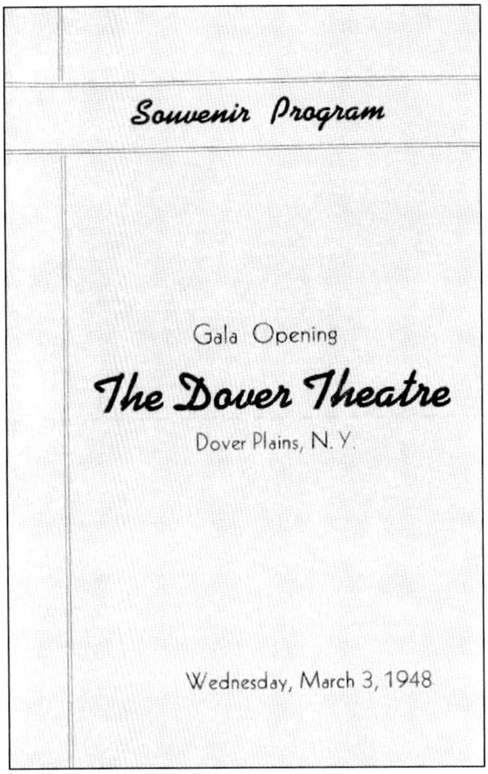

The Dover Theatre gala opening took place on March 3, 1948. Anthony Boscardin and Frank Knickerbocker proudly opened their luxurious 700-seat theater. Architecturally designed by a theater specialist and decorated by sound, stage, and interior design professionals from New York City, the theater boasted an elegant atmosphere, large screen, modern acoustics, and luxury seating. The main feature starred Walter Brennan in *Driftwood*. Today the remodeled theater building is known as Ketcham's Corner. (DRH.)

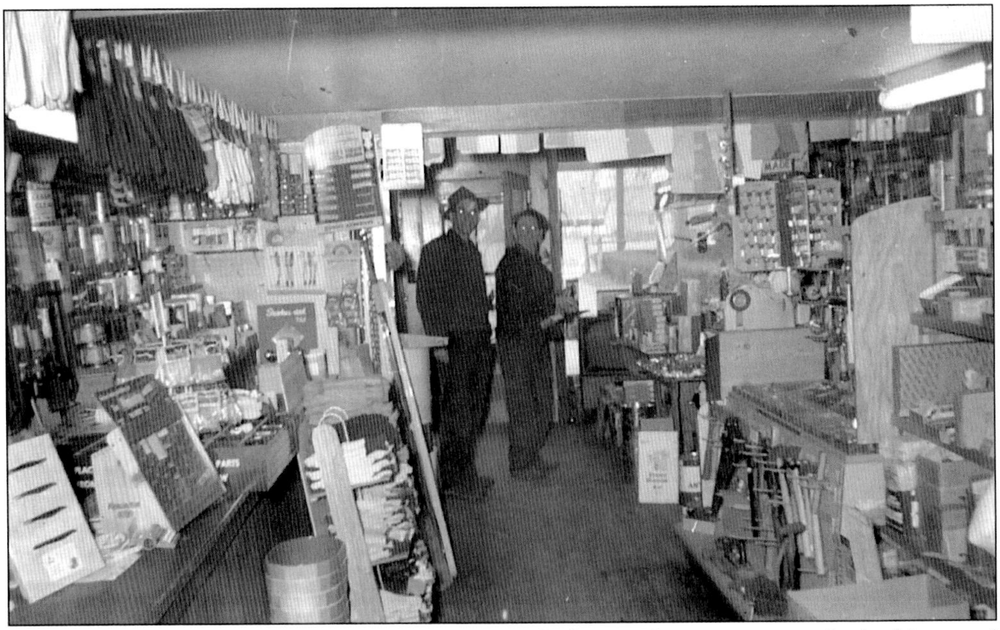

The Anthony L. Wathley Lumber Company stocked everything necessary for building and working the farm, from wood to flypaper. In this 1956 photograph, Frank (left) and his father, Tony, look back along countless displays into the store. Their air freshener was freshly sawn lumber. An ancient scale sits on the crowded counter. Nearby, a seven-toed calico cat guarded the old-fashioned cash register. The buildings burned in 1975. (PW.)

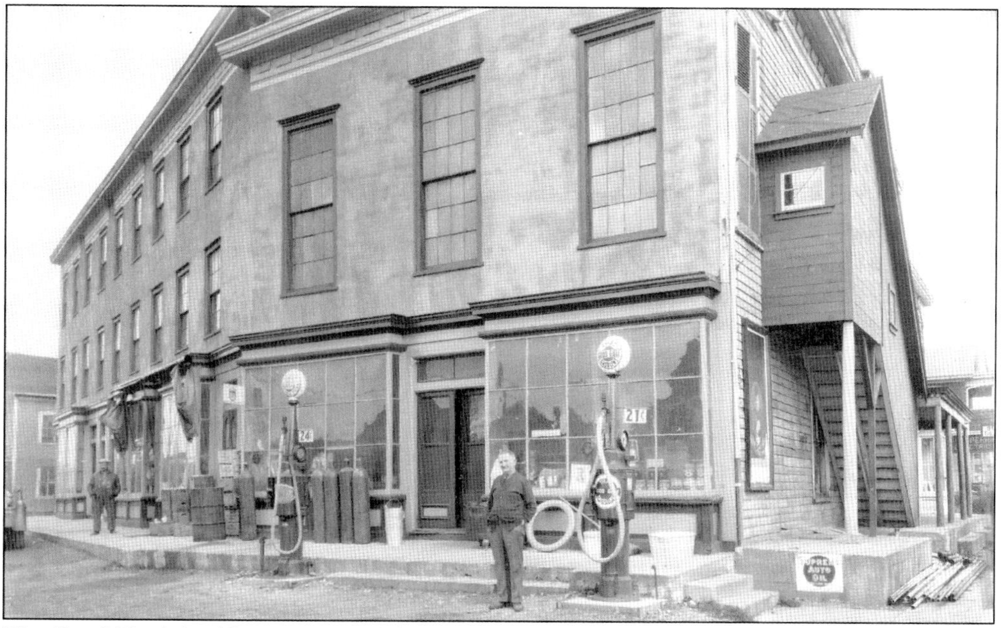

The Reed Block building sat east of the railroad tracks across from the Dover Plains National Bank. In this 1920s photograph, plumber Michael P. Brady stands in front of his plumbing and hardware store. The former tinsmith also sold wood and coal stoves, Supreme Motor Oil, and Gulf gasoline, which was 21¢ and 24¢ per gallon. Up Railroad Avenue, Joe "Rich" Cutolo stands in front of his grocery store. (ELB.)

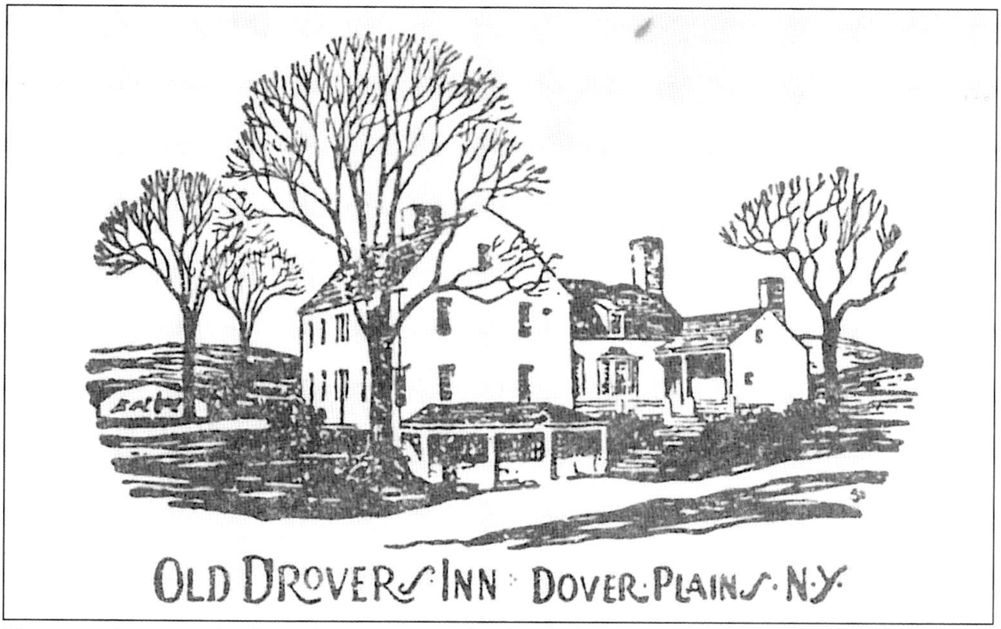

Gone are the trees of today. This yesteryear sketch of Old Drovers Inn appeared on a postcard in the 1950s. Shown is the original basement entrance for the inn and the gambrel-roofed addition. The postcard reverse included recipes for either key lime pie or the inn's world-famous cheddar cheese soup. Written and left at the inn, the owners mailed the postcards, compliments of the host. (DPH.)

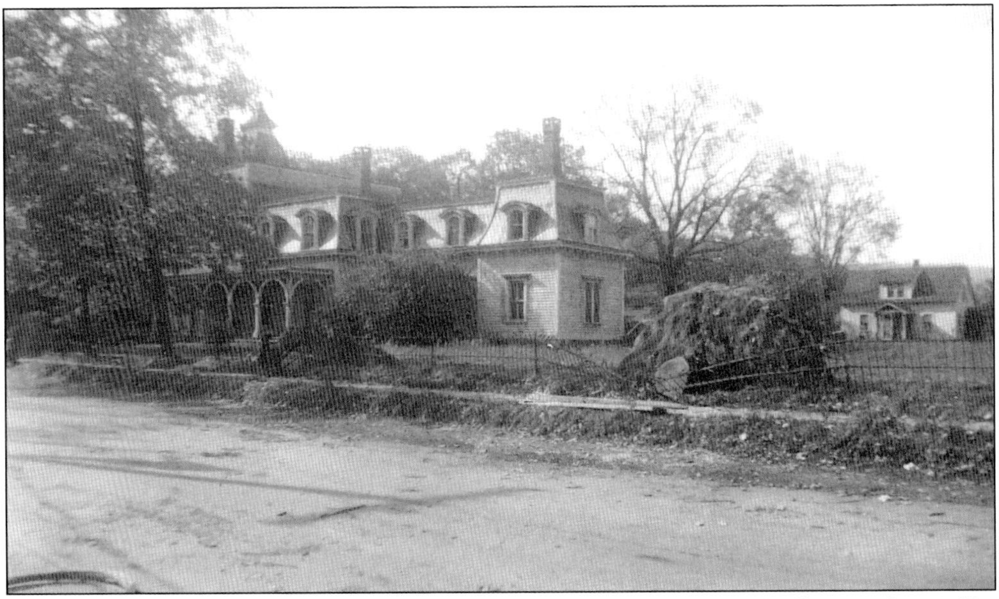

After Congressman John Henry Ketcham's death in 1906, his family gradually moved away. For a while, his former home was known as the Plymouth Inn. After 1929, like many large homes, upkeep was too expensive, and it fell into disrepair. The tenant house, which was located in the northwest corner of the Ketcham estate, was purchased by the Boscardin family in 1951, and plans were made to move it north. (FB.)

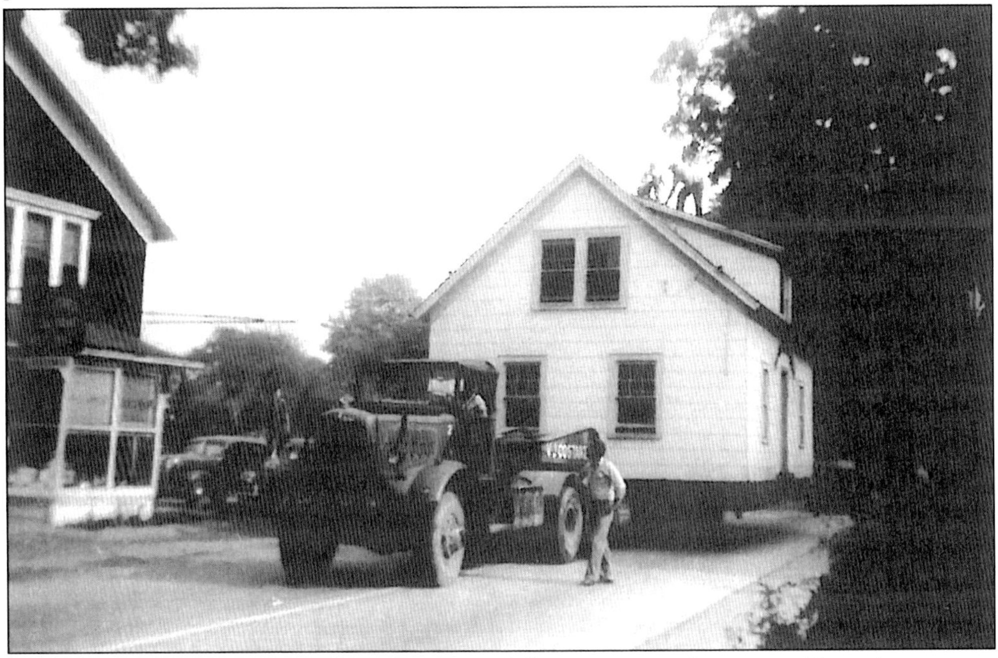

The Boscardin house was prepared for a move. Cellar areas were dug out, and huge beams were run under the house. Leveled, jacked up, and moved onto a frame, the house was pulled onto Mill Street and a half mile north on Route 22. This photograph shows the move when the house was opposite the bowling alley in 1952. Today Frank and Carolyn Boscardin own the charming home on Route 22. (FB.)

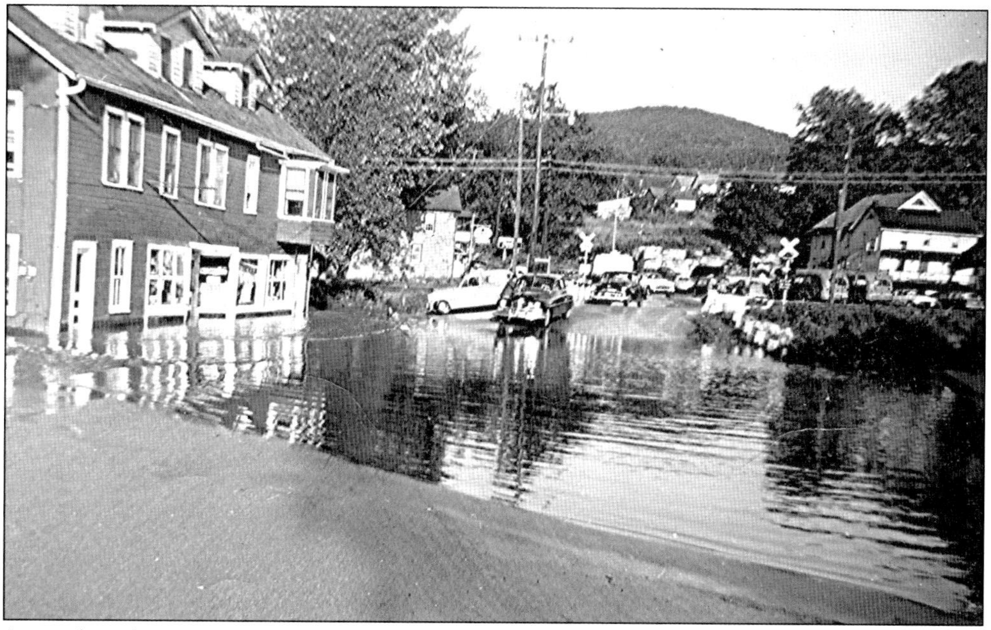

Around mid-August in 1955, Hurricanes Connie and Diane struck with damaging winds and torrents of rain. Upstream, many dams overflowed and then failed. The Ten Mile River overflowed to record heights, damaging houses, buildings, and roadways. The Swamp River overflowed its banks, flooding Wingdale just west of the railroad tracks between the bridge and the old Garrison's Store and Post Office building. (IH.)

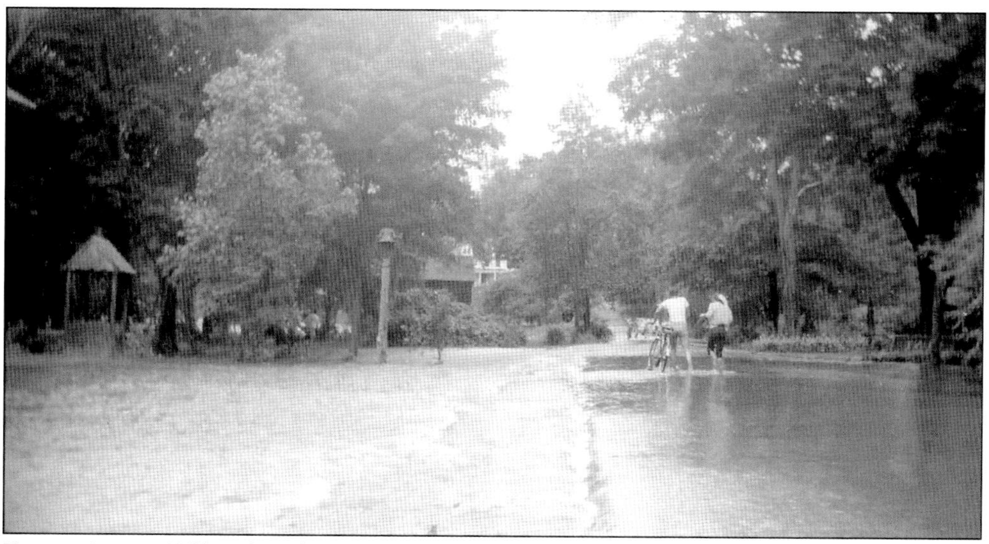

During August 1955, in less than a week, Hurricanes Connie and Diane dropped over 20 inches of rain. Rivers rose to record levels, causing widespread flooding and damage. The photograph of the road by Hunt's Country Furniture shows water backed up over the road to the showroom building on the far left side. Dover residents were without power and were isolated for days by raging waters. (IH.)

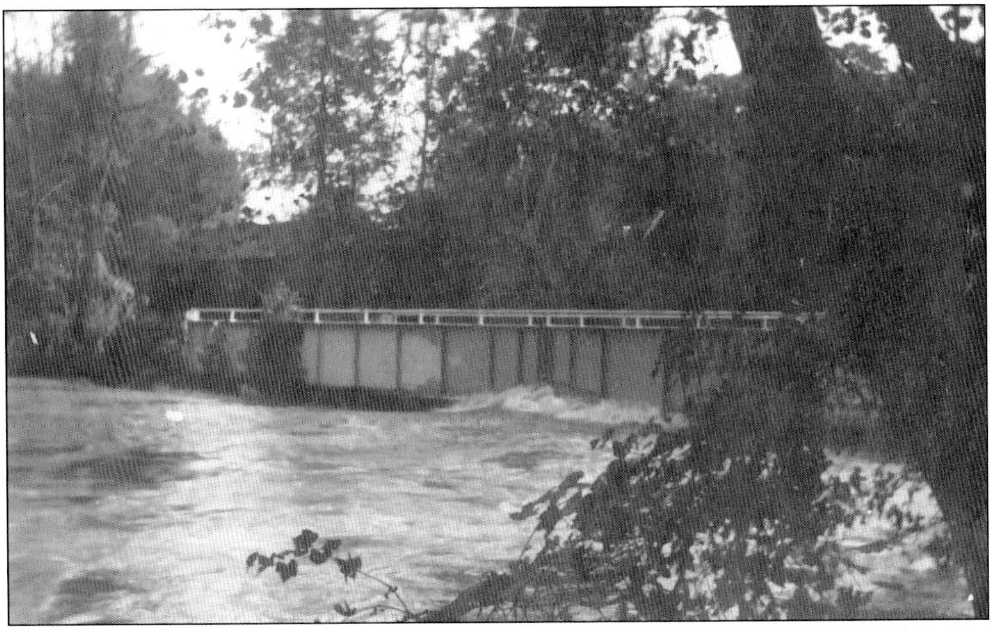

Priscilla Hunt Van Horn snapped this photograph from upriver as water levels raged against the center support on the bridge built around 1935. Beyond the bridge on the left, the Hunt's Country Furniture showroom outline can be seen through the rain. The bridge continued to deteriorate through the 2005 and 2007 floods. On March 31, 2008, the bridge closed. Demolition began to remove and replace the structure. (RV.)

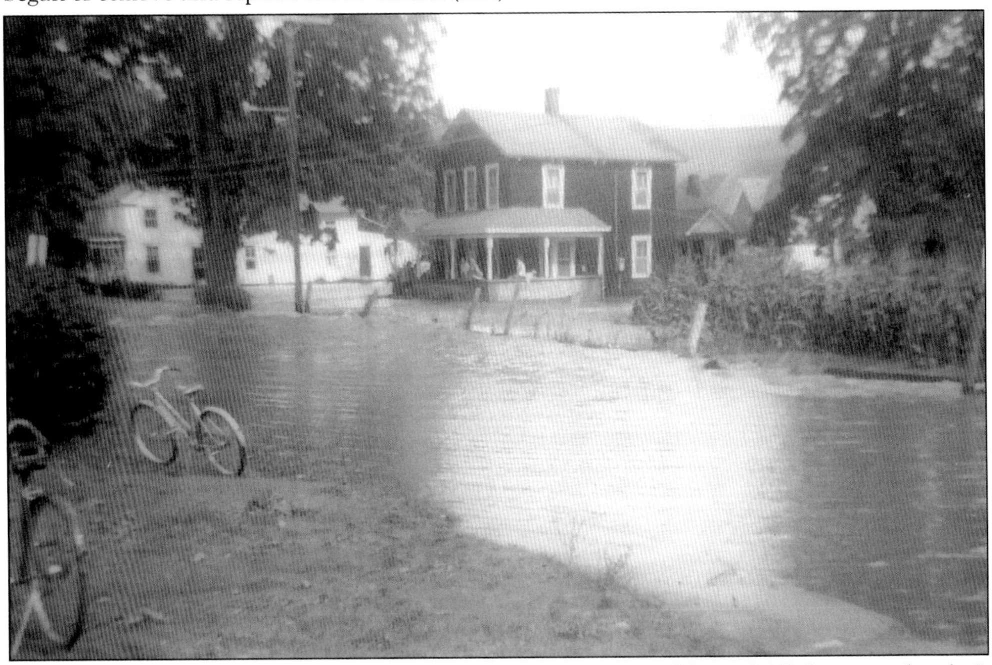

In the 1955 flood, dams washed out upstream and water covered lower Mill Street and today's Powell Park almost to the Powell Road intersection. These houses below the rectory on the other side had mud halfway up the first-floor stairs. Below Dover Plains at the southern end of Limekiln Road and today's Craig Lane area were under six feet or more of water. (DRH.)

Eight

The Need for Speed

Although drag racing may have started on some flat roadbeds in California, after drivers began running the clock in 1949, they focused on acceleration, and the sport took off.

By 1953, the National Hot Rod Association had run its first official race. Drag strips became a destination. When deejay "Cousin Brucie" Morrow advertised the Dover Drag Strip on 77WABC Radio, the 72-mile trip was a Sunday outing. For Craig Breedlove's *Spirit of America*, the *Batmobile*, or a recent race winner, traffic was lined up back to Pawling as fans came from all over New York and Connecticut. Anybody could race, and the early cars were souped-up street machines where alterations reduced weight. Fans lined the track and watched as cars, engines, and driving styles evolved and speed barriers fell.

The legionnaires from the Wingdale American Legion post saw the drag strip as a way to raise funds by selling food and refreshments. For those who wanted drinks and dinners, new restaurants appeared. For those who wanted peace and quiet, the weekends on Pleasant Ridge Road were noisy. During the 15 years the Dover Drag Strip operated, the local economy was stimulated, drag racing legends were born, and some fans and participants found a calling.

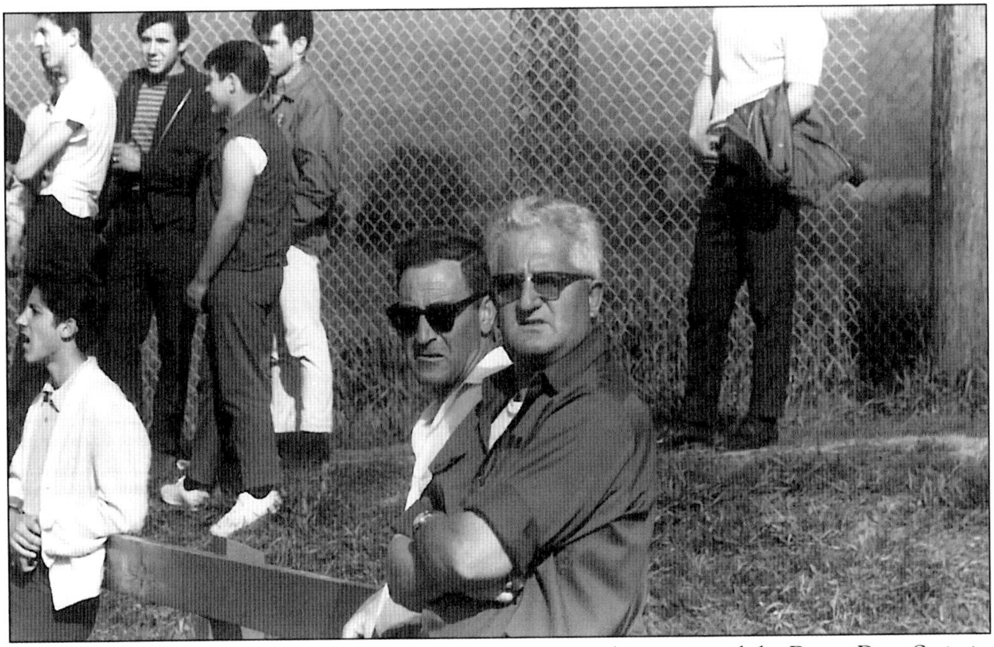

On May 14, 1961, owners Chet Anderson (left) and Joe Archiere opened the Dover Drag Strip in Wingdale. It cost $2 for spectators and $3 for the pit area. More than 7,000 fans saw 450 cars race weekly. During the 1960s, WABC Radio deejay "Cousin Brucie" Morrow routinely announced upcoming competitions at the Dover Drag Strip on Route 22 in Wingdale, 72 miles north of the George Washington Bridge. (BPM.)

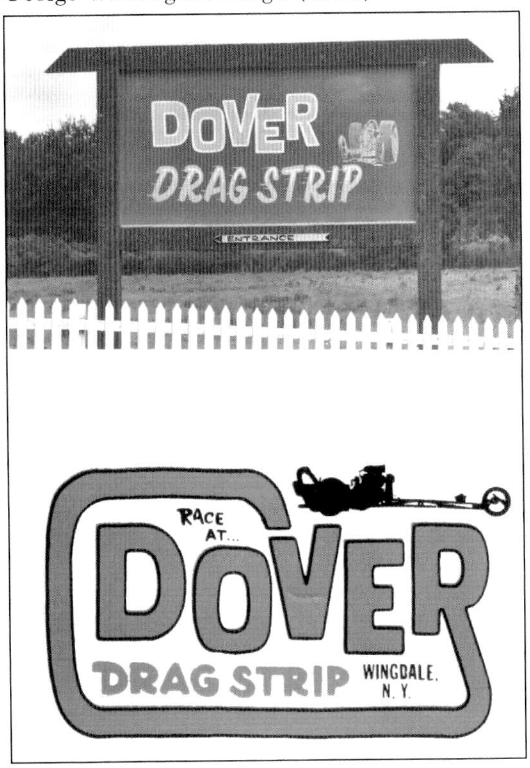

Dean (Dino) Lawrence created the track sign design and class-win stickers. Commuting to the School of Visual Arts in New York City, he designed the wraparound *R* track logo. Lawrence hitched to Dover and said he wanted to announce. When the first announcer left, Archiere let him try. Lawrence announced from 1965 until 1970. Today he owns Carolina Signworks. His brother Ted was the track tech inspector and events coordinator. (BPM.)

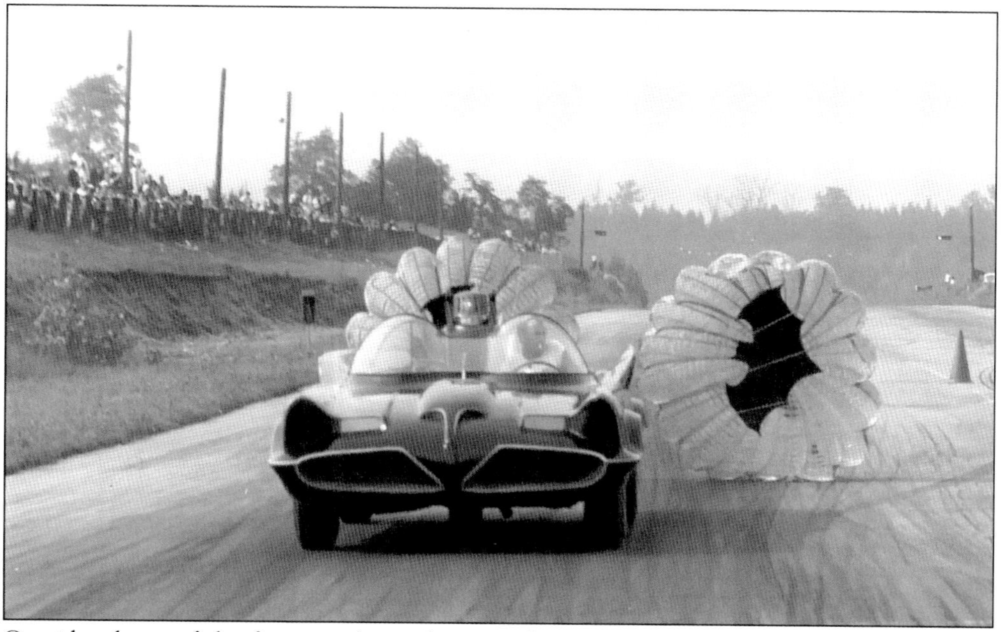

Considered one of the finest tracks in the east, the Dover Drag Strip received National Hot Rod Association sanction by 1971. The 3,400-foot-long track was 70 feet wide and paved with epoxy-based asphalt. No expansion joints interfered with the racing. As the track was cut nine feet below ground level, track seating provided spectacular views and spectator safety. On this day, racing and show cars included the original *Batmobile*. (BPM.)

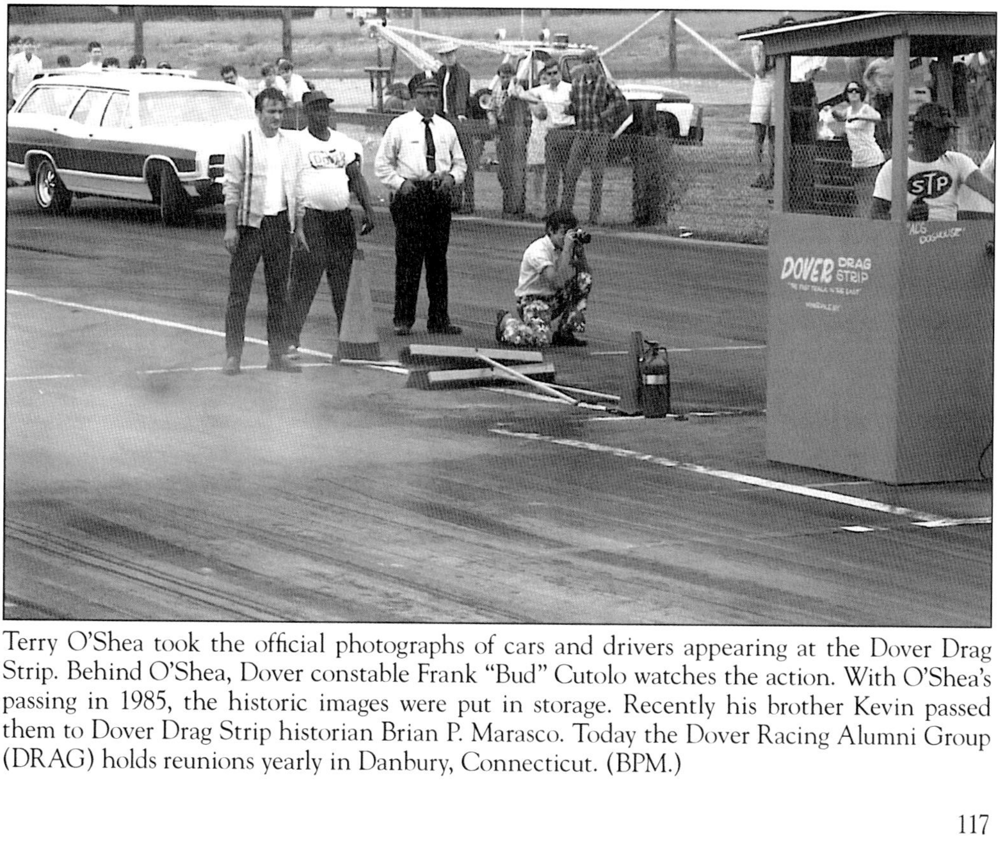

Terry O'Shea took the official photographs of cars and drivers appearing at the Dover Drag Strip. Behind O'Shea, Dover constable Frank "Bud" Cutolo watches the action. With O'Shea's passing in 1985, the historic images were put in storage. Recently his brother Kevin passed them to Dover Drag Strip historian Brian P. Marasco. Today the Dover Racing Alumni Group (DRAG) holds reunions yearly in Danbury, Connecticut. (BPM.)

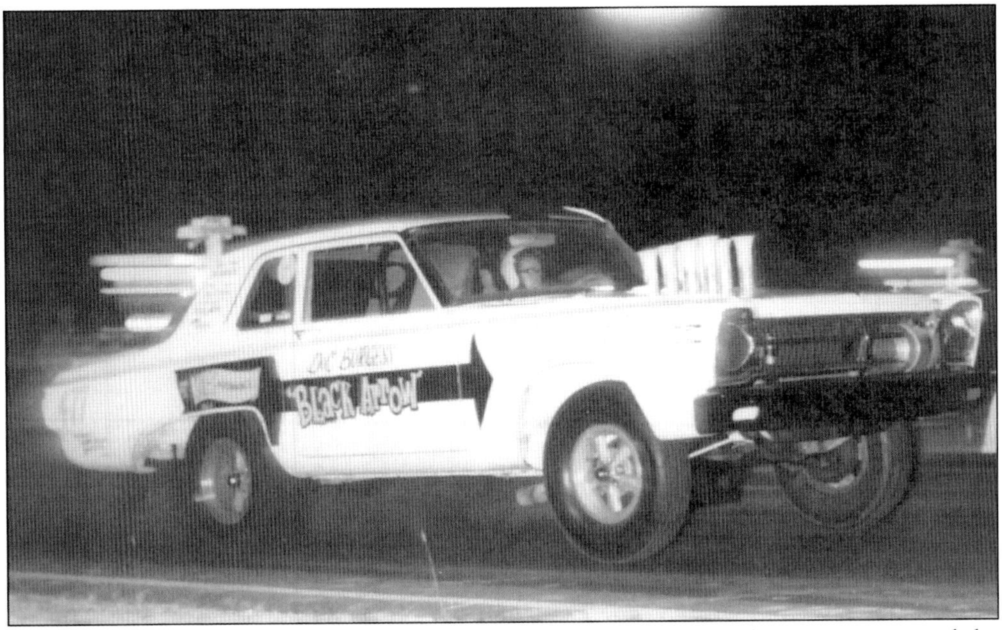

Victories of the *Black Arrow* depended on the skilled driving of Richard "Doc" Burgess and the mechanical expertise of Fred Murphy. When racing went to different weight classes, they modified the car, changing fenders from steel to fiberglass. Murphy shortened the wheelbase, relocated and resized the batteries, and used fiberglass to replace other parts. These cars were the forerunners of the funny cars known today. Recently a *Black Arrow* model car was released. (FM.)

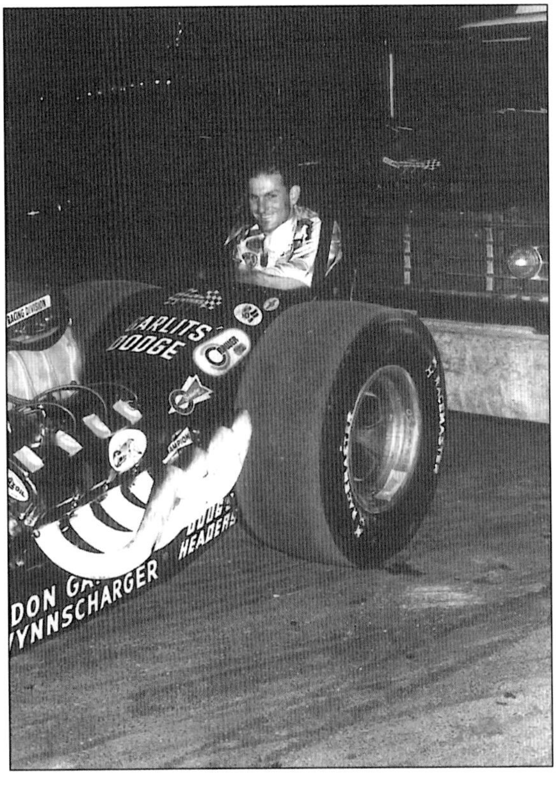

Dover Drag Strip ran Fuel Dragsters, funny cars, gassers, hot rod, pro-stock, and street-legal cars. Craig Breedlove exhibited his *Spirit of America*. Drag racing legends that raced here included "Big Daddy" Don Garlits, Shirley "Cha-Cha" Muldowney, Paula Murphy, Ronnie Sox and Buddy Martin, Don "Snake" Predone, and Dick Morose. Some of the greats developed products while others built corporations and dynasties based on their early experiences. Many are hall of fame members and are still racing. (BPM.)

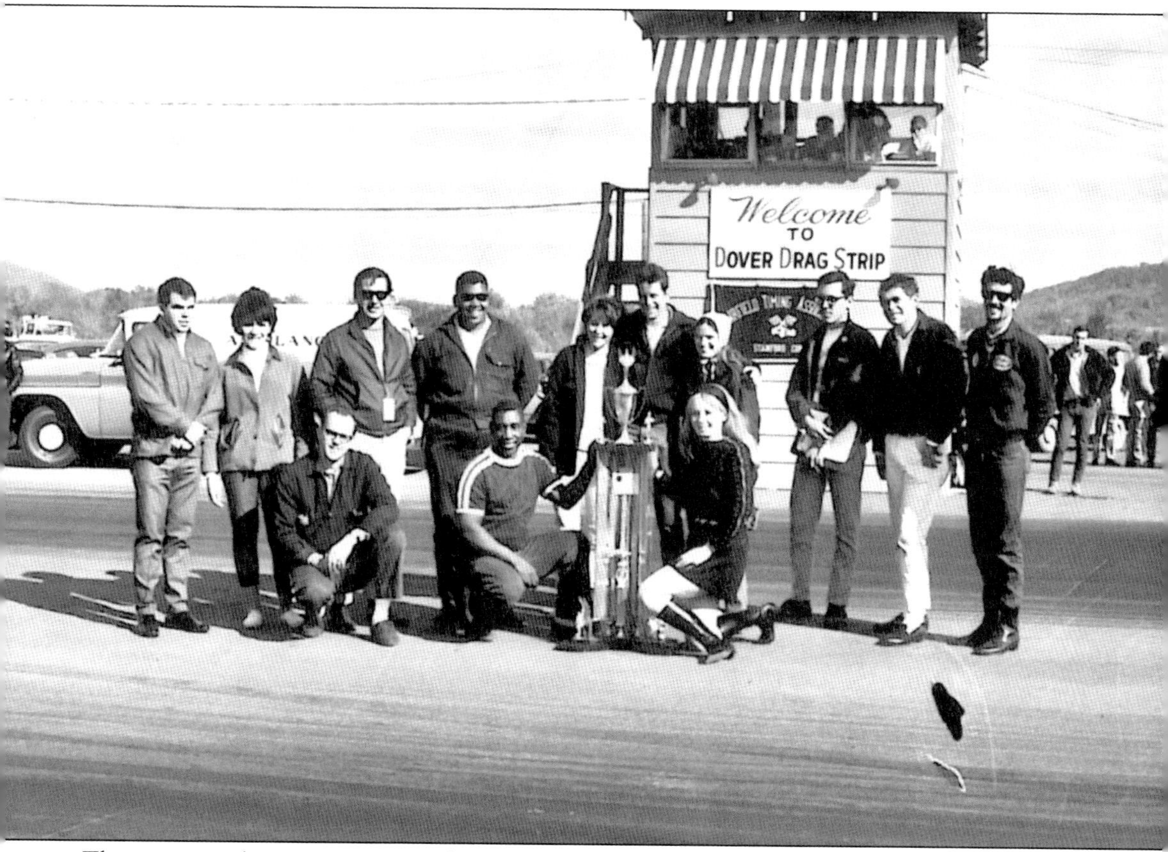

The most popular racing group at the track was the Fairfield Timing Association (FTA), which raced competitively at other drag strips. The FTA team logo is posted directly under the welcome sign. At the 1967 end-of-the-year awards, Barbara Lombardo presents the Pepsi Cola Trophy to Joe Tanner. His son Charlie is behind him. Other team members include Ron Frost and Skip North. (BPM.)

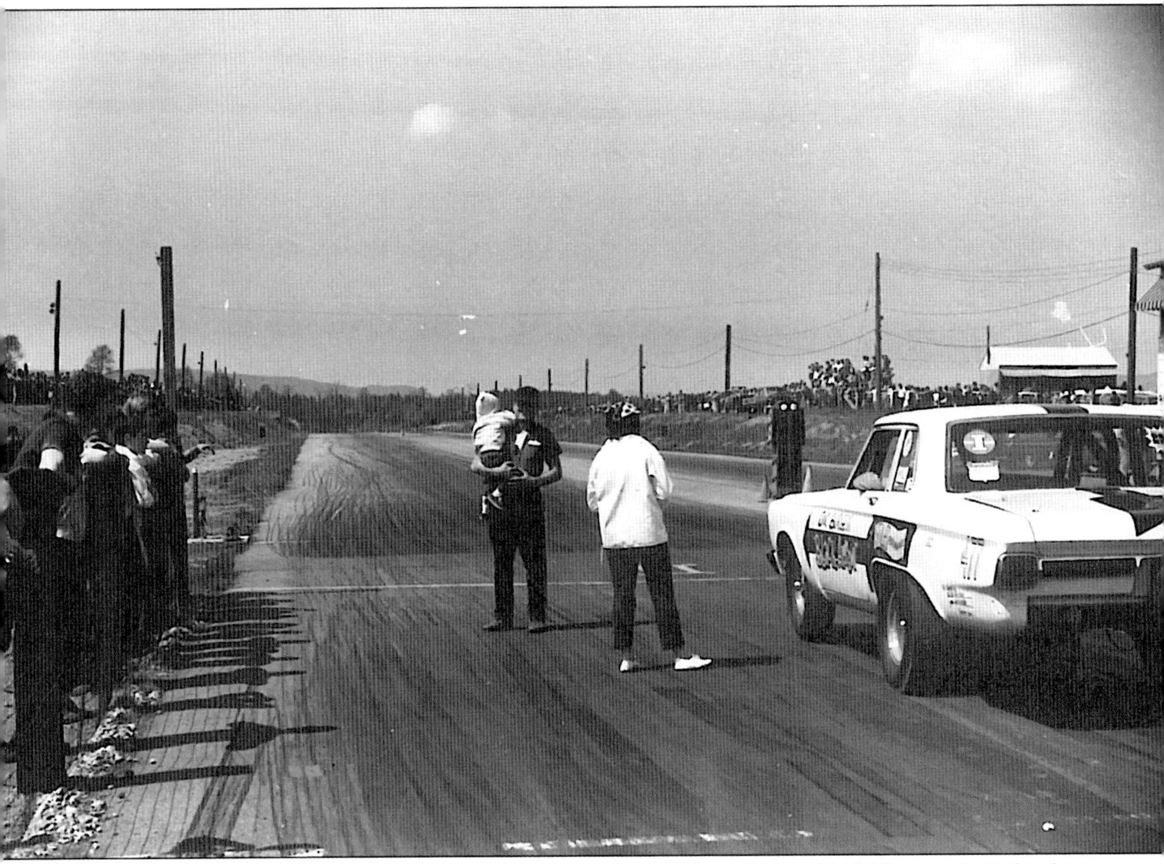

In 1966, Dover's veterinarian Richard Burgess Sr. purchased the 1965 Plymouth Belvedere nationals winner from Bill Jenkins. Mechanic Fred Murphy altered the wheelbase and added a Hillborn Hemi engine. The dragster averaged 130 miles per hour in the quarter mile. In this 1966 photograph, Doc Burgess waits between races, chatting with his wife, Helen. Starter Al Svarplaitis holds young Rich Burgess Jr. Today Richard Burgess Jr. crews for NASCAR's Richard Childress Racing Team. (BPM.)

Nine

Between Today and Tomorrow

In the last 50 years or so, Dover has seen many changes. Through the 1960s, Dover prospered as numerous new businesses were opened, including a branch of the Dover Plains National Bank. Then changes in mental health philosophy and laws made the phasing out and closure of Harlem Valley State Hospital inevitable. As the valley's major employer, the impacts were devastating. By 1980, the Department for Youth had taken over some buildings on the campus, providing jobs and retraining for many. Some employees found new jobs or changed careers. Others moved away. Meanwhile, a partnership formed by the affected towns and grant funding supported marketing studies. The town revised its master plan and zoning to enhance and support future development and has maintained an economic redevelopment zone on the parcel for over a decade. Today a new proposal is under consideration for the campus.

New development did come. A slow but steady stream of people from the south increased as homeowners from New York City and Westchester County discovered, bought, and built in Dover. By 1976, the town celebrated the American bicentennial with a huge celebration. The historical society, galvanized by the state's destruction of a Colonial inn, took steps to save the deteriorating Connell house, today known as the Tabor Wing House. Population continued to increase, but the new residents commuted. The emergency services partnered with town government to stretch their dollars and provide better services. Despite struggles with severe weather and massive flooding in 2005 and 2007, the town has managed to develop its parks, recreation programs, and government offices. The Dover Stone Church and access way were acquired for open space parkland through collaboration with the owner, adjacent developer, Friends of the Dover Stone Church, Dutchess County, and the state. It was another award-winning project that gained state recognition. When the historical society gave the town the Tabor Wing House, grant funding restored and adapted it for offices. The town won awards for the building in 2005 from Dutchess County and in 2006 from the Best of Hudson Valley. Today the town is evaluating plans for the redevelopment of the Harlem Valley State Hospital campus and looking forward to moving ahead.

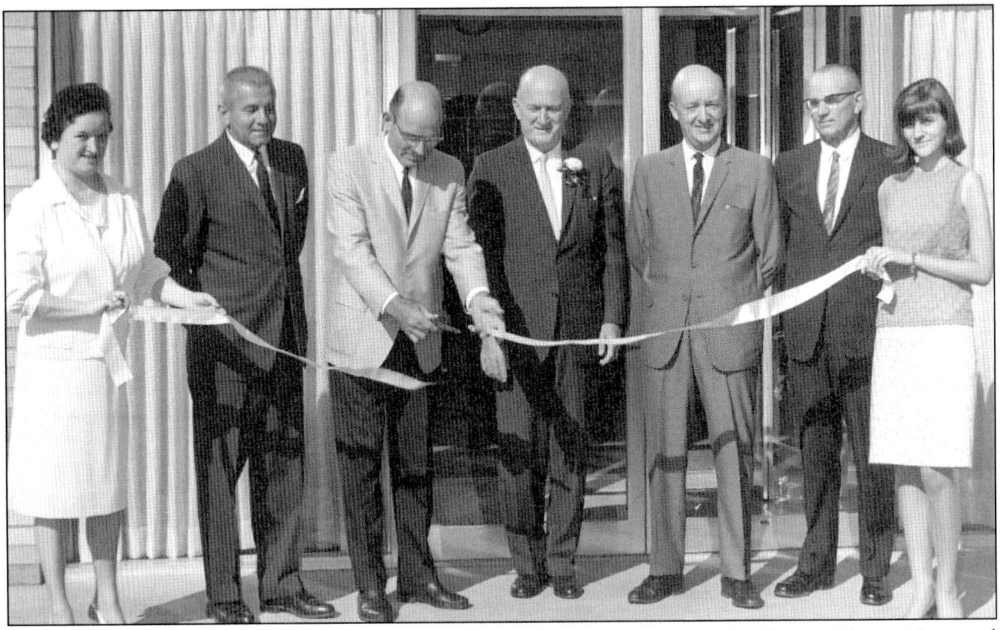

In 1964, bank president Thomas J. Boyce led the ribbon cutting at the Dover Plains National Bank branch located in the Wingdale Plaza. Shown from left to right are Jean Faix, William Schreiber, town supervisor Armando Mostachetti, Tom Boyce, Dr. Arthur Sullivan, Kenneth Vincent, and Jean Ann Maserio. After the psychiatric center closed, the bank closed the branch. Today the Wingdale Post Office occupies the site. (TDHS.)

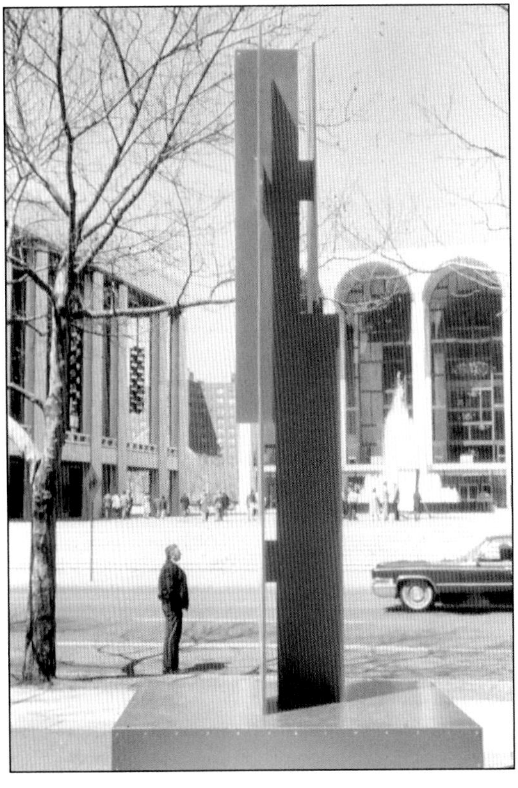

Roger H. Bolomey taught art at Dover Elementary School during the late 1950s and early 1960s. His sculptural works emphasized the vertical, upright, standing positions of four slabs of steel while drawing attention to the center. Each slab stood separate but unified within the individual work. According to the sculptor, he enjoyed the Wingdale area, naming a work in its honor. *Wingdale* is in a small park opposite Lincoln Center. (New York City Department of Parks and Recreation.)

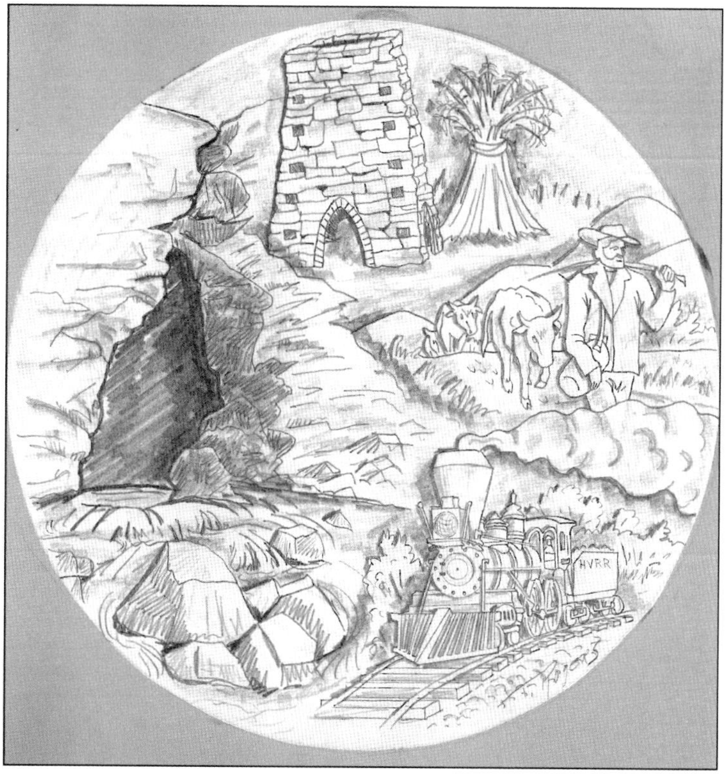

For the 1976 bicentennial, the Town of Dover Historical Society sold a medallion to raise funds for the celebration. The medallion was created by Thomas D. Rogers, who created the soaring eagle on the 2000 golden Sacagawea dollar. This sketch was one of three preliminary drawings made for the medallion. (TDHS.)

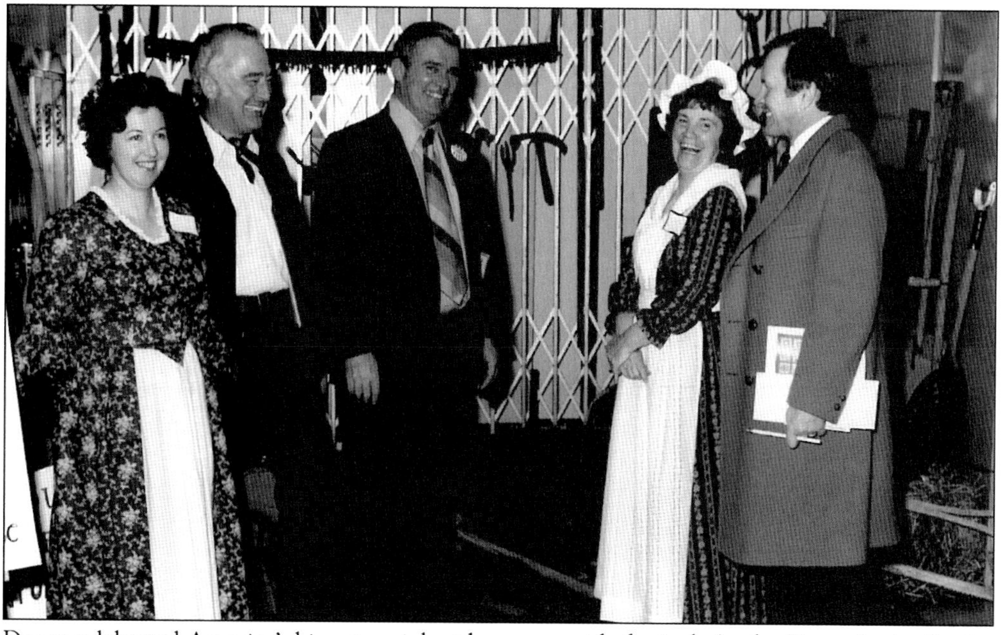

Dover celebrated America's bicentennial with a town-wide festival. At the Dover Junior-Senior High School, educational displays focused on local history. From left to right at the early farming implement exhibit are historical society members vice president Caroline Rogers Reichenberg, Pres. Donald B. Dedrick, town supervisor Augustus O'Neill, and teacher Mary Benson Wamsley. The unidentified person (right) is a visitor at the display. (TDHS.)

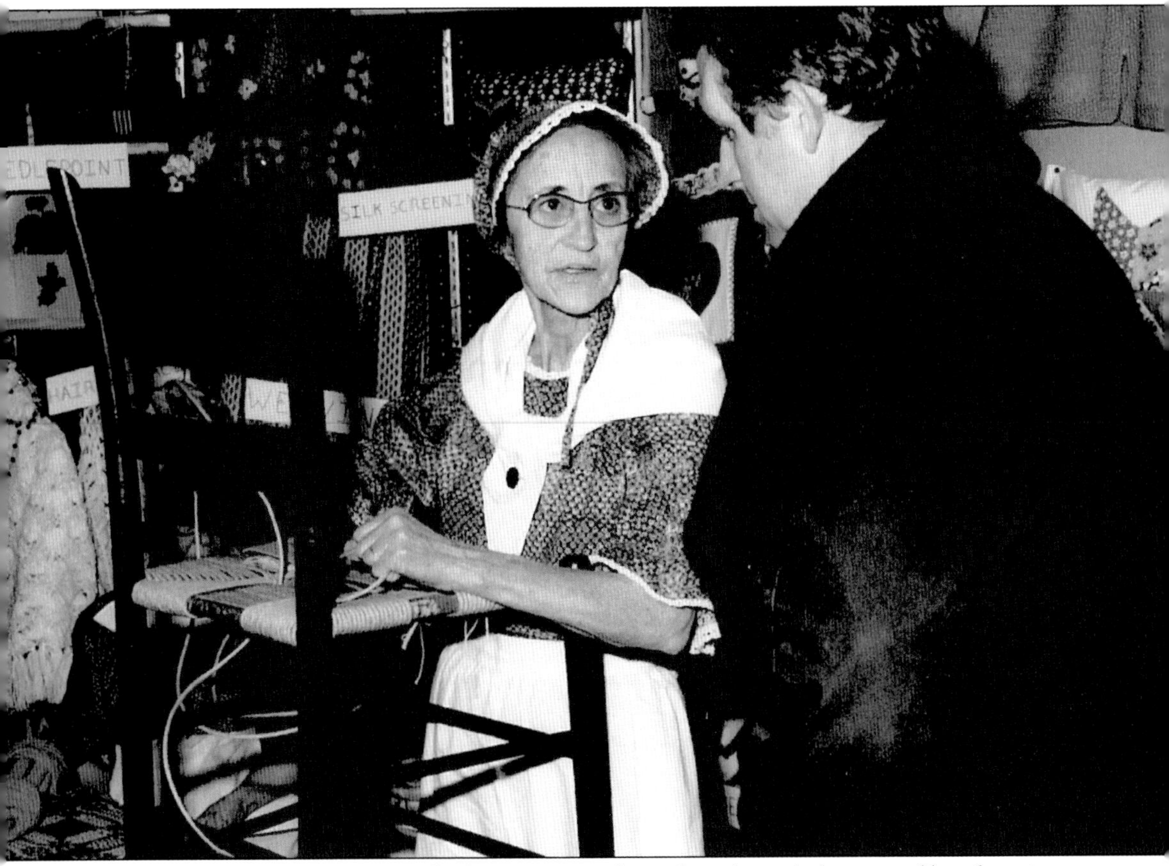

Florence Reimer demonstrates the historic, complicated, and nearly lost art of hand caning to Robert Humeston. Reimer was the high school nurse and mentor to a multitude of students. For years, she hosted regular gatherings of the Dover Doers. There, women of all ages met to socialize, knit, crochet, stitch, and quilt items for gifts and charitable causes. She was honored as citizen of the year in 1980. (TDHS.)

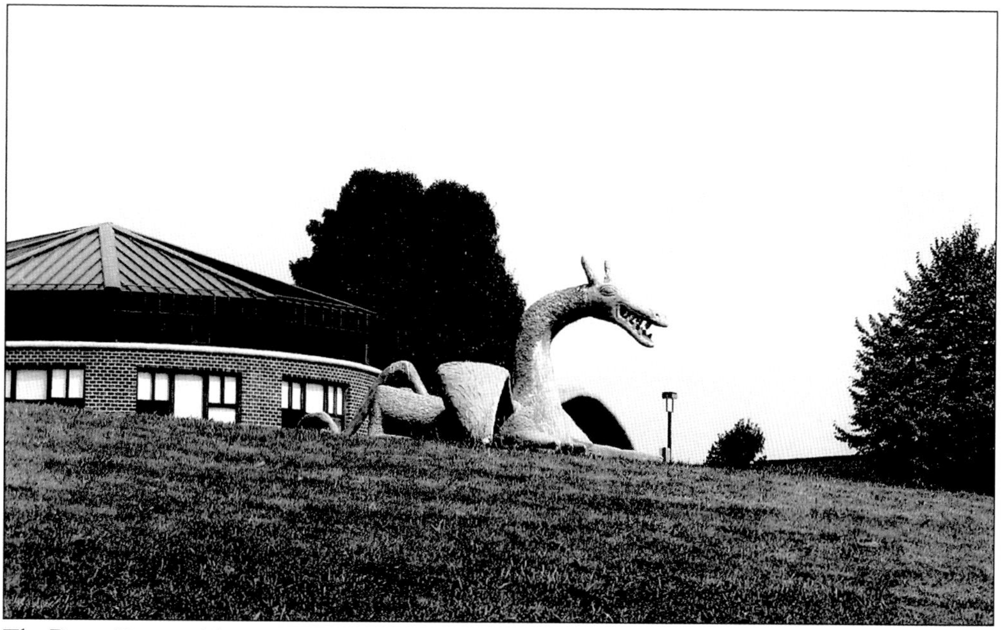

The Dover Dragons' dragon greets visitors to Dover Middle-High School. Donated by John Emerson, the dragon was loaded on a truck and driven 30 miles to its new home in 2001. Dover graduates have gone on to challenging and successful careers. A highlight of the sports program came when the 1997 Dover football team won the New York State Class C championship. (DPH.)

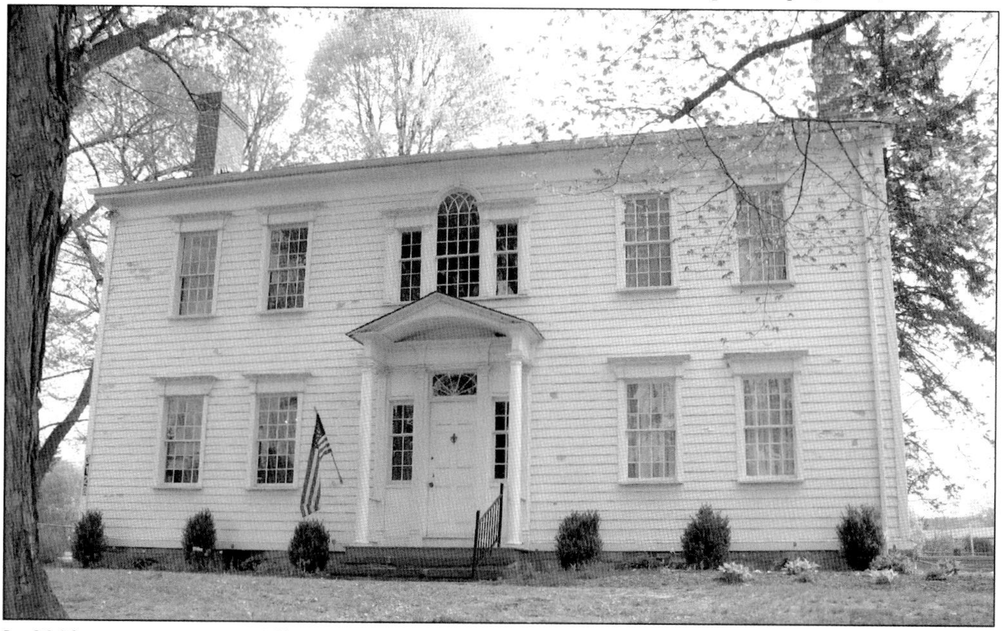

In 2003, town supervisor Jill Way applied for historic preservation grant funding. The Tabor Wing House restoration won the 2005 Dutchess County Department of Planning and Development Award for best adaptive reuse of a historic structure. In 2006, the editor of *Hudson Valley* magazine visited the Tabor Wing House. Having seen many government offices from New York City to Albany, he named the Tabor Wing House the best government offices in the Hudson Valley. (TDHC.)

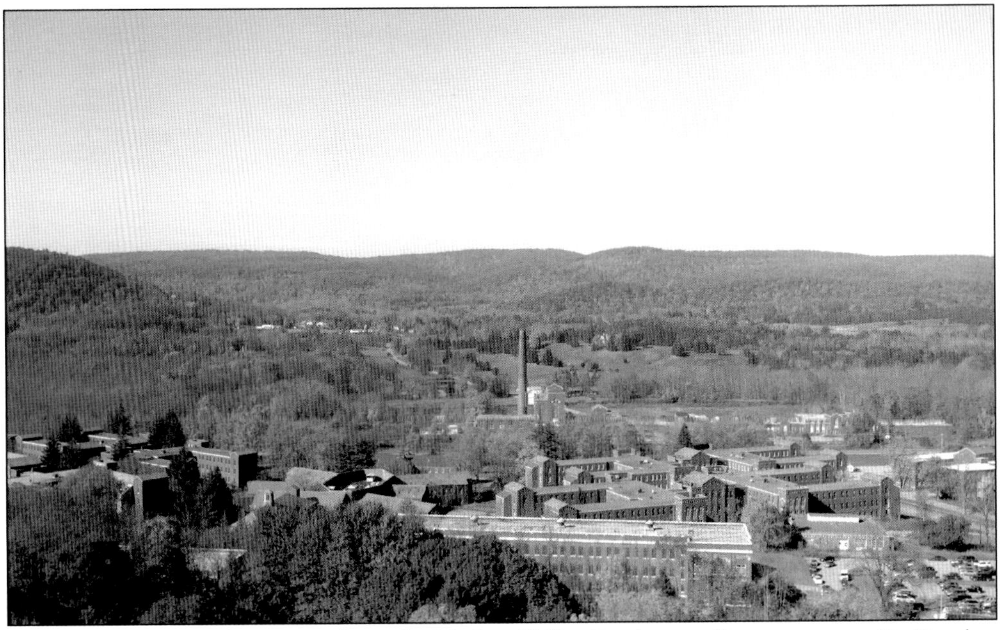

In 1993, steps were taken to purchase the Harlem Valley Psychiatric Center campus. By October 2003, the site was in private hands. This photograph looks westward from atop building 85. Below, the symmetrical design and layout of the campus are apparent. Across Route 22, the powerhouse chimney divides the golf course area, and the Manor House and gardens crown the golf course hill. (The Benjamin Companies.)

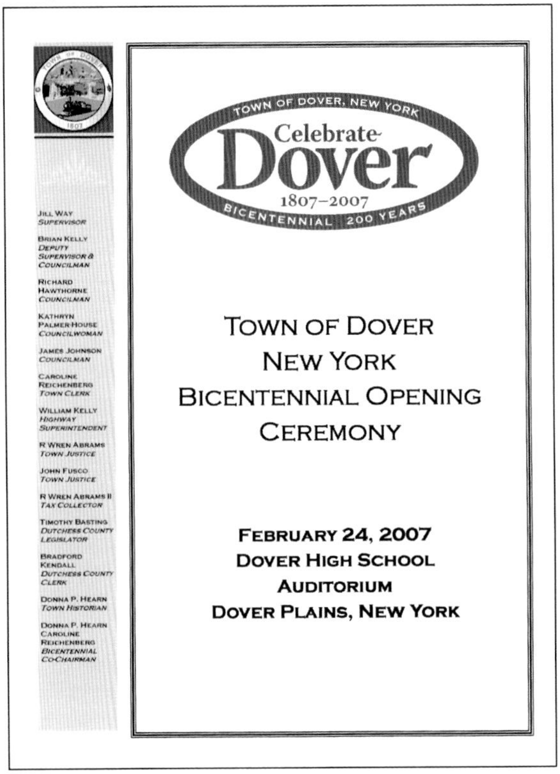

Jill Way
Supervisor

Brian Kelly
Deputy Supervisor & Councilman

Richard Hawthorne
Councilman

Kathryn Palmer-House
Councilwoman

James Johnson
Councilman

Caroline Reichenberg
Town Clerk

William Kelly
Highway Superintendent

R Wren Abrams
Town Justice

John Fusco
Town Justice

R Wren Abrams II
Tax Collector

Timothy Basting
Dutchess County Legislator

Bradford Kendall
Dutchess County Clerk

Donna P. Hearn
Town Historian

Donna P. Hearn
Caroline Reichenberg
Bicentennial Co-Chairman

Town of Dover, New York
Celebrate Dover
1807–2007
Bicentennial 200 Years

Town of Dover
New York
Bicentennial Opening
Ceremony

February 24, 2007
Dover High School
Auditorium
Dover Plains, New York

Bicentennial opening ceremonies were held at the Dover High School auditorium. The program highlights included the return of the 1807 minutes book and a rendition of "Put on Your Old Gray Bonnet." Participants viewed photographs and exhibits, tasted local restaurant offerings, and had their postmarks stamped and then signed by the engraver. A summer festival was held at Boyce Park with fireworks and a parade, and a November gala ball ended the year. (TDHC.)

BIBLIOGRAPHY

Bowen, Clarence Winthrop. *The Boundary Disputes of Connecticut*. Boston, MA: James R. Osgood And Company, 1882.

Cook, S. G., M.D. and Charles E. Benton, eds. *The "Dutchess County Regiment" (150th New York State Volunteer Infantry) in the Civil War, Its Story as Told by Its Members*. Danbury, CT: The Danbury Medical Printing Company, 1907.

Maher, Richard H. *Historic Dover*. Second Edition, 1908.

Poucher, J. Wilson, M.D. and Helen Wilkinson Reynolds. *Old Gravestones of Dutchess County, New York*. Poughkeepsie, NY: Dutchess County Historical Society, 1998.

Reed, Newton. *Early History of Amenia with Impressions of Amenia by Dewey Barry*. Amenia, NY: Harlem Valley Times, 1985.

Scott, Kenneth. *Counterfeiting in Colonial America*. New York: Oxford University Press, 1957.

Smith, James H. *History of Dutchess County, NY with Illustrations and Biographical Sketches of Some of its Prominent Men and Pioneers*. Syracuse, NY: D. Mason and Company, 1882.

Smith, Philip H. *General History of Dutchess County from 1609–1876*. Pawling, NY: self-published, 1877.

State of New York. Senate document No. 165. April 10, 1857.

Town of Dover Historical Society. *A History of Dover Township*. Dover Plains, NY: Town of Dover Historical Society, 1982.